OVERCOMING DEPRESSION

OVERCOMING
DEPRESSION

Demitri F. Papolos, M.D.
and Janice Papolos

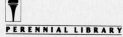

PERENNIAL LIBRARY

Harper & Row, Publishers, New York
Cambridge, Philadelphia, San Francisco, Washington
London, Mexico City, São Paulo, Singapore, Sydney

First PERENNIAL LIBRARY edition published 1988

Designed by C. Linda Dingler
Illustrations by Kim Llewellyn

Library of Congress Cataloging-in-Publication Data

Papolos, Demitri F.
    Overcoming depression.

    "Perennial Library."
    Bibliography: p.
    Includes index.
    1. Depression, Mental—Popular works.   2. Manic-
depressive psychoses—Popular works.   I. Papolos,
Janice.   II. Title.   [DNLM: 1. Depressive Disorders—
popular works.   2. Manic Disorders—popular works.
WM 171 P218o]
RC537.P36   1988   616.85'27   86-46094
ISBN 0-06-091488-2 (pbk.)

88 89 90 91 92 FG 10 9 8 7 6 5 4 3 2 1

For Alexander

CONTENTS

FOUR
COMING FULL CIRCLE

APPENDICES

PREFACE

Although mood disorders have always been a part of human experience, the past ten to fifteen years have seen such advances in their treatment that people no longer have to struggle through crippling sieges of depression or uncontrollable mania. With proper diagnosis and treatment, mood swings can be prevented or diminished in severity. In fact, so many advances have been made in such a short period of time that a lag in communication has developed—people aren't aware that psychiatry has a new understanding of recurrent mood disorders and that available treatments can dramatically improve the quality of their lives. An update is in order.

In the pages that follow, we explore the nature and course of depression and mania and describe the medications used in their treatment—the benefits as well as the complications. We summarize and explore the current scientific concepts of the underlying causes of mood disorders: first, because they're interesting and important and second, because they are the scaffolding for the research that should result in new and more sophisticated treatment in the future. While the research findings presented throughout the book were culled from the major scientific and clinical journals in the fields of psychiatry and the basic sciences, we have made an effort to make this information accessible to the layperson without oversimplifying or overstating the present state of knowledge. We tried not to let the ascendant biomedical model of psychiatry become an opportunity to gloss over the difficult psychological and social issues pertinent to mood disorders. These conditions involve periodic disturbances in mood, concentration, sleep, activity, appetite and behavior and they profoundly affect an individual's functioning, social relations, life-course and self-esteem. Major sections of this book are devoted to exploring what happens to a person who suffers recurrent episodes of depression or mania as well as the impact of these illnesses on family members. In these sections we outline ways in which everyone concerned might better cope with the problems the episodes present.

In order to broaden the scope of the book and provide a three-dimensional picture of the realities of these disorders and of a patient's interactions with the mental health profession, we devised a rather extensive questionnaire and distributed it nationally through the manic-depressive support groups. Many people responded with moving and informative accounts of their experiences during cycles of illness. They told us their concerns and problems and urged us to convey to others the methods they had found to cope with these disorders.

Knowledge is a great balancer, and informed individuals can and do respond more constructively to the problems of illness. It is our intention to aid in the early recognition of depression and manic-depression, to reinforce and supplement the information given by the consulting psychiatrist or physician and to clear away some of the mysteries from the field of psychiatry and its treatment of the major mood disorders. We want to let people know what to expect so that they can better assess their treatment and act in their own best interest. It is our hope, then, that this book will be a resource that will make living with the illness easier for all concerned.

Demitri F. Papolos, M.D.
Janice Papolos
New York City

ACKNOWLEDGMENTS

Throughout the writing of this book, we were privileged to have the special counsel of Ross J. Baldessarini, M.D. He put his enormous store of experience and knowledge at our disposal, and his attention to the manuscript contributed countless improvements.

We would also like to acknowledge the other professionals who responded generously to our requests for information and assistance. They are: Olivia H. Baker, R.N., Miron Baron, M.D., Judith Berenson, M.S.W., Judith Bernz, Wade Berrettini, M.D., Joseph Biederman, M.D., Vernon R. Bruette, Debra M. Cassel, Johnine Cummings, M.S.W., Linda K. Franz, M.S.W., Gary Goldsmith, Rosalie Greenberg, M.D., Marian C. Harkavy, Artie Houston, Stephen B. Kahn, Esq., Thomas Kranjac, M.D., Dulcie E. Lewis, R.N., Elizabeth Mackintosh, Ph.D., David Moltz, M.D., Eric J. Neutzel, M.D., Grace Oettinger, O.T., William Parsons, Ph.D., Richard Satkin, Maggie Schie, Bruce J. Schwartz, M.D., Delores Segal, Scott Sherrill, Esq., Andrew E. Skodol, M.D., Jorge L. Tapia, D.D.S., Kenneth G. Terkelsen, M.D., Maryellen Walsh and Marilyn Weiss.

Special thanks are owed to the many members of the manic-depressive support groups across the nation who answered our questionnaire. Their voices have added an immediate and vital perspective to these pages.

Pam Bernstein, our agent and friend, encouraged this project from the start, and Carol Cohen's keen eye and intelligent editing brought clarity to the manuscript and kept us on course.

Finally, we wish to acknowledge the people who were most directly involved with the evolution of this volume, and who offered us crucial and unfailing support: Rose B. Albicocco, Laurie Scandurra Ball, Rosalie Snyder Bate, Richard L. Hauger, M.D., Mervyn M. Peskin, M.D., Stephen P. Reibel, M.D., Barbara L. Sand, Barbara Solomon, Herman M. van Praag, M.D., Ph.D., and Kevin Walz.

ONE

ABOUT THE ILLNESS

The purpose of this book is to make you aware of psychiatry's progress in the study and treatment of the major mood disorders. Proper diagnosis and the treatment of depression and manic-depression require an expert. You should consult only with a highly qualified physician about questions specific to yourself.

All names, characteristics, backgrounds and other details about the people described in the case examples in this book have been changed.

1
THE PERSONAL EXPERIENCE

When we first told friends and people outside the psychiatric field that we were writing a book on depression and manic-depression, we expected polite but lukewarm interest. That wasn't what happened. Instead, one person after another confided to us: "I've had experience with it, my mother and brother are bipolar"; "My grandmother and younger sister were just put on lithium"; and, "My adopted son suffers from recurrent depression. . . . I don't know if his real parents had it." These people were stating what clinicians have always observed: depression and manic-depression are very common illnesses and tend to concentrate in families.

Mood disorders are the "common cold" of major psychiatric illnesses, and more than twenty million Americans will suffer an episode of depression or mania during their lifetimes. One in five families will directly feel their impact. Those who have manic-depression will veer from periods of superactivity, manic elation and grandiose schemes to periods of despondency, immobility, guilt and inability to experience pleasure or even to think normally. The people who experience these highs and lows have what psychiatrists now call *bipolar disorder*. Those who suffer recurrent severe depression without the highs are said to have *unipolar* or nonbipolar major depression. The psychiatric profession groups these mood disturbances under the rubric *major affective disorders*. At first glance the term "affective" doesn't send the mind traveling, but it's a word philosophers and psychologists have traditionally used for emotion or one's "spirits."

Whatever these disorders are called—affective, manic-depressive illness, recurrent mood disorders, unipolar or bipolar depression—

they've been affecting mankind throughout the centuries. Some very familiar individuals figure among the victims: King Saul of the Bible (who needed David's music to soothe his despondency), King George III (the last English king to rule the American colonies), Abraham Lincoln, Winston Churchill and Theodore Roosevelt. The writers and poets Honoré de Balzac, Virginia Woolf, Ernest Hemingway, Robert Lowell and Anne Sexton suffered mood swings, as did the composers George Frederick Handel, Robert Schumann, Hugo Wolf, Hector Berlioz and Gustav Mahler. These people are well known and respected, so it may seem that the illness fuels a certain kind of drive and creativity. But a study of their lives would also reveal searing anguish, shattered relationships, psychosis and even suicide.

Mood changes are hallmarks of the human experience, and mood has a powerful evolutionary value: it regulates our disposition to action and behavior, and keeps us involved in life and yet relatively safe. If a person is too pessimistic, he may not realize his potential— someone who is depressed will step back from life and not participate. On the other hand, a person with too optimistic a mood may place himself at risk—someone experiencing a manic episode can get carried away with an exalted sense of power and self-importance and act impulsively and recklessly. An immoderate mood disposition can cause life to be fragmented, disorganized, painful and potentially dangerous.

Mood also has a strong influence on what a person thinks about from moment to moment and therefore significantly influences the way someone feels about himself. When depressed, a person often dwells on exaggerated memories of losses or failures, or focuses on the morbid and negative aspects of his life to the exclusion of all other things. Negative thoughts or perceptions about oneself can erode self-esteem, resulting in an unrealistic sense of worthlessness and the feeling of being a burden to others. A person may experience persistent feelings of sadness and emptiness, become tearful for no apparent reason or become irritable and hostile.

The depressed person may be slowed down, lack energy and have fewer ideas. Decisions are next to impossible to make, and everyday tasks and challenges become intimidating. Some severe types of depression may include irrational, psychotic or delusional symptoms. Since these episodes may last for several months or longer, one's morale or self-esteem can become seriously impaired. Prolonged periods of depression can lead to the wish to die and to thoughts of killing oneself.

In contrast to this bleak picture, the person experiencing the "highs" of manic-depression often describes feeling better than at any other time in his life. He cannot understand why anyone would call his experience abnormal or part of an illness. His rate of thinking is markedly increased; one thought after another bursts into consciousness demanding expression. During a manic episode a person feels more excited, has surges of energy and describes feeling more active, more creative, intelligent and sexual than he ever thought possible. Sleep seems unnecessary, and he's ready to "take on the world." It is not unusual for a person in a manic state to decide to try to write the great American novel or to embark on audacious and risky business ventures.

The seemingly boundless energy and enthusiasm that is often a part of the manic swing can be infectious at first. Those witnessing a person charged with exuberance and confidence are often quite intrigued. Mania is not a state to be envied, however. Decisions made during a manic high are typically reckless and impulsive. Spending sprees and sexual indiscretions are common, and some people experiencing the disorder find the excess energy and excitement unbearable. They may turn to alcohol or drugs to calm the agitation or irritability. As the manic throttle is pushed, the person becomes more argumentative, intrusive and insistent about getting his own way. Others around him then become confused, angry and alarmed.

While some people experience a more controlled state of mania with elation and excessive activity called *hypomania,* others lose contact with reality as their thinking becomes fragmented, disorganized and delusional. The person may envision himself as the savior of the world, or he may experience paranoia and respond to others with extreme irritability and anger. In this psychotic stage the disorder can be confused with schizophrenia. Eventually the manic episode runs its course, though, and the person may be plunged into the depths of depression—surrounded by the shards of his life, career and relationships.

The person who experiences out-and-out manic episodes alternating with periods of depression is referred to as having *bipolar I* disorder. The person who suffers very mild hypomanic periods as well as severe depression is said to have *bipolar II* disorder. There are also some people who experience only the manic highs, or recurrent bouts of acute psychosis, and little or no depression, and they are referred to as having *unipolar mania*.

The onset of the first episode of an affective disorder may not always be obvious. Some people have brief, mild episodes infrequently without seeking treatment or even knowing that they are ill. Since we all experience periods of sadness, disappointment and grief, it is difficult to know when a depressed mood becomes a medical condition. While there continues to be debate about this question, it may be useful to conceptualize the state of depression as developing along a continuum from mild to severe.

When a person experiences some major disappointment in a career or relationship, the loss is usually followed by a few days of sadness, withdrawal, sleep disturbance and anxiety, but it is not long before the normal mood is reestablished and the person regroups and goes on with life. When, however, the depressed mood persists and the isolation from others continues, and the individual loses a sense of pleasure and meaning in life and begins to develop physical symptoms such as loss of appetite, a marked interruption in the regular sleep cycle and a marked decrease in the ordinary level of activity, these signs signal the onset of a "clinical depression." The person has moved across the boundaries that demarcate normal mood fluctuations to a medical condition. (It should be noted that the clinical syndrome of depression can present itself without any noticeable precipitants such as loss or disappointment.)

Typically, episodes of illness are time-limited: they come and go, last from several weeks to several months and are followed by periods of relatively normal mood and behavior. Untreated, the average depressive episode lasts about four months, the average manic episode about three months. Periods of depression, however, can last for twelve months or more without remitting.

Not all people who experience a major depression will suffer a recurrence, but studies suggest that between 50 and 85 percent of patients who seek treatment for depression at university medical centers will have at least one subsequent episode of depression in their lifetimes. The lifetime average for depressive episodes is five to seven, but as many as forty episodes have been reported.

Bipolar illness is definitely a recurrent or episodic disorder: a 1973 study examined nearly four hundred patients who had a manic-depressive episode, and only two failed to have a recurrence. Without treatment, the frequency and severity of the illness tends to increase over the years, but usually reaches an eventual plateau.

The unipolar form of the illness is more common than the bipolar, and it is estimated that two-thirds of the individuals who experience a mood disorder have depressions only. However, 10 to 15 percent of the people who first experience one or more depressive episodes go on to experience a hypomanic or manic episode and thus are reclassified as bipolar. It is not unusual for a relative to have the unipolar form of the disorder and a descendant to have the bipolar form, or vice versa.

Manic and depressive episodes present differently in different persons, but there are two basic types of episode:

1. Periods of depression are characterized by:
   - Poor appetite and weight loss, or the opposite, increased appetite and weight gain
   - Sleep disturbance: sleeping too little, or sleeping too much in an irregular pattern
   - Loss of energy: excessive fatigue or tiredness
   - Change in activity level, either increased or decreased
   - Loss of interest or pleasure in usual activities
   - Decreased sexual drive
   - Diminished ability to think or concentrate
   - Feelings of worthlessness or excessive guilt that may reach grossly unreasonable or delusional proportions
   - Recurrent thoughts of death or self-harm, wishing to be dead or contemplating or attempting suicide
2. Periods of hypomania or the more severe state of mania are characterized by:
   - Persistently "high" (euphoric) or irritable mood states
   - Decreased need for sleep
   - Appetite disturbance
   - Increased activity, sociability and sexual drive
   - Pressured speech
   - Racing thoughts
   - Loss of self-control and judgment

It's a discomforting, unhappy menu of symptoms with much potential for misery and shame. This can be compounded by a lack of understanding of what actually is going on inside—on the part of both the patient and those closest to him. When someone doesn't understand that he is in the throes of a depression, he is likely to ascribe the symptoms to erroneous causes, thereby delaying medical treatment. Not only is he confused, he also doesn't have an adequate explanation for those who are witnessing the changes, and the situation is ripe for myth, misunderstanding and distortion. Over and over again you hear families say: "I thought he was an alcoholic with big ideas"; "We thought he was just lazy and wouldn't get out of bed"; and, "How can she be unhappy? She has so much to be grateful for in life. Why can't she pull herself up and get going?" What they don't realize is that these illnesses are insidious, and once they take hold the victim is without the power to lighten or temper his mood or symptoms.

If someone had cancer and were promised a cure in a far-away clinic, nothing would stop that individual from getting on a plane to seek out that cure. But Dick Cavett put his finger on the very thing that separates depression from any other illness. When speaking of his own experience with a severe depression, he said: "What's really diabolical about it is that if there were a pill over there, ten feet from me, that you could guarantee would lift me out of it, it would be too much trouble to go get it."

Tragically, only one in three people suffering from a major mood disorder seeks help, and only one in ten seeks help from a psychiatrist trained to diagnose severe psychiatric disorders and treat them medically. Today, thanks to lithium, antidepressant and anticonvulsant medications, these disorders are eminently treatable. It is estimated that over 80 percent of people suffering from depression and manic-depression can achieve substantial relief from their crippling symptoms. Stigma and a lack of knowledge as well as the often insidious nature of these disorders are a lethal combination.

It is crucial that people recognize the symptoms and understand the nature of these severe, recurring illnesses. But a list of symptoms alone is not sufficiently telling. It does not capture the human experience. Therefore, we've used patients' accounts and descriptions from literature to allow a more intimate look into these variable mood states.

WHAT DOES IT FEEL LIKE TO BE DEPRESSED?

A person who enters a depressive episode often describes his mood as sad, hopeless, down in the dumps, irritable and black. But there is another dimension to the depression experienced by a significant number of people—an anxious, restless, anguished feeling. Some people seem to be trapped in an agitated state of arousal as Robert Burton describes in his 1621 *Anatomy of Melancholy:* "They are in great pain and horror of mind, distraction of soul, restless, full of continual fears, cares, torment, anxieties, they can neither drink, eat, nor sleep for them, take no rest, neither at bed nor yet at board. . . ."

Many patients report a change in their thought patterns, in both the rate and content of thoughts. There is a paucity of ideas and a loss of the natural capacity to imagine a future. When the mind is laid barren of thought, the imagination cannot make the necessary leap into the future, and the individual experiences himself as out of time and isolated from the ongoing current of life. He cannot reconnect. One person described it this way:

> The most awful thing was that I realized my days had been com-posed of little moments of anticipated pleasure: that first cup of coffee in the very early morning, the inner thoughts that made me chuckle, a browse through a bookstore, the satisfaction of a job or chore completed. . . . Now these moments failed to hold the crest of pleasure—everything was flat and gray. Life seemed locked away from me and I was filled with unspeakable dread.

One young woman who was forced to leave college after her freshman year explained how terrified she was by the sense of inner strangeness and isolation she felt during her first encounter with depression:

> When I came home I was in a severe state of depression and anxiety, and my family was at a complete loss. I felt very isolated, unable to communicate. I felt I had let them down incredibly and I had this tremendous guilt.
> But I couldn't talk to them. I felt like my brain wasn't func-tioning. I had a hard time just carrying on a conversation. The

depression was really scary, because I felt that some incredible, horrible thing had happened to me, but there were no signs on the outside. I couldn't explain to people that inside I was completely different. I felt estranged, bizarre, weird. My thoughts were much slower. It was terrifying to be in college and sit through a whole lecture and be unable to remember a word of what the professor had said. Or, I'd sit down and read the textbook and I couldn't absorb any of it. I felt like some bizarre trick of fate, that something terribly wrong had happened to me on the inside, but nobody would understand.

It is common for people in the throes of a depression to feel that the world is drained of color—that everything is stale and empty, and that there is no "light at the end of the tunnel." Previously enjoyed activities hold no interest or pleasure for them, and they are said to have the clinical symptom known as *anhedonia*. The word doesn't in any way reveal the awfulness of the symptom. Author Maryellen Walsh describes what it's like to witness its appearance in a loved one:

Joy, affection, desire, pride, humor are all drained away. What makes life worth living disappears slowly, relentlessly until nothing seems to be left. . . . Anhedonia creeps in and claims the person who once laughed with you, who once hugged you, who once loved to be first on the hill to catch the new powder snow. The lights go out one by one. It is the death of the spirit.

Major depression is more than an anguished mood or the loss of the capacity to experience pleasure. It is accompanied by severe disturbances in appetite and sleep patterns—the so-called biological or vegetative symptoms. Usually a person complains of having no appetite—food just doesn't taste good anymore. One man was able to pinpoint the onset of his depression when he recalled sitting at a table in a restaurant with friends listening to them rave over food he felt tasted like sawdust.

In the case of a severe depression, the person may lose a great deal of weight. Sometimes, as in an *atypical* depression, the opposite may occur: the person actually develops a craving for sweets and carbohydrates and begins to put on weight. (This type of depression is frequently associated with the bipolar form of the disorder.)

Some people notice a change in their sleep pattern before any other signs of depression appear. They may have trouble going to sleep at night (initial insomnia), wake up during the middle of the night and find it difficult to get back to sleep (middle insomnia) or find themselves awakening early, around four or five A.M., and are overtaken by anxious, guilty thoughts they cannot quell. Journalist Percy Knauth chronicled his battle with depression in *A Season in Hell,* and had this to say about the sleep disturbance:

> As the lack of sleep wore me down, a sense of hopelessness enveloped me. I knew that nothing I did could change the situation. There was nothing I *could* do. I was convinced that I was laboring under some kind of curse so that any efforts of my own to fight this situation were foredoomed to failure.
>
> More realistically, I understood that the only tool I could fight with—my mind—was the very part of me that was affected. Can a legless man get up and walk even if he knows that only walking will save his life? My mind was going; how could I use it to extricate myself from my despair?
>
> With this hopelessness came the final stage in my loss of self-esteem: in my own eyes I became worthless. In long night sessions, I reviewed my life and saw everything that I had done wrong. Not even the most trivial detail escaped this deadly scrutiny. I remembered arguments I had had with my older children when they were very young, in my first marriage, and I realized what a poor excuse for a father I had been. I recalled the details of my divorce, and I understood precisely why my wife had left me for another man: I had never really filled the role of husband. Viewed in the merciless gloom of this early-morning self-analysis, even my work appeared to me to have been a fraud. At last I was being showed up for the hapless faker that I was, and this was my punishment.

Because there is no sense of the future in depression, the past, as Dr. Leston Havens says, "becomes fixed, immovable, bad, the place of irredeemable mistakes."

Although the majority of depressed people report some kind of insomnia, approximately 15 to 30 percent feel the need to sleep excessively (hypersomnia) and never feel rested, even after twelve or fourteen hours of sleep. In addition to the mood, appetite and sleep disturbances of depression, people may experience bodily pains such as headaches, backaches, constipation or stomach problems. And sexual appetite, as one man described it, is "the first to go . . . you don't even remember what it felt like."

Physicians describe the changes that occur in a depressed patient's activity and mental processes as *psychomotor agitation* or *retardation*. Things are either speeded up or very slowed down. Some individuals experiencing depression can't sit still: they pace, wring their hands and pull at their hair or clothing. Others seem suspended in slow motion, so drained of energy that the capacity to initiate any activity is all but extinguished. Speech, like everything else, is deadened, and the person may speak in a low, monotonous voice with long pauses before answering.

The capacity to participate in life, to interact with others, to take pride in past accomplishments and to initiate and complete everyday tasks—the means by which one maintains a sense of worth or value—seems forever lost in depression. The emotion of sadness can become so pervasive, so compelling, that it eclipses any consideration of past achievement or success. Like Percy Knauth, the depressed person may wrestle constantly with punitive thoughts and self-accusations. He or she may magnify minor failings or transgressions, experience excessive guilt and feel that some terrible punishment is deserved. The person may actually believe that he does not deserve to be helped:

> The power that overcame me did so with a peculiar thoroughness. It was unknowable and untouchable and it worked by robbing me of all self-esteem. Every horrible feeling that had ever been buried inside my psyche now surfaced and distilled into a self-image of pure loathing. I was worthless, and any momentary energies I would occasionally muster and that might have enabled me to seek help were twisted by this power into relentless thoughts of self-destruction.

The sense of worthlessness and guilt may reach delusional proportions. A person in a psychotic depression may be convinced that he is being persecuted and is to be held accountable for some imagined wrongdoing, or that a life-threatening disease is wracking his body when all the evidence is to the contrary. These delusional ideas are held with absolute and unshakable conviction—virtually all efforts to convince a person of their unreality are unsuccessful.

Some patients may experience what are called *nihilistic delusions*—they are convinced that the world is going to end by Armageddon or holocaust. These delusions reflect the patient's overwhelming sense of helplessness and hopelessness. Hallucinations, especially of voices, may also be present in these psychotic depressions. They are usually related to the content of the particular delusion. For instance, if the delusion is one of being persecuted, the voices are usually berating or derogatory and blaming. If the delusion is nihilistic, the voice or voices may threaten doom and destruction.

Clearly, there are a host of terrible symptoms that can be manifested during a depressive episode, but most subside as the episode remits. However, the illness is not over when the symptoms clear. A person's confidence in himself, his relationships and his future may be shaken seriously by the experience, his career or job advancement may have been jeopardized, and he may have resorted to alcohol or drugs to help numb the unbearable feelings. He may recover only to find that he is now dependent on these substances. In the worst of all possible scenarios, the person may not survive the depression. The appalling feelings of hopelessness and worthlessness can lead to suicidal thoughts or actions. He or she may become obsessed with finding a way out of the misery. Van Wyck Brooks, in his book also called *A Season in Hell,* describes it thus:

> I had always been possessed by this idea or that, usually the notion of the book I happened to be writing, which I pursued like a beagle with his nose to the ground; and I was possessed now with a fantasy of suicide that filled my mind as the full moon fills the sky. It was a fixed idea. I could not expel this fantasy that shimmered in my brain and I saw every knife as something with which to cut one's throat and every high building as something to jump from. A belt was a garotte for me, a rope existed to hang oneself with, the top of the door was merely a bracket for the rope, every rusty musket had its predestined use for me. . . .

Approximately 15 percent of untreated or inadequately treated patients with an affective disorder commit suicide. (Paradoxically, many complete the plans just as the depression is lifting and they become more energized and active.)

In the following passage from Patricia Bosworth's superb biography of the photographer Diane Arbus, Diane's mother, Gertrude Nemerov, recalls her own depression and the one that caused her daughter to end her life:

> All I know is that I had everything in life that a woman wants and I was miserable. I didn't know why. I simply could not communicate with my family. I felt my husband and my children didn't love me and I couldn't love them. I stopped functioning. I was like a zombie. My friend May Miller had to take me shopping and help me try on clothes. I wasn't able to take them off the hangers I felt so weak.
>
> That night I remember putting on my prettiest evening gown and we went up to the dining room. I forced myself to laugh and act as if I was having a marvelous time—inside I was absolutely choked. Panicked. *Because I could not define my depression. . . .*
>
> . . . I felt no better and remained depressed the entire summer and into the fall. Then slowly, very slowly, I came out of it. I don't quite know how. A year went by and I was all right again. I was exhausted. I felt as if I'd recovered from a hideous disease and had finally healed.
>
> I tell you this because Diane, I think, was concerned for me; she observed me during those painful months. We never talked about what was troubling me, of course, but years later when she contracted hepatitis and had to go into the hospital, she fell into a ghastly, unending depression that went on for three years—until her death. Periodically she would call me on the phone in Florida and cry, "Mommy—Mommy—tell me the story of your depression and how you got over it." And although I had no real answer—no solution—I would repeat my story and it seemed to reassure her. That if I had gotten well, so could she. . . .

WHAT DOES IT FEEL LIKE TO BE MANIC?

A person experiencing hypomania, or the first stage of a manic episode, feels imbued with energy, optimism and self-confidence. Ideas and conversation flow easily and the mood is euphoric, expansive and often infectious. One woman explained that she felt a "kinship with the effervescence of Dom Perignon." People who are hypomanic seem enthralled with themselves and the universe; they are captivated by their own sense of power and virtuosity. Many people describe feelings of being reborn—as if they are for the first time recognizing their true potential. As one individual put it:

> I experienced a sudden feeling of creative release before my illness, was convinced that I was rapidly attaining the height of my intellectual powers, and that for the first time in my life, I would be able to function up to the level of my ability in this direction. . . . I also had a sense of discovery, creative excitement, and intense, at times mystical inspiration in intervals where there was relief from fear. . . . My capacities for aesthetic appreciation and heightened sensory receptiveness, for vivid grasp of the qualities of living, and for imaginative empathy were very keen at this time. . . .

In the manic state a person is caught up with the ideas that pour into his mind. Association after association occurs to him, and his speech can be full of jokes, plays on words and amusing irrelevancies. The following poem, written in a few moments by a woman while in a hypomanic state, illustrates the punning and infectious humor:

God Is a Herbivore

Thyme passes, mixed with long grasses of herbs in the field.
Rosemary weeps into meadow sweeps
While curry is favored by the sun in its heaven.
The glinting scythe cuts the mustard twice
And the sage is ignored on its rock near the shore.
Hash is itself—high by being.
The law says shallots shall not—so they shan't.
  But . . .
The coriander meanders, the cumin seeds come
While a saffron canary eats juniper berry
Ignoring the open sesame seeds on the ground.

Sometimes a person in a manic state chooses words not because they are logical, but because they sound alike or rhyme. These kinds of associations are called clang associations. The eighteenth-century

English poet Christopher Smart wrote his poem "Jubilate Agno" ("Rejoice in the Lamb") while manic and in an insane asylum. A section of it reads:

> For the instruments are by their rhimes,
> For the shawm rhimes are lawn fawn and the like.
> For the shawm rhimes are moon boon and the like
> For the harp rhimes are sing ring and the like
> For the harp rhimes are ring string and the like.
> For the cymbal rhimes are bell well and the like.
> For the cymbal rhimes are toll soul and the like.

Speech during a manic episode is very striking. There is a push of words, they are spoken rapidly, and the voice is loud and intense. There is an insistent, nonstoppable quality to it—it brooks no interruption from others—and is called *pressure of speech*. During the more muted hypomanic state, the enthusiasm and intensity conveyed can be compelling and even engaging to others. But eventually the conversation comes undone. As the hypomanic state escalates closer to mania, the person's thoughts begin to race, and he leaps from topic to topic. He cannot complete one thought before another grabs his attention. The rules of logic that would normally govern a person's verbal production are unhinged in the manic state and there is a scattershot quality to the phrases. This *flight of ideas,* as it is called, is described by one patient thus:

> My trouble is that I've got too many thoughts. You might think about something, let's say that ashtray, and just think, oh! yes, that's for putting my cigarette in, but I would think of it and then I would think of a dozen different things connected with it at the same time.

Another patient explained it this way:

> My thoughts get all jumbled up. I start thinking or talking about something but I never get there. Instead I wander off in the wrong direction and get caught up with all sorts of different things that may be connected with the things I want to say but in a way I can't explain. People listening to me get more lost than I do.

Speech is not the only thing that revs up in the manic state. There is a great increase in activity, an urge to get going. A person may pace up and down, move about constantly or plan sudden, exotic trips. There is a decreased need for sleep, and the individual may go to bed for only short periods of time and awaken full of energy, or go for days with no rest at all. Ernest Hemingway once went through a forty-two-day period where he slept only two-and-a-half hours a night.

Appetite may be increased, and frequently the taste is for bizarre things, as this patient reveals:

I have often in manic states eaten ordinary cabbage leaves or new brussels sprouts picked straight off the plants with such relish that they appeared to me the greatest delicacies—a kind of manna from Heaven. Even common grass tastes excellent, while real delicacies like strawberries or raspberries give ecstatic sensations appropriate to a veritable food for the gods.

Many patients speak of a heightening of all the senses, especially the way they perceive colors and light:

The first thing I note is the peculiar appearances of the lights— the ordinary electric lights in the ward. They are not exactly brighter, but deeper, more intense, perhaps a trifle more ruddy than usual. Moreover, if I relax the focusing of my eyes, which I can do very much more easily than in normal circumstances, a bright star-like phenomenon emanates from the lights, ultimately forming a maze of iridescent patterns of all colours of the rainbow, which reminds me vaguely of the Aurora Borealis. . . . Connected with these vivid impressions is a rather curious feeling behind the eyeballs, rather as though a vast electric motor were pulsing away there.

This patient also describes a sensation that often occurs early in a manic phase: a kind of oceanic feeling, a desire to merge or be at one with the universe:

One night I woke up and started feeling good again. I felt I could do more with my time, that anything was possible. I felt alive and vital, full of energy. My senses seemed alive, colors were very bright, they hit me harder. Things appeared clear-cut, I noticed things I had never noticed before. There was a feeling of exhilaration, a sense of union with the whole world.

Time slowed down, much more experience could be crowded into a brief time span. Sexually I felt awakened, competent, responsive. I seemed to notice symmetry and harmony, and I wanted to experience everything. I could concentrate on a speck of something and just stare at it. A whole new world opened up, and I felt more secure than ever before. . . .

One patient noted that she loved "the sunrise, the sunsets, people, life"; another said he felt like hugging people he passed in the street. There is a compelling desire to be involved and interact with people and the environment. Often this mood prompts the person to call friends at all hours of the night and regale them with details of the new and exciting projects he is planning. The poet Robert Lowell wrote to the Nobel laureate T. S. Eliot after a manic episode:

I want to apologize to you for plaguing you with so many telephone calls last November and December. When the 'enthusiasm' is coming on me it is accompanied by a feverish reaching to my friends. . . .

Accompanying this increased sociability is an increased sexual drive (hypersexuality). It is not uncommon for the person to "fall in love" and impetuously pursue a love affair or a string of affairs, possibly jeopardizing an established relationship or marriage.

During these periods of manic elation, people are suffused with a sense of specialness and purpose. They are so overly optimistic and their mission is so compelling that they lose the sense that their actions have consequences. For them, there is no day of reckoning. Buying sprees are a common feature of manic episodes, and it is not unusual for the person to go out and purchase outlandish things. One respected businessman left his office in Hong Kong one afternoon, went shopping and wrote a purchase order for four hundred rickshas. Months later they arrived at a New York port, and he couldn't fathom what had possessed him to buy them. A young woman from Chicago wrote to us that in one week she bought $27,000 worth of clothes and furs. After spending her money, she decided to organize things at work. "I ordered a $100,000 computer that we didn't need and couldn't afford," she revealed. "One day I decided our firm needed a little more space, so I decided to buy the Xerox building."

Unfortunately, the upbeat, indefatigable quality of the mood cannot be maintained. Within minutes the euphoria can dissolve into irritability and anger. During such periods a person might talk exuberantly and outline all his current plans and thoughts. The listener may be fixed in rapt attention, unprepared for the sudden shift of tone and intention. Abruptly, and without provocation, the mood may turn irritable or hostile. The patient can become belligerent and suspicious, and launch into an angry and effusive tirade.

These dramatic shifts of mood and behavior, termed *labile affect,* are characteristic of the manic state and often leave others perplexed and baffled. If the hostile outburst is directed toward the listener (as it usually is), he or she may experience this symptomatic behavior as a personal attack, become alienated and withdraw.

A telling account of one man's switch from depression into mania is presented in *Mood Disorders: Toward a New Psychobiology* by Drs. Peter Whybrow, Hagop Akiskal and William McKinney. Here, a young man chronicles the characteristic lability of mood as well as the changes in perception and thinking that occur in these states:

> It was in the spring that I first began to be plagued by sleeplessness for which I sought medical advice and was given at various times Elavil and Librium (I think). I was drinking, not heavily but steadily, both socially and in order to help the sleeping problem. It also served to break the boredom of my job. For the first time I felt it was becoming unmanageable. I disliked the sycophancy demanded of the workers—disliked is not strong enough here—I despised any expression of authority, whether it applied to me or not. I was becoming angry over little things, feeling I could run the place better, more efficiently, more humanely. Everything seemed static, futile, even though I was earning a reasonable wage and intended to leave for Europe within weeks.
>
> Retrospectively I suspect I was a little depressed. I know I was anxious about not sleeping, as I kept telling people about it, wanting to acquaint them with my difficulties. Then during

the week or two before departing for Europe, my mood lightened quite suddenly. Things seemed almost humorous at the office and my colleagues like so many robots. I believe I was increasingly anxious to get everything under way, growing tense waiting to be in Europe and relying on more than the prescribed dose of Elavil in order to gain some calm. One evening after having only two glasses of beer (I remember the amount precisely), I sat on the corner of a street downtown and found myself laughing and crying simultaneously. I was struck by the ludicrous nature of the simple actions performed by other people: looking both ways before crossing the road, for instance. People tended to ignore me, and this made the entire situation all the more comical. I began to feel a great sense of energy and a wish to move. I began to defy the traffic, running in and out (I had a sense of fear, but also power which seemed to allow me to take enormous risks). The whole street seemed brilliantly lit, as though from an arc lamp, and I felt wonderful and yelled epithets at the motorists, who stopped and screamed at me.

Also my increased strength was not imaginary. After I got back to my apartment, I smashed down the kitchen door, although it was locked and although I had the keys with me. I simply kept butting it with my shoulder until I tore it from its hinges. I didn't sleep much, if at all, that night, feeling a great pressure and a sense of elation. I decided to leave for Europe immediately rather than in a week's time as planned and indeed did so only two days later.

The laughing episode did not return, but I went to Europe with a good deal of energy and buoyancy. I was not there long (a week or two) when I became irascible and difficult to live with. (I had met a girl on the plane and we were touring together.) I felt that she didn't appreciate me, either for my sexual prowess or for my wit. Anyway, I felt I had an idea for a novel and it was imperative for me to return home to line up a publisher.

I think I remember these episodes in retrospect with more coherence than they had at the time. Some things are just lost. I remember being shocked later, for example, how much money I had spent, even though my stay in Europe had been but a few days. On my return I was trying to write, something I had always wanted to do.

The work I produced was appalling, however—fragmented, no discipline, sporadic, and uneven. I felt "other worldly" and under pressure, aware that something must give but convinced I was a genius. There were also short periods of calm, an overwhelming sense of euphoria that was rather nice really, almost mystical. But my emotions weren't all happy, they seemed to fluctuate tremendously: self pity, hatred (I was probably capable of doing physical injury), a diffuse and general love, abject helplessness, hopelessness, and guilt. These last three began to predominate, even though for a time it seemed that whenever I hit a record "low" some bright and incredible idea came to offer hope temporarily. But decline from each of these plateaus left me deeper in despair, with less capacity to halt the downward trend even temporarily. My inability to confront people reached a pitch. There was a sinking of all my faculties.

Most people who have the disorder experience the mood and behavioral changes we have been describing. Some, however, proceed so far as to become psychotic. Those that do may experience paranoia, hear voices or see visions, as well as express bizarre or delusional thinking sometimes considered to belong to the realm of schizophrenia alone. (Indeed, even today, patients seen at this stage of mania are often misdiagnosed as schizophrenic. The difficult diagnostic distinction between these two disorders is explored in the next chapter.)

Some manic patients suffer grandiose delusions: they may become convinced that some special force has empowered them to save the world from catastrophe, or that they have a special relationship to God or some national or international figure. Others exhibit more paranoid features and feel that they are being watched, controlled, persecuted or attacked. A man who loaded his family into a car and raced through several states to warn the Commissioners of Public Works that the Communists were poisoning the reservoirs was experiencing a delusion that was both paranoid and grandiose: America was being attacked; only he could save the country from disaster.

The following account illustrates the evolution of a paranoid psychotic state. The patient scans the environment as if everything relates to him alone. As the ordinary constraints of logic dissolve, sounds, objects and conversations take on a multitude of hidden meanings:

> I got up at 7 A.M., dressed, and drove to the hospital. I felt my breathing trouble might be due to an old heart lesion. I had been told when I was young that I had a small ventricular septal defect. I decided that I was in heart failure and that people felt I wasn't strong enough to accept this, so they weren't telling me. I thought about all the things that had happened recently and could be interpreted in that light. I looked up heart failure in a textbook and found that the section had been removed, so I concluded that someone had removed it to protect me. I remembered other comments. A friend had talked about a "walkie talkie," and the thought occurred to me that I might be getting medicine without my knowledge, perhaps by radio. I remembered someone talking about a one-way plane ticket; to me that meant a trip to Houston and a heart operation. I remembered an unusual smell in the lab and thought that may be due to the medicine they were giving me in secret. I began to think that I might have a machine inside of me which secreted medicine into my bloodstream. Again I reasoned that I had a disease that no one could tell me about and was getting medicine for it secretly. At this point I panicked and tried to run away, but the attendant in the parking lot seemed to be making a sign to motion me back. I thought I caught brief glimpses of a friend and my wife so I decided to go back into the hospital. A custodian's eyes attracted my attention; they were especially large and piercing. He looked very powerful. He seemed to be "in on it," maybe he was giving medicine in some way. Then I began to have the feeling that other people were watching me. And, as periodically happened throughout the early stages, I said to myself the whole thing was absurd, but when I looked again the people really were watching me.

Another hallmark of psychosis, auditory hallucinations, is a not uncommon experience in severe mania or in psychotic depressions. The voices are experienced as real, and often have extraordinary influence over the individual. They may be heard only occasionally or continuously during an episode. There may be one voice or even several that carry on a conversation. The manic person may simply overhear the voices, or the voices may make direct statements to him. For instance, they may inform him of some dire consequences of his behavior or thoughts, or command allegiance or some action. Often the directive will be in concert with a delusional idea, as in the case of the patient who believed that the Communists were poisoning the water supplies. In his case, the voices gave him his itinerary by telling him which Commissioners of which states to approach and convincing him of the need for his intervention.

In the majority of cases the voices are disturbing, accusatory or derogatory, although at times the voices may be pleasant or even humorous:

> At first I'd had to strain to hear or understand them. They were soft and working with some pretty tricky codes. Snap-crackle-pops, the sound of the wind with blinking lights and horns for punctuation. I broke the code and somehow was able to internalize it to the point where it was just like hearing words. In the beginning it seemed mostly nonsense, but as things went along they made more and more sense. Once you hear the voices you realize that they have always been there. It's just a matter of being tuned to them.
>
> The voices weren't much fun in the beginning. Part of it was simply my being uncomfortable about hearing voices no matter what they had to say, but the early voices were mostly bearers of bad news. Besides they didn't seem to like me much and there was no way I could talk back to them. Those were very one-sided conversations.
>
> But later the voices could be very pleasant. They'd often be the voice of someone I loved, and even if they weren't, I could talk too, asking questions about this or that and getting reasonable answers. There were very important messages that had to get through somehow. More orthodox channels like the phone and mail had broken down.

Every day, millions of people throughout the world experience these signs and symptoms of mania and depression. Recently, some alarming findings were reported by the National Institute of Mental Health. Apparently depression of all kinds has been found to be increasing in incidence among the age group, or cohort, born since 1940. More people are getting depressed and at a much younger age. Attempts to explain this so-called "cohort phenomenon" range from the effects of urbanization to the radical shifts in traditional male and female roles, but there are no definitive answers yet. Researchers admit being baffled and concerned.

However sobering these statistics may be, there is still much cause for optimism. Today, a person no longer has to be overwhelmed by the symptoms and the social problems that arise from depression and manic-depression. Acute episodes can be attenuated and lithium and antidepressant drugs prevent or moderate the recurrence of the episodes. Other drugs offer new hope to those who do not respond to lithium, and psychotherapy can help a patient contend with the illness and the confusion and terrible feelings it engenders.

Accurate diagnosis is the starting point for the treatment of all illness, and the 1980s have seen the development of reliable diagnostic systems for mood disorders that ensure more specific treatment and more focused research. It is to this that we turn next.

2

DIAGNOSING
THE DISORDERS

If a person has a persistent cough with an accompanying fever, he or she will very likely see a doctor. The physician listens to the lungs with a stethoscope and, if crackling sounds at the base of the chest are detected, orders a chest X-ray. Should a shadow appear on the film, the doctor can order a sputum culture and often establish the precise organism that is producing the pneumonia. Moreover, the culture determines which antibiotic is prescribed. Equipment, lab tests, X-rays and tangible points of reference that can be seen and measured are the building blocks upon which a diagnosis is made in most areas of medicine.

This is generally not the case with psychiatric disorders. There are no lab tests that undeniably pinpoint a diagnosis, symptoms of many disorders overlap, and each person experiencing an illness expresses it through the unique filter of mind and personality. The patient's report of symptoms, observable behavior, the clinical course of the disorder and family history are the main instruments the psychiatrist has. And they are more subjective than objective. Yet it is vital to the patient's well-being that the correct diagnosis be made, since the proper diagnosis guides the treatment, provides the patient and family members with an informed idea of outcome and facilitates professional communication and research efforts.

HISTORICAL ATTEMPTS AT DIAGNOSIS

Although the written description of mood disorders dates back forty centuries to Pharaonic Egypt, it is only very recently that we've had a reliable, structured diagnostic system.

The diagnosis of mental disorders has been a problem historically. Since there were no scientific treatments, and no understanding of the causes, the physicians who attempted to deal with them were up against a host of handicaps. With very little to go on, and few treatments in all of medicine, the same treatments were applied to the array of mental problems. Although attempts were made to classify the illnesses, the lack of effective treatments made diagnosis rather academic.

In the 1950s, however, the discovery of antimanic and antidepressant medications galvanized the psychiatric community. "The right medication for the right patient" became the admirable and exciting mission, but the lack of an objective system for describing and grouping these patients was all too apparent. Psychiatry looked to a medical model, and the paterfamilias of this view was a German physician who lived and wrote in the late nineteenth and early twentieth centuries, Emil Kraepelin.

Kraepelin spent countless hours with the mentally ill, carefully noting their symptoms and the course of their illnesses. He felt that proper classification, diagnosis and prognosis were extremely important, and he began to focus his attention on two groups of patients. Those who had symptoms of euphoria and an excess of energy at times, followed by periods of depression and a lack of energy, and who tended to recover, he labeled as having manic-depressive insanity. Those who exhibited bizarre symptoms such as hallucinations and delusions and who tended to become ill earlier in life and follow a deteriorating course, he labeled as having dementia praecox (or precocious dementia, to separate it from senility). Later this illness concept was renamed schizophrenia and broadened by Eugen Bleuler.

Kraepelin organized his clinical data and psychiatric observation in his very successful textbook *Psychiatrie: Ein Lehrbuch für Studierende und Aertze*. He laid the foundations for modern psychiatry by meticulously describing the symptoms of mental illness, chronicling case histories and emphasizing the *course of illness* as a major distinction between dementia praecox and manic-depressive illness.

In the 1950s and 1960s, amid the vast changes taking place in psychiatric thought and delivery of care, a group at Washington University in St. Louis picked up the Kraepelinian mantle and began again to focus on diagnosis, rigorous classification and the biological underpinnings to mental disorders. Although Sigmund Freud himself had felt that psychiatry would become more biological in the future, his psychodynamic approach to the mind had been dominant in the United States since the 1930s. The St. Louis group—led by Eli Robins, Samuel Guze and George Winokur—began to push for a diagnostic framework for psychiatry that was squarely within a medical model and that concentrated its efforts on a distinct classification system based on objective criteria. The more that psychiatric research could accomplish, and the more data that could be generated thanks to new techniques in neuroscience, the more vital it became that a psychiatrist in California who cited a case of manic-depressive illness or schizophrenia be understood by a colleague in West Virginia or West Germany.

But this was not the case. Two international studies whose results were made public during the 1970s—the International Pilot Study of Schizophrenia (the IPSS) and the US–UK Study—identified the lack of consensus about diagnosis within the profession. The IPSS was spearheaded by some British psychiatrists who wanted to study the symptoms of schizophrenia in different countries. They used standardized interviewing and evaluating methods and diagnosed patients in the United States, England, Taiwan, Colombia, the USSR, and other countries. Eventually it became clear that the physicians in the Soviet Union and the United States diagnosed schizophrenia more often than those in any of the other countries.

The American psychiatric profession received an even sharper view of its diagnostic tendencies when Drs. Robert Kendell and John Cooper and several other British psychiatrists designed the US–UK Study to compare the diagnostic practices of American psychiatrists to those of the British. They videotaped diagnostic interviews with eight patients and then showed the tapes to psychiatrists throughout the British Isles and to psychiatrists from east coast cities in the United States. There were glaring differences in the diagnostic practices of the two groups: again the American psychiatrists saw schizophrenia in the majority of the cases, whereas the British psychiatrists diagnosed personality or affective disorders.

This American tendency to be overgenerous with the schizophrenic label was a noticeable and knotty problem, and the "neoKraepelinians" of the St. Louis group decided to attack it head on. Under the direction of John Feighner, they developed a standardized set of definitions for fourteen psychiatric illnesses and specified which symptoms and how many of them had to be present in order to make a particular diagnosis. These became known as the Feighner or "St. Louis" criteria, and as more research groups and clinicians began to see the logic of the idea and employ its methods, the American Psychiatric Association (APA) decided to overhaul its *Diagnostic and Statistical Manual* (one edition had been published in 1952 and a second in 1968). In June 1974, the APA appointed a task force under the leadership of Dr. Robert Spitzer of New York, and work began on what was to become known as the DSM–III.

The people involved had their work cut out for them. They set out to develop a classification system that would reflect the current state of knowledge about mental disorders, maximize its usefulness for both clinical practice and research studies and ensure that the new nomenclature was as compatible as possible with the ICD–9— the ninth version of the *International Classification of Diseases, Injuries and Causes of Death* developed by the World Health Organization.

There were meetings, hundreds of memos, telephone conversations and more than one hundred advisors; there were drafts and revisions of drafts. At a special convention, scores of experts from the biological, psychoanalytic and behavioral schools of thought gave speeches and made their points about the definitions and diagnosis of mental disorders. Feelings ran hot and high as the arguments continued. But six years after the APA task force appointments, and after more than eight hundred clinical psychiatrists field tested the material in 212 psychiatric facilities with over twelve thousand patients, the APA published the DSM–III. So many copies were sold in the first year, 1980, that it was the best selling nonfiction book after the Bible and the *Fannie Farmer Cookbook*. The demand caught the APA by surprise, but it powerfully emphasized the need for the DSM–III within the psychiatric community.

A BRIEF LOOK AT THE DSM–IIIR

The DSM–III is not a catechism; it is a tentative working system of classification that is intended to undergo change and refinement as it keeps pace with the new developments in psychiatry. Because the scientific underpinnings of psychiatric diagnosis are far from complete, DSM–III's contents were sometimes pushed by the winds of politics and personalities; still, its debut was groundbreaking and impressive. In its 494 pages it brought clarity and order to some 187 disorders, and it not only defines the disorders, but, taking its cue from the Feighner criteria, it also provides inclusion and exclusion criteria that enhance diagnostic agreement among clinicians. (Because the DSM–I and II and the ICD–9 had not provided such precise guidelines, the doctor was left to his own resources when it came to defining the content and boundaries of the diagnostic categories.) A revised edition of the DSM–III (dubbed the DSM–IIIR) was published in May 1987, and the DSM–IV is projected for the early 1990s.

In the DSM–IIIR, Mood Disorders are divided into Depressive Disorders and Bipolar Disorders. There are four criteria that must be met before the diagnosis of a major depressive episode can be made. (Our comments appear in italic.)

Diagnostic Criteria for Major Depressive Episode

NOTE: A "Major Depressive Syndrome" is defined as criterion A below.

A. At least five of the following symptoms have been present nearly every day during the same two-week period and represent a change from previous functioning; at least one of the symptoms is either (1) depressed mood, or (2) loss of interest or pleasure:
   1. Depressed or irritable mood most of the day
   2. Markedly diminished interest or pleasure in all, or almost all, activities most of the day
   3. Significant weight loss when not dieting or weight gain, or decrease or increase in appetite (in children, consider failure to make expected weight gains)
   4. Insomnia or hypersomnia [*sleeping excessively*]
   5. Psychomotor agitation or retardation
   6. Fatigue or loss of energy
   7. Feelings of worthlessness or excessive or inappropriate guilt (which may be delusional) and is not merely self-reproach or guilt about being sick
   8. Diminished ability to think or concentrate, or indecisiveness
   9. Recurrent thoughts of death (not just fear of dying), recur-

rent suicidal ideation without a specific plan, or a suicide attempt or a specific plan for committing suicide

B. 1. It cannot be established that an organic factor initiated and maintained the disturbance.

[*This criterion cautions the psychiatrist to rule out the possibility that the depressed mood is caused by some other illness or drug (see pages 32–33 and 130).*]

2. The disturbance is not a normal reaction to the death of a loved one (Uncomplicated Bereavement). NOTE: Morbid preoccupation with worthlessness, suicidal ideation, marked functional impairment or psychomotor retardation, or prolonged duration suggests bereavement complicated by Major Depression.

C. At no time during the disturbance have there been delusions or hallucinations for as long as two weeks in the absence of prominent mood symptoms (i.e., before the mood symptoms developed or after they have remitted).

[*Criterion C helps distinguish depression from schizophrenia. Sometimes people who are severely depressed have psychotic symptoms—they suffer hallucinations and delusions. This criterion, then, helps distinguish a psychotic depression from schizophrenia because it says that the patient who is depressed does not hear voices or hold firm to untrue beliefs when the episode of depression has passed, and that he or she was not troubled by these symptoms before the episode started. People who suffer from schizophrenia are often troubled by these kinds of symptoms and often exhibit bizarre behavior before episodes of acute illness and afterwards as the acute episode remits.*]

D. Not superimposed on Schizophrenia, Schizophreniform Disorder, Delusional Disorder, or Psychotic Disorder.

[*This criterion states that a person cannot suffer from both depression and schizophrenia.*]

Diagnostic Criteria for Manic Episode

NOTE: A "Manic Syndrome" is defined as including criteria A, B, and C below. A "Hypomanic Syndrome" is defined as including criteria A and B, but not C, i.e., no marked impairment.

A. A distinct period of abnormally and persistently elevated, expansive, or irritable mood.

B. During the period of mood disturbance, at least three of the following symptoms have persisted (four if the mood is only irritable) and have been present to a significant degree:

  1. Inflated self-esteem or grandiosity
  2. Decreased need for sleep, e.g., feels rested after only three hours of sleep
  3. More talkative than usual or pressure to keep talking
  4. Flight of ideas or subjective experience that thoughts are racing
  5. Distractibility, i.e., attention too easily drawn to unimportant or irrelevant external stimuli
  6. Increase in goal-directed activity (either socially, at work or school, or sexually) or psychomotor agitation
  7. Excessive involvement in pleasurable activities which have a high potential for painful consequences, e.g., the person engages in unrestrained buying sprees, sexual indiscretions, or foolish business investments

C. Mood disturbance sufficiently severe to cause marked impairment in occupational functioning or in unusual social activities or relationships with others, or to necessitate hospitalization to prevent harm to self or others.

D. At no time during the disturbance have there been delusions or hallucinations for as long as two weeks in the absence of prominent mood symptoms (i.e., before the mood symptoms developed or after they have remitted).

[*Criterion D helps distinguish between a manic episode and schizophrenia. Patients in a manic state may act bizarrely and suffer delusions and hallucinations, but once the manic episode passes, these symptoms disappear. Schizophrenic patients, on the other hand, may be preoccupied with delusional thoughts before and after an acute episode of illness.*]

E. Not superimposed on Schizophrenia, Schizophreniform Disorder, Delusional Disorder, or Psychotic Disorder.

[*This criterion states that a person cannot be diagnosed as having mania and schizophrenia at the same time.*]

F. It cannot be established that an organic factor initiated and maintained the disturbance.

[*Since a disorder such as temporal lobe epilepsy, drugs such as amphetamine, cocaine, and hallucinogens and steroids such as cortisone can cause symptoms that resemble mania, this criterion asks the psychiatrist to rule out the possibility that the manic mood is a result of another illness or a response to a drug.*]

As a number of the DSM–IIIR criteria caution, there are a variety of medical conditions that can mimic or masquerade as depression or mania. The following chart lists such conditions, which range from hormonal disorders and neurological syndromes to malignancies and diseases of the blood.

Hormonal and Metabolic Disorders

Hypothyroidism
Hyperthyroidism
Addison's disease
Cushing's disease
Wilson's disease
Diabetes
Hyperparathyroidism
Hypoglycemia

Infectious Diseases

Influenzas
Mononucleosis
Hepatitis
Viral pneumonias

Venereal Disease

Syphilis

Cancers

Pancreatic
Central nervous system tumors

Autoimmune Disease

Systemic lupus erythematosus

Neurological Disorders

Parkinson's disease
Dementia
Temporal lobe epilepsy
Multiple sclerosis
Huntington's chorea
Stroke

Blood Diseases

Iron deficiency anemia
Acute intermittent porphyria

Metal Intoxications

Thallium
Mercury

Almost all of these medical conditions can be ruled in or out by careful physical examination coupled with laboratory studies. Therefore, it is extremely important that the diagnosing physician take a careful patient and family medical history as well as request that the patient have a complete physical examination and routine blood tests. Thyroid function studies should be conducted also. Only then should a primary depressive or manic episode—one that is not secondary to or caused by a primary medical condition—be diagnosed.

SCHIZOPHRENIA, MANIA AND SCHIZOAFFECTIVE
DISORDER: THE LACK OF CERTAINTY

DSM–III helped remove much confusion from the field of psychiatry, but it didn't clear up all diagnostic dilemmas. Even with the more rigorous criteria, there is still controversy about the diagnosis of patients who have psychotic symptoms. Are they schizophrenic, are they manic, do they have a severe depression with psychotic symptoms, or is their condition better described by the term *schizoaffective*—a hybrid category that overlaps the criteria for schizophrenia and mood disorders?

As mentioned earlier, Kraepelin drew boundaries between manic-depressive psychosis and dementia praecox and emphasized the difference in the *course* of the illnesses as well as their form. In 1911, Eugen Bleuler, the Swiss physician, rechristened dementia praecox as schizophrenia and focused on its *symptoms*. He described a concept of schizophrenia with very elastic boundaries—so elastic, in fact, that they stretched to encompass a large portion of patients that Kraepelin would have called manic-depressive. Bleuler believed that schizophrenia was characterized by a disorder of the thought processes. Manic-depressive illness, on the other hand, was characterized by problems in mood.

In 1960 the German psychiatrist Kurt Schneider composed a list of symptoms that he felt strongly suggested a diagnosis of schizophrenia. He termed them "first-rank" symptoms, and they included auditory hallucinations, hallucinations of touch, the feeling that thoughts are being inserted into one's mind or that one's thoughts are being broadcast and the feeling that all of one's actions are under the control of others. It became diagnostic tradition to assume that even short-lasting delusional, bizarre and psychotic thinking established one firmly as a schizophrenic.

But is this so? Gabrielle Carlson and Frederick Goodwin of the National Institute of Mental Health reported in 1973 that there seemed to be three stages of mania. In the third, and most extreme, stage the patients experienced hallucinations, bizarre beliefs and paranoia. Drs. Carlson and Goodwin felt that the patients would have been diagnosed as schizophrenic if they hadn't appeared clearly manic both earlier in the course and later as the episode was resolving.

Dr. Harrison Pope of Harvard Medical School's McLean Hospital in Belmont, Massachusetts, reviewed twenty studies that showed that the so-called schizophrenic symptoms (including visual and auditory hallucinations, thought broadcasting and experience of influence) occur among 20 to 50 percent of patients with well-validated cases of manic-depressive illness. "The evidence," he writes, "suggests that the presence of cross-sectional 'schizophrenic' symptoms is of little differential diagnostic value. Such symptoms merely establish that the patient is psychotic, and are of little help in distinguishing whether the patient has manic-depressive illness or schizophrenia."

Dr. Pope and Dr. Joseph Lipinski teamed in 1977 to write what has become a seminal article in the psychiatric literature. Entitled "Diagnosis in Schizophrenia and Manic-Depressive Illness: A Reassessment of the Specificity of 'Schizophrenic' Symptoms in the Light of Current Research," it takes rigorous issue with the traditional concept that psychosis and schizophrenia are synonymous. Whereas Bleuler stated that a diagnosis of manic-depressive illness should be made only by elimination of the diagnosis of schizophrenia (thus directing doctors to look for schizophrenic symptoms first), Pope and Lipinski and a growing number of other thoughtful clinical investigators who share their point of view make the argument that schizophrenia should be diagnosed only after exclusion of manic-depressive illness. Their tack is that the symptoms are not as important as the family history, the patient's functioning before the onset of illness, the course of the disorder, the response to treatment and the eventual outcome. Since DSM–IIIR "schizophrenics" rarely respond to lithium, and approximately 70 percent of manic-depressives do, a trial of lithium would be a valuable test.

The family history is an important clue, however. Genetic data suggest a low familial cross-over between affective disorders and schizophrenia: the illnesses tend to breed true. Thus, if the family history reveals manic-depression, depression or alcoholism, it would appear highly unlikely that the patient is schizophrenic.

Schizophrenia is still overdiagnosed in young people. Historically the name dementia praecox—*early-occurring* dementia—emphasizes that schizophrenia affects people at a young age. This is true—three-quarters of all cases start in the sixteen to twenty-five age group. Although affective disorders typically occur later in life, major affective illnesses are being recognized in young adults, adolescents and even elementary school-aged children. Nevertheless, chances are that if a fifteen to nineteen year old entering the hospital for the first time is manic and acutely psychotic, it is likely that he will be diagnosed schizophrenic.

Dr. Peter Joyce conducted a study at the Sunnyside Hospital in New Zealand and found that although the *mean* age of first hospitalization with an affective syndrome was 30.8 years, the most *common* age of onset was fifteen to nineteen years and that over 70 percent of these young people received an initial diagnosis of schizophrenia.

But the problem is even more complicated. There are patients whose symptoms and poor response to lithium seem inconsistent with the diagnosis of bipolar illness. They seem to present a confusingly mixed group of symptoms that straddle the definitions of schizophrenia *and* mood disorders. For example, these patients' symptoms fulfill criteria for depression or mania but their hallucinations or delusions are not related to the disordered mood—they are "mood incongruent"—and thus are more characteristic of schizophrenia. Even after the resolution of the affective symptoms, these patients continue to have disturbances in thinking and perception.

The inadequate solution to this diagnostic problem has been the creation of a controversial intermediate disease category called *schizoaffective disorder*. The DSM–IIIR admits that its description of the disorder is not definitive but instructs psychiatrists to consider the category for "conditions that do not meet the criteria for either schizophrenia or a mood disorder, but that at one time have presented with both a schizophrenic and a mood disturbance, and, at another time, with psychotic symptoms but without mood symptoms." Some of the questions that fuel the controversy are: (1) Is schizoaffective disorder a variant of schizophrenia? (2) Is it a variant of affective disorders? (3) Is it a third independent psychosis, a transitional state between schizophrenia and affective psychosis? (4) Is it a combination (mixed form) of schizophrenia and affective psychosis? or (5) Is it a heterogeneous syndrome including different conditions?

Many psychiatrists would respond affirmatively to number 2—schizoaffective disorder is a variant of affective disorders. They reason that perhaps the patient is nonresponsive to lithium (or only partially responsive) and that a combination of lithium and an antipsychotic medication or lithium and the anticonvulsant medication carbamazepine treats this subtype of the affective illness and that maybe a drug will be found that will be more specific. The truth is that at present no one really knows for sure. No doubt scientific developments in the years ahead will bring some clarity to many of these diagnostic dilemmas.

SUBTYPES OF MOOD DISORDERS

This chapter has for the most part focused on the rather classical manifestations of the mood disorders, but there are several subtypes of the illness that have been identified and that need to be discussed. (Note: The medications mentioned in this section are thoroughly described in Chapter 5.)

Rapid Cycling

Patients who experience frequent and continuous recurrences of depression and mania are said to have a rare subtype of bipolar illness called *rapid cycling*. Drs. Ronald Fieve and David Dunner coined the term "rapid cyclers" and defined the subtype for those who have four or more episodes of illness in a one-year period.

The treatment of these patients is difficult. They often respond poorly to lithium, and the drugs used to treat depressive cycles may, in some cases, actually contribute to rapid cycling. The tricyclic antidepressants may flip a patient into mania and/or shorten the intervals between episodes. There have been anecdotal reports that monoamine oxidase (MAO) inhibitors and perhaps even lithium can do the same thing.

Carbamazepine (Tegretol), an anticonvulsant medication, may be a useful treatment approach, alone or in combination with lithium. Another anticonvulsant drug, sodium valproate (Depakene), is also being used to treat this condition. Electroconvulsive therapy (ECT) can be effective during either the manic or depressive swings.

Because an underactive thyroid can contribute to rapid cycling, thyroid function studies should be done, and thyroid supplementation considered as a treatment option.

Mixed States

Patients who simultaneously display significant symptoms of depression and mania are said to be in a *mixed state*. There are various theories as to the causes of the mixed state: one is that it is a transitional phase in which depression "switches" to mania and the patient becomes trapped in the switch state. This theory leaves much unexplained, but it is generally well accepted that patients who experience mixed states are more difficult to treat than those people who have manic episodes well separated from their depressive ones.

The following case history demonstrates a kind of mixed state:

F. L. was a sixty-year-old woman who came to the hospital with all the signs and symptoms of a psychotic, agitated depression. This was her fourth episode during the last twenty-one years. For two of the episodes she had received electroconvulsive therapy (ECT). For the third she had received an antidepressant medication and experienced improvement without remission. The remission finally occurred on its own a year later.

The present episode had begun with obsessive concerns about her invalid husband. She continually worried about mistakes she had made in her husband's diet and care and began to feel that death lurked everywhere. She became apprehensive, then agitated. She had trouble falling asleep and awoke early in the morning, her obsessive concerns whirling in her head. But throughout this typical melancholic picture ran another thread of delusional idea. On occasion she would experience an upsurge of exhilaration and energy. She would begin to sing religious songs and, if others were around, preach to them vigorously and intrusively. She would then smile beatifically saying that she was suffused with the love of God because she and Jesus were saving the world. But through it all her facial expression looked depressed and she was always on the verge of tears. Family history showed paternal uncles who were gamblers and alcoholics while she had two sisters who had experienced typical agitated depressions.

Three weeks of treatment in the hospital with the antidepressant that had finally worked in the earlier episode ended her agitation and apprehension, but her religious talk and depressive mood continued. In the out-patient clinic it was decided that she was suffering the effects of a mixed manic-depressive state and she was started on lithium. After two weeks she was in remission and has remained symptom-free on maintenance lithium alone for three years.

Although the patient might have been thought to have a unipolar "agitated depression" with psychotic features, the presence of manic symptoms in the midst of severe depressive symptoms is a clue to recognizing the mixed state. F. L.'s grandiose, radiant, beatific religious delusions were out of tune with the patient's misery. The correct diagnosis of a mixed state was extremely important because rather than receiving electroconvulsive therapy when the antidepressant, imipramine, failed, F. L. received lithium and improved rather rapidly.

Cyclothymia

A milder manifestation of manic-depressive illness is *cyclothymia*. People who receive this diagnosis experience short and irregular cycles of depression and hypomania. The episodes are not of sufficient duration or severity to qualify as a major affective disorder as the cycles typically last for days, not weeks. The cycles often begin in the teens or early childhood, and the problem may appear to be a personality disorder or hyperactivity. The mood states can change so frequently that patients often remark that they awaken with a distinctly different mood than they had the day before.

Dr. Hagop Akiskal, the director of the Affective Disorders Clinic of the University of Tennessee, and his colleagues feel that cyclothymia has a two-phased course and that people with the disorder have certain identifiable problems in their behavior and relationships. These are summarized as follows:

Two-Phased Course

1. There is an increased need for sleep alternating with decreased need for sleep (although intermittent insomnia can also occur).
2. The self-esteem is shaky. It can alternate from a lack of self-confidence to a naive or grandiose overconfidence.
3. There are periods of mental confusion and apathy, alternating with periods of sharpened and creative thinking.
4. There is a marked unevenness in quantity and quality of productivity, often associated with unusual working hours.

5. There is uninhibited people-seeking (which may lead to excessive sexuality) alternating with introverted self-absorption.

Typical Behaviors

1. Irritable-angry-explosive outbursts that alienate others
2. Episodic promiscuity; repeated failures of marriages or romances
3. Frequent changes in careers, academic pursuits and future plans
4. Alcohol and drug abuse as a means of self-treatment or augmenting excitement
5. Occasional financial extravagance

The family pedigree of people with cyclothymia is often "loaded" with all types of affective and "related" disorders, including depressive and manic-depressive illness, alcoholism and drug dependence and suicide.

Approximately 60 percent of the patients diagnosed with cyclothymia respond to lithium. However, much remains to be explored about this bipolar subtype and its treatment.

Chronic Depression

Although a majority of patients have major depressive episodes that are separated by periods of normal functioning, 15 to 20 percent of patients do not recover fully from any given episode and have symptoms of depression that persist for at least two years. They are said to have *chronic depression*. The painful symptoms of the acute episode fade into an emotional aridity and these patients live without any positive feelings. Their mood is low, they lack energy and their outlook on the future is generally bleak.

DSM–III defines *dysthymia* as a depression in which a person is bothered most or all of the time during a two-year period by a depressive syndrome or symptoms of depression that are not of sufficient severity or duration to meet the criteria for a major depressive episode. The DSM–IIIR excludes from this category patients whose chronic depressive symptoms were preceded by a major depression. It is thought that a significant number of Americans suffer from dysthymia, which can begin early in life or have a late onset.

Unfortunately, not a lot is known about the classification and treatment of these milder disorders. This is perhaps because the people who suffer them don't end up in emergency rooms or hospitals and are thus rarely the subjects of research. Also, many psychiatrists have not commonly viewed these long-term depressive syndromes as mood disorders but rather as personality disorders. Recently, investigators have begun to explore the use of antidepressants and different kinds of psychotherapies for these milder depressions. Such studies may lead to a better understanding of these disorders and further define their treatment.

Patients with *double depression* are those who go a full two years in a low-grade state of depression—the dysthymia mentioned above—but who then go on to have a major depressive episode. The period of time during which the major depressive episode is layered over the dysthymic symptoms is called double depression. Often the dysthymic symptoms continue even after the resolution of the major depressive episode, and there are high rates of relapse to recurrent major depressive episodes. In fact, the longer the patient remains chronically ill before recovering from the major depression, the greater the likelihood of relapse. For these reasons, patients with double depression should receive intensive treatment during and after recovery from the major depressive disorder.

There are severe deficiencies in our knowledge of how best to treat chronic depressions. More studies need to be conducted in order to assess the efficacy of antidepressants, lithium, electroconvulsive therapy and psychotherapy. One thing seems sadly certain: the patient who remains chronically depressed over time has a reduced chance of recovering.

SYNDROMES WITH FEATURES OF MOOD DISORDERS: ANOREXIA, BULIMIA AND OBSESSIVE-COMPULSIVE DISORDER

Researchers, in investigating the symptoms, genetic patterns, neuroendocrine disturbances and pharmacological responses of the eating disorders and obsessive-compulsive disorder, have found some similarities between them and the affective disorders. *Anorexia nervosa* is a disorder characterized by a disturbed body image, severe weight loss and an intense fear of becoming obese that does not diminish as the weight loss progresses. *Bulimia* is a disorder characterized by binge eating followed by attempts at purging the food consumed—either by vomiting or laxative abuse. Both illnesses are classified as eating disorders by DSM–IIIR, but there are many unknowns surrounding the classification. For instance, some researchers consider bulimia to be a symptom of anorexia rather than a separate illness, as bulimic behavior has been noted in 16 to 47 percent of patients who have anorexia.

A significant percentage of patients with anorexia nervosa and bulimia also have symptoms of depression. They describe dysphoric moods, low self-esteem, hopelessness, suicidal thoughts, and suffer from insomnia, weight loss, constipation and reduced libido. Several studies found that 35 to 75 percent of bulimic individuals had a diagnosis of affective disorder during the acute stage of the illness, and follow-up studies examining patients four to ten years after treatment found that approximately 44 percent were diagnosed as having an affective disorder. Data has also revealed that there is a higher rate of affective disorders in the first-degree relatives of patients with eating disorders than in those of normal controls.

Further evidence of the link between eating disorders and affective disorders is seen when certain laboratory tests—the dexamethasone suppression test (discussed on page 70) and the thyrotropin-releasing hormone test—are administered to anorectic and bulimic patients. These tests reveal a dysfunction in the neuroendocrine system in a significant number of patients with mood disorders and patients who have anorectic and bulimic features.

In the 1970s, investigators began to report some encouraging results when patients with anorexia and bulimia were treated with tricyclic antidepressants and MAO inhibitors, the medications used to treat depression. Today these drugs are known to be beneficial to some patients with anorexia, but even more so to patients with bulimia.

There is definitely evidence to suggest considerable overlap between the eating disorders and the affective disorders, but it is presently unclear whether eating disorders are a variant of mood disorders, or whether the symptoms of mood disturbance result from an eating disorder.

There may also be a relationship between mood disorders and *obsessive-compulsive disorder* (OCD). People suffering from this psychiatric illness have recurrent and intrusive thoughts that cause discomfort and anxiety and depression. The obsessive thoughts can be allayed only by some compulsive act. Anyone who locks up the house and goes back to make sure the stove is turned off so the house won't burn down has some idea what it's like to act compulsively on an obsessional thought. Most people can stop after the second check; the person with OCD, however, must repeat a compulsive action over and over, without knowing why and often with the understanding that it is senseless. Still, there is a sense of pressure and the anxiety is partially relieved by the action.

Many patients with OCD describe obsessions about dirt or contamination (of one's self or others), and it is not uncommon for their fear to have an element of disgust to it—often it is focused on urine, feces or semen. A great many patients describe handwashing or showering rituals in which they wash their hands over eighty times a day or spend hours attempting to shower themselves clean.

There are several links between OCD and depression. Many of the symptoms such as guilt, indecisiveness, low self-esteem, exhaustion and sleep and hormonal disturbances are common to both. Although OCD has traditionally been difficult to treat, the same class of drugs used to treat depression—the tricyclic antidepressants—has been found to reduce some of the obsessional symptoms. (A drug called chlorimipramine has been studied with good results but has not yet been approved for use in the United States.)

In the April 1986 issue of the *Journal of Clinical Psychiatry,* Drs. Steven Dilsaver and Kerrin White further bolstered the relationship between mood disorders and OCD when they reported on the family of a seventeen-year-old girl with affective disorder. Not only did three generations of the family have major affective disorders, but the girl and her two brothers exhibited obsessive-compulsive behavior during episodes. Interestingly, the seventeen year old and three of her cousins suffered from bulimia also, and she and quite a few of her relatives suffered from panic attacks. This pedigree implicates associations between bipolar disorder, bulimia, panic attacks and obsessive-compulsive disorder. The authors of the article suggest that such a pedigree study offers a potentially powerful method for determining whether there is an association between these various types of disorders.

3

THE SEARCH FOR
GENETIC MARKERS

As we mentioned at the opening of this book, rarely did a person speak of only one family member with depression or manic-depression. More often there were two or more relatives affected, as these illnesses tend to concentrate in families. Familial tendencies suggest a genetic transmission, but since genetic theories don't survive on hints and suggestions, intense scientific inquiry has lately been focused in this direction. The next few years should yield some heady things about the genetics of mood disorders, but right now researchers are looking for a gene and its location and a possible mode of transmission. And they are searching hard for a genetic marker that would identify those who are at risk.

Current research indicates only that the vulnerability to these disorders is "passed down" (inherited) in families—the way a physical illness such as diabetes shows up in a family pedigree. Family studies continue to show that the relatives of people who have manic-depression or depression have a significantly higher rate of these disorders—perhaps two to three times higher—than occurs in the general population. But how does a scientist disentangle the subtle strands of heredity from those of environmental influences? Is the problem one of nature or of nurture? To solve this puzzle the researchers turned to two classic investigative techniques in genetic research: twin studies and adoption studies.

Twins are particularly rich territory for the geneticist. Identical twins develop from a single fertilized egg and thus are genetic carbon copies of each other; fraternal twins develop in the womb together, but from two separate fertilized eggs (like any sibling pair, they share only 50 percent of their genes). If a trait is 100 percent genetically determined and one partner of an identical pair develops a disorder, then the other twin will develop it also. Their "concordance rate" or rate of similarity would be 100 percent. If, then, the concordance rate of identical twins is higher than the concordance rate of fraternal twins for the same disorder, researchers begin to assume that there is an underlying genetic component.

The results of seven twin studies conducted in the United States, England, Germany, Norway and Denmark pegged the combined concordance rates for identical twins with affective disorders at 76 percent and found that 19 percent of the fraternal twins were concordant for affective disorders. These results support the general case for a genetic factor in affective disorders, but they still fail to tease apart the skeins of heredity and environment. This is because nearly all of the twin pairs were raised together in the same homes and it is known that a twin's behavior has a major influence on his or her partner.

Adoption studies attempt to separate more precisely the influences of heredity and environment. A summary of all the reports in the psychiatric literature of identical twins raised apart from their partners revealed that eight of twelve pairs, or 67 percent, were concordant for unipolar and bipolar illness. This established that the intrapair concordance rate for twins raised apart was approximately the same as for twins reared together. Again the data attested to a genetic component. On the other hand, it also suggested that the disorder is not wholly genetic (approximately 33 percent of the identical twins were *not* concordant for the illness). Some environmental or social factors must interact in some way with the genetic trait.

A report published in 1977 by Drs. Julien Mendlewicz and John Rainer described a study they had conducted in Belgium. They looked at the biological and adopting parents of adopted adults who had been diagnosed as manic-depressive. They also examined three comparison groups: the parents of nonadopted adult manic-depressives, the biological and adoptive parents of normal adults and the biological parents of adults with polio. The parents of the patients with polio were included in order to determine whether or not a chronic disabling disorder in a child may induce depression in his parents.

Rainer and Mendlewicz found that there was a greater degree of affective illness in parents biologically related to the manic-depressive adoptees than in parents who adopted and raised these same individuals. Nature was indeed having its say over nurture, at least to a certain degree. This study bolstered previous research implicating genetic factors in bipolar illness, but that's about all that can be concluded from the "observed-from-the-outside" type of data that adoption and twin studies offer. More specific information will have to be coaxed from the genes themselves.

THE AMISH: A NATURAL LABORATORY
FOR THE STUDY OF AFFECTIVE DISORDERS

Another approach used to mine information about affective disorders is to examine multigenerational pedigrees of very large affected families. Dr. Janice Egeland of the University of Miami School of Medicine is conducting an important and imaginative study, here in this country, with the Old Order Amish of Lancaster County, Pennsylvania, a group of people who dress in plain clothes and live much as they did when they came to America in the eighteenth century. The Old Order Amish are an ultraconservative religious sect with many settlements throughout the United States. This project, now in its eleventh year, continues to reveal some intriguing things about affective disorders—both genetically and epidemiologically.

In many ways the Amish community provides a natural laboratory for all genetic research. They are a well-defined, closed population numbering some twelve thousand people, with little migration into or out of the community. They can trace their ancestry back to thirty progenitors, and they maintain extensive genealogic records. The community encourages a high birth rate, so a researcher can study large families. It is also important that this community prohibits the use of alcohol and drugs, substances known to complicate diagnostic assessment. Finally, the Amish were extremely cooperative with Dr. Egeland because of a long-standing, trusting relationship. Without a doubt this is an outstanding milieu in which to conduct an affective disorders study. (It should be noted that the Amish have no more mental illness than the rest of the population, but the social values mentioned above do make illnesses easier to diagnose.)

Dr. Egeland and her research staff began to look closely at several large, multigenerational families with a significant number of members who suffered from bipolar disorder. Originally they were looking to see if mood disorders tend to occur with other known genetic markers such as color blindness or certain blood types.

It is estimated that there are over 100,000 genes, but the locations of only about 1,500 are currently known. Researchers do know, however, where the genes for color blindness and certain blood types reside, and they assume that if the gene for an affective disorder is near one of the known genetic markers, the two traits would be inherited together. Studies of this kind are called linkage studies.

No linkage could be established in the preliminary Amish studies. The case could not be made that the gene for bipolar disorder traveled in the company of those known genetic markers. It was fortunate, therefore, that at that point molecular biologists developed a remarkable technique of gene probing using recombinant DNA that allowed investigators to continue the linkage studies.

This new method of getting genetic markers came about when scientists discovered that they could produce DNA in the laboratory. (DNA is the stuff chromosomes are made of.) Each chromosome has a unique sequence of "rungs," known as bases, and a gene is a short segment of the ladder-like DNA. These researchers found that if they came up with a piece of manufactured DNA that happened to match a segment of the natural DNA, the two pieces would stick together. Probing with the synthetic DNA, they discovered that chromosomes are studded with interesting variations. Each variation is unique to a particular point on a specific chromosome in an individual's cells. These variations have been named restriction-fragment-length polymorphisms (RFLPs); geneticists refer to them affectionately as "riflips."

By using the riflip probes, geneticists are mapping the human genetic structure. They are searching the blood cells of families who have certain inherited diseases. If a specific riflip, or variation, is present primarily in people who have bipolar disorder, it may be assumed that the riflip is close to a gene that may play a part in the illness's manifesting itself. In other words, if a marker—a riflip—can be found that shows that it segregates with the disorder, that would mean that the gene for that disorder is located in the DNA close to that particular marker.

In order to conduct these genetic linkage studies, large families are needed. The search was on again since Dr. Egeland and her colleagues realized that they could apply the new molecular genetic techniques by establishing cell lines for Amish families. The large families and stable population of the Amish have made it possible for them to find enough ill and well family members to begin tracking the fate of the riflip landmarks through three generations. In 1983, Dr. Egeland collected blood samples from fifty-one subjects and established permanent cell lines for one large pedigree—Pedigree #110—at the Coriell Institute for Medical Research in Camden, New Jersey. The DNA from those cells is then available for repeated genetic probing. The goal is to link the gene that carries the code for the illness to a trackable landmark from which it rarely gets separated.

The laboratories of Drs. David Housman and Daniela Gerhard at the Massachusetts Institute of Technology and Kenneth Kidd and David Pauls at Yale University have been typing individuals in Pedigree #110 for riflips over the past several years and performing genetic linkage analyses on a number of markers.

How feasible is it that this method will eventually yield a genetic marker for bipolar disorder? Very feasible. This same method of gene mapping was applied to a heritable illness called Huntington's chorea. This is a terrible disease in which a person begins to deteriorate neurologically, becomes demented and then dies (this is the disease that killed the folk singer Woody Guthrie). Each child of an affected parent has a 50 percent chance of inheriting the dominant gene and of getting the illness. Another cruel factor in its transmission is that the disease doesn't appear until a person reaches the age of thirty to forty. So for half a lifetime a person lives under the most awful sort of Damoclean sword. Whether or not one should have children or whether or not those one already has will be affected are frightening unknowns. Not too long ago, though, American families with Huntington's disease were invited to supply data on their family tree and on all aspects of the disease in their family—age at onset, clinical syndrome, and so on. These data were kept on record and the largest of the families were asked to supply blood and skin samples for the search for the Huntington's chorea gene. Dr. James Gusella and his research team at the Massachusetts General Hospital in Boston and Dr. Nancy Wexler of Columbia University began to study first the

Pedigree #110

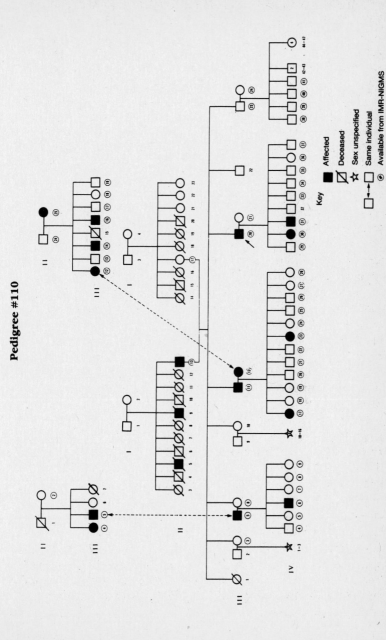

Key

■ Affected
⊘ Deceased
☆ Sex unspecified
□ Same individual
◉ Available from IMR-NIGMS

Reprinted with permission from the Coriell Institute for Medical Research.

blood samples of the American families and then the quickly-flown-in samples of a large family that lives along the shores of Lake Maracaibo in Venezuela. Working with hunches and the riflip techniques, they made an extraordinary breakthrough and located the chromosome *and* the area of the gene. It is now possible to tell some of these family members whether or not they have inherited the Huntington's gene.

Hopefully we're not far away from a breakthrough in the area of affective disorders. In 1979, when the first blood samples were drawn, only one riflip was known to exist in humans. By 1983 over four hundred riflips had been described. The discovery of new probes mapped to specific chromosomes has continued at an unprecedented rate. At present over eight hundred riflips have been reported, and new ones are pinpointed every week. At the 1984 International Workshop on Human Gene Mapping, it was predicted that the human genome might be mapped within a decade.

These rapid and continuous advances provide a very strong impetus toward the identification by genetic linkage of the site of a major locus for bipolar disorder. Dr. Egeland and her coworker Dr. David Pauls of Yale University have been working to address the question of the mode of inheritance in these families. From an analysis of thirty-two bipolar Amish families, they have developed strong evidence of a single, dominant gene for predisposition to the illness. The evidence that there was a dominant gene contributing to expression of the illness further inspired the search for a linked marker.

Dr. Gerhard and Dr. Housman began to focus their attention on the short arm of chromosome 11, and preliminary evidence strongly supports the possibility of a genetic marker for that region. These findings are currently undergoing further investigation and replication.

Even if a major gene locus is found, environmental and other genetic influences do modify the expression of the illness. There is significant clinical variation in the illness and there may be more than one major gene locus found among other people with other varying forms of the disorder. MIT's Dr. Housman is confident they're on the right track, though. When interviewed by the *Wall Street Journal,* he noted: "If there is a gene or several genes at work in manic-depression, we're going to find them. It's just a matter of time."

A number of extremely promising potentials can be expected if this gene is found. Diagnosis would become more accurate, and the face of genetic counseling would be changed. We would gain information on how the gene and the environment interact. We would have a better idea which nongenetic factors are related to the onset and course of the disorder. Finally, the information should help to determine the specific biochemical defect and origin of the disorder. Since genes control and regulate the production of enzymes and biologically important proteins, a problem at the level where genetic information is translated could alter the structure and function of a protein, an enzyme, a neurotransmitter or a receptor site (see the next chapter). This vulnerability within the central nervous system may underlie the sequence of events that results in manic or depressive symptoms. Identifying the gene and what it codes for would be a revolutionary breakthrough in understanding the functional changes that accompany manic-depressive illness. From there the future might bring better drugs and medical treatments, perhaps even a way to correct the problem in utero or after. Reaching these potentials is predicated on first locating a genetic marker.

THE EPIDEMIOLOGY OF MOOD DISORDERS

The Amish studies will undoubtedly tell us much about genetics, but they have already yielded some surprising data in the field of epidemiology (the branch of medical science that studies the incidence and distribution of disease in communities and whole countries). Previously the epidemiological studies on the illness in the general population reported anywhere from a 10:1 to a 3:1 ratio of unipolar depression to bipolar depression. But Dr. Egeland found an equal 1:1 ratio in the families she studied. In her opinion, past studies based on hospital records tended to miss the hypomanic and even manic features that preceded or followed a serious depressive episode. Therefore, many people who were diagnosed during a depressive episode and recorded in studies as unipolar might actually have had bipolar illness. Of course, new studies in the general population will have to be conducted to confirm or refute a higher frequency of bipolar illness.

Dr. Egeland discovered another nonconforming ratio, this one involving the comparison of men to women with the disorder. The universal sex ratio for bipolar and unipolar disorders combined shows a preponderance of women—usually 2:1. This ratio reflects the reported 3:1 female to male ratio for major depression and the approximately equal—1:1—rate for bipolar disorder. The Amish study varies from the traditional statistic because it came away with a much closer female to male ratio of 1:1 for major affective disorders. Dr. Egeland notes the importance of several factors for this finding, explaining that the Amish culture prohibits the use of alcohol and drugs—substances that might mask the expression of affective disorders. It is suspected that many men self-treat the symptoms of an affective disorder with alcohol or drugs and thus find themselves added to the epidemiological roll calls of alcoholics or drug abusers. Since alcohol and drugs are culturally prohibited to the Amish, the unmasked symptoms of a primary affective disorder will manifest themselves—they will not be obscured—and a proper diagnosis can be made. Also, since crime and sociopathy are practically unknown among the Amish, none of the men are lost to the epidemiological study due to imprisonment. Everyone in the community is accounted for, and any manifestation of mental illness is usually observed and attended.

These are exciting times. Future reports from southeastern Pennsylvania will no doubt do much to expand our knowledge of the causes and course of mood disorders.

GENETIC COUNSELING

So, in the meantime, what would help identify those at risk for the disorder as well as calm many fears about it? The answer is, genetic counseling. In various areas of the country there are doctors in the field of genetic research who can examine a family's history, explain the risk estimates and alleviate the anxieties a family lives with.

Actually, more and more people in this country are availing themselves of the services and science of genetic counselors: pregnant women who have amniocentesis routinely have a genetic counseling session, and people with diabetes and their families often talk with counselors. In the affective disorders field, even while we wait for further clarification of the nature of inheritance or possible genetic markers, the counselor can still explain the empirical risk estimates. These are percentages culled from the pooled results of large family studies that show the rate at which any given mental disorder occurs in each of the different classes of relatives of an affected patient. While these estimates are not totally accurate, they are at least informative. Until further progress is made on the molecular biology or psychosocial fronts, they're the best figures available.

We asked geneticist and psychiatrist Dr. Miron Baron of the New York State Psychiatric Institute in New York City how families react to the knowledge that an affective disorder seems to have a genetic basis, and how they react specifically to genetic counseling. "Most people are relieved," he answered. "The information puts an end to self-blame and guilt. Often, in the fearful playground of the mind, people tend to exaggerate the risk factors, and counseling helps inject reality into the situation and puts things in perspective. As a matter of fact, sessions like this allow the families to vent a lot of concern and work through some of their anxieties. Genetic counseling shows a family how to retain a quiet attentiveness but go on with the business of living."

Most counseling is done in one session, and it is important that all family members come. In this way everyone can contribute personal recollections about relatives and themselves, and the counselor can be sure everyone understands the disorder and the statistical and medical information.

The counselor questions the family as to the number and order of relatives, parental age, ethnic background, possible occurrence of stillbirths or deaths, and lists the ages, sex and health of living brothers, sisters and children. Grandparents, aunts, uncles and cousins are noted also. Then the counselor draws up a pedigree and gets an idea of the patterns of recurrence. One factor that must be considered in the determination of risk is that the spouses of people who have an affective disorder also have a relatively high rate of affective illness (approximately 20 percent). This may be because of a phenomenon known as *assortative mating*—the tendency of married couples to manifest similar genetically influenced traits. There is no real explanation for this at present, although some researchers hypothesize that people with the same disorder may have personality traits or similar life histories that may attract them to each other. If both parents are indeed ill, however, the risk to the children increases significantly.

A client has the right to expect that a genetic counselor will be emotionally supportive, sensitive and tactful, noncoercive and competent. The counselor should speak in terms a layman can understand and yet offer up-to-date information about genetic, biological and epidemiological research in the field of affective disorders.

Psychiatrists who specialize in genetic counseling are not common across the country. For the most part they are found at large medical or research centers and at university teaching hospitals. A psychiatrist may be able to recommend a counselor, or you can call the department of psychiatry at one of the centers just mentioned and ask for a recommendation.

Before we close this chapter, we'd like to point out one more time that while manic-depression and depression are familial disorders and seem to have an underlying genetic component, other factors that have yet to be identified modify or possibly mask their occurrence. No one is doomed by a visit to a genetic counselor—a session usually does more to alleviate than agitate. It can also stave off a great deal of future suffering. For example, if people know that they have a genetic background and perhaps a predisposition to develop an affective disorder, they may take better care of themselves and seek help earlier. This limits the damage an episode can cause and helps prevent a chronic course from developing.

As with Huntington's chorea, the search for a genetic marker for bipolar disorder is a collaborative effort that involves clinicians in the field, molecular geneticists and, most important, families. The cooperation of concerned families is helping science to get to the bottom of so many of the disorders that affect humankind. Never forget that you are indeed a part of the whole, a valued and vital part of the ongoing search for the causes of the affective disorders.

4
WHAT CAUSES
THESE DISORDERS?

We want to warn you at the outset that this chapter will require concentration as it contains some of the most recent scientific information about mood disorders. Our object, however, is not to strain eyes or tax minds, but to outline how much new knowledge is accumulating from research efforts, and how many new research and therapeutic efforts are being prompted by this new knowledge.

The progress made in the study of the major affective disorders during the past decade is unmatched by that in any other area of psychiatric research. These advances have been especially visible in the areas of clinical diagnosis, epidemiology, genetic studies, sociology and psychology of depression and mania. The rapid accumulation of knowledge in part reflects changes in the methods of study. Patient studies have shown a marked shift away from anecdotal observations and speculations of single-case reports to more rigorous scientific studies examining groups of patients and using standard diagnostic systems.

Equally impressive advances have been made in the neurosciences. Researchers can measure the brain's electrical impulses and determine some of its chemical components and interactions. Modern technology now allows us to peer beneath the bony vault of the skull and visualize the brain with positron emission tomography (PET) and nuclear magnetic resonance imaging (MRI).

Our knowledge about these disorders has expanded exponentially, and our understanding should continue to grow. Yet, with all these recent advances, there is still no answer to the question: what causes these disorders?

Genetic, biological and psychological studies provide clues, but clues only. There is a plethora of findings, and a number of theories that are guiding the research efforts, but few of the findings have achieved the status of fact and none of the theories provides a broad enough framework to encompass the findings. However, there is good reason to believe that genetic and environmental forces operate in varying degrees to influence the development and course of affective disorders.

In this chapter we explore this research and outline a few of the hypotheses constructed around the clues. The starting point for this discussion is the nerve cell itself, and the fact that depressed people have lower levels of specific neurochemicals. Then we look at the endocrine system and the hormone cortisol, which plays a critical role in the individual's response to stress and which has been found to be abnormally elevated in many patients suffering with depression. Next we'll explore studies that reveal a relationship between stressful events, such as separation and loss, and the biological changes that accompany those events. Finally, we examine circadian rhythms, the twenty-four-hour schedules of bodily activity, which seem to be disregulated in depression and mania. We begin with the brain's architecture and the mechanisms by which the brain communicates with itself, the body and the world around it.

INSIDE THE BRAIN:
THE LIMBIC-DIENCEPHALON

The brain sits above our spines, is about the size of a grapefruit and weighs about three and a half pounds. Packed into this space are perhaps one hundred billion brain cells. It is said that the number of possible interconnections between the cells is greater than the number of atoms in the universe.

Near the center of the brain is the area on which most affective disorder researchers focus—the *limbic-diencephalic system*. This is comprised of the limbic system, the hypothalamus, and the brain stem (including the reticular activating system, the locus coeruleus and raphe nuclei). The limbic system, as the mediator of human feelings, receives and regulates information of an emotional nature,

The Limbic-Diencephalic System

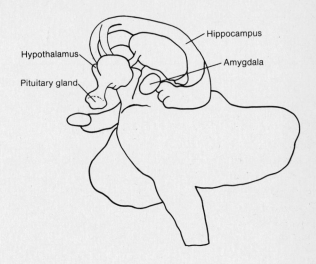

Hypothalamus

Pituitary gland

Hippocampus

Amygdala

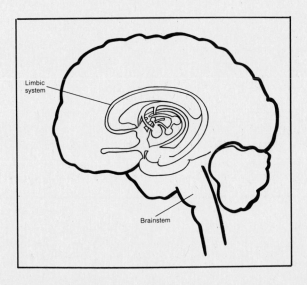

Limbic system

Brainstem

and governs sexual desire, other appetitive and consummatory behaviors and the self-protective mechanism of fight or flight.

By far the most important structure of the limbic system is the
four-gram, walnut-sized hypothalamus. This "brain" within the brain
regulates a host of human processes, including appetite, thirst, sleep,
sexual desire and body temperature, and it activates the reaction of
the organism to stress, as well as the *timing* of many other basic
functions on an hour-by-hour or daily basis. The hypothalamus also
controls the master gland of the brain, the pituitary.

The hippocampus and the amygdala are the other major centers
of the limbic system. They are both involved with memory formation,
but they are also known to gauge emotional reactions such as elation,
excitement, anxiety, agitation, rage and aggression, as well as modulate the capacity to start and stop behaviors associated with these
emotions.

The limbic forebrain provides a key integrating system for se-
lectively modulating emotion and responses to sensations. Its unique
location within the forward part of the brain enables it to correlate
and integrate every form of internal and external perception.

One other structure in the brain is particularly interesting for
the affective disorders researcher: the pineal gland. The pineal projects down above the back of the brainstem. Information about light
is brought by special nerve pathways from the eyes to the pineal
gland where it affects sleep and the secretion of the hormone
melatonin.

All of these interconnected areas govern mental activities and
bodily functions that are known to be disturbed during manic and
depressive episodes. Recent advances in the neurosciences are gradually revealing the central nervous system to look more and more
like an interactive network of oscillating nuclei (centers) that exchange information across spatial and temporal boundaries within a
hierarchical organization.

How do these structures process information, communicate with
each other and generate behavior? Through the actions of the billions
of brain cells or neurons we mentioned above.

A neuron, the basic cell of the nervous system, consists of a cell
body, a long, thin tube jutting from the cell body (the axon) and a

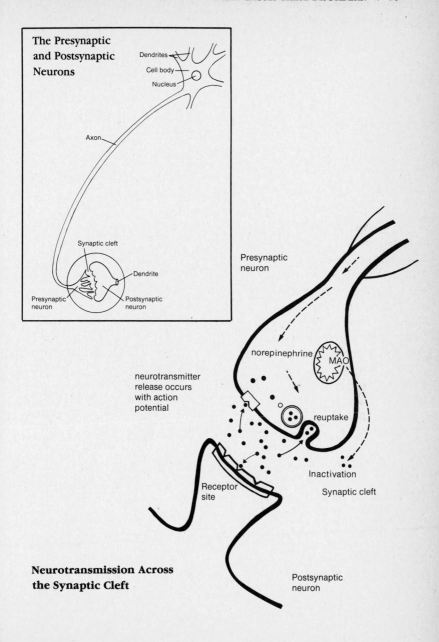

The Presynaptic and Postsynaptic Neurons

Dendrites

Cell body

Nucleus

Axon

Synaptic cleft

Dendrite

Presynaptic neuron

Postsynaptic neuron

Presynaptic neuron

norepinephrine

MAO

neurotransmitter release occurs with action potential

reuptake

Inactivation

Receptor site

Synaptic cleft

Neurotransmission Across the Synaptic Cleft

Postsynaptic neuron

set of shorter fibers (dendrites) that branch and reach out to receive impulses from other nerve cells. A nerve impulse travels electrically down the axon until it cannot continue farther due to a tiny gap— the synaptic cleft—that separates it from other cell fibers. Little sacks or vesicles at the end of the axon spill out chemical transmitter molecules that ferry the impulse across the gap and attach to the cell membrane on the other side. Each of these chemicals, or neurotransmitters, has a certain shape and seeks out a molecule, or *receptor,* on the adjacent cell membrane into which it fits—like a key and its complementary keyhole. Depending on the type of transmitter, and the type of reception it gets from the receptive cells on the other nerve cell, the chemical will either excite the next cell to fire and continue the communication or inhibit it (in this case the message is "there is no message"). These neurotransmitters include amines such as *serotonin, norepinephrine, acetylcholine* and *dopamine;* amino acids; glutamic acid, GABA; and peptides such as substance P and endorphins.

The synaptic cleft is about twenty millionths of a millimeter wide, and it takes less than one-five-thousandth of a second for the neurotransmitter to leap the gap and arrive on the opposite shore. Each nerve cell evaluates all of the excitatory and inhibitory neurotransmitter inputs and decides whether or not to generate the impulse. Then the transmitter molecule responds to the constant vibration and motion going on around it and pulls off the receptor site. Back in the synaptic cleft its future lies in one of two directions: either it will be "inactivated"—split into smaller molecules by an enzyme such as monoamine oxidase, acetylcholinesterase or a peptidase—or, in a process known as "reuptake," it will be sponged up into the presynaptic nerve terminal from which it had been originally released. These two processes clear the site for the arrival of the next chemical messenger.

Two neurotransmitters have most often been implicated in depression and mania: norepinephrine and serotonin. The small cluster of norepinephrine nerve cells originates in an area of the brainstem called the *locus coeruleus* ("blue area") and projects up through the midbrain and extends throughout the cerebral cortex. The serotonin system begins in an area in the midbrain and brain

The Norepinephrine System

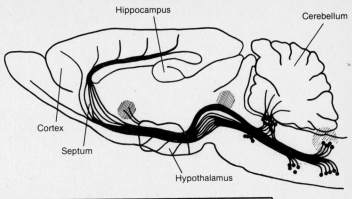

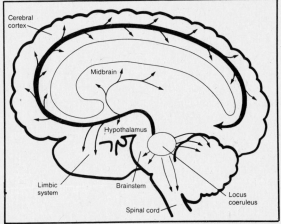

stem called the *raphe nuclei* and projects its nerve pathways to the thalamus and to the gray matter of the cerebral cortex. This pathway is also involved with large parts of the limbic system and hypothalamus. These two neurotransmitter networks reach many parts of the brain that are responsible for a variety of functions disturbed in depression and mania, namely mood, sleep, appetite and sexual activity.

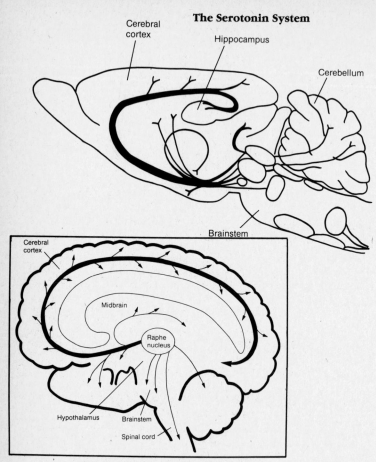

The Serotonin System

Cerebral cortex

Hippocampus

Cerebellum

Brainstem

Cerebral cortex

Midbrain

Raphe nucleus

Hypothalamus

Brainstem

Spinal cord

The Biogenic Amine Hypothesis

The first modern biological theory of depression was formulated after scientists observed that certain drugs had mood-altering properties. Some patients taking a drug called *reserpine* to lower their blood pressure became depressed; a number of patients taking *iproniazid* for tuberculosis found their mood improving. When researchers explored what these drugs were doing at the level of the nerve cells, they found that reserpine caused norepinephrine to leak out of the storage vesicles, whereupon it was destroyed by the monoamine oxidase enzymes. Thus, there were too few molecules of norepinephrine to support neurotransmission. Iproniazid, on the other hand, inhibits the enzyme monoamine oxidase, which breaks down norepinephrine and serotonin. This inhibition increases the number of neurotransmitters that can be released when a nerve impulse arrives. These events at the cell level led to the formulation of the *biogenic amine hypothesis.*

The biogenic amine hypothesis postulates that in the state of depression there are too few norepinephrine or serotonin neurotransmitter molecules being synthesized and released, and therefore not enough molecules to ferry the impulse across the synaptic cleft. Depression results. Conversely, it was held that too many transmitter molecules in the synaptic cleft might cause mania. The tricyclic antidepressant drugs (discussed on pages 105–10) were thought to be effective in treating depression because they block the reuptake of the neurotransmitters and help keep their concentration at a high enough level in the synaptic cleft that they can transmit the impulse and activate the receptor. The monoamine oxidase inhibitor drugs (discussed on pages 110–13) inhibit the enzyme in the synapse that splits the amine neurotransmitters into inactive by-products. This reduces the neurotransmitter breakdown and therefore ensures a high enough concentration of neurotransmitters in the synaptic cleft to maintain a steady flow of impulses.

However, it was later discovered that certain of the tricyclic antidepressants worked to prevent reuptake of serotonin as well as norepinephrine. Thus, an elaboration of the hypothesis evolved: there must be two different types of depression—one based on a disorder of the norepinephrine metabolism, the other involving serotonin.

These theories came under fire as well. New, "atypical" antidepressants such as mianserin failed to inhibit significantly the reuptake of serotonin or norepinephrine and yet produced an antidepressant effect. Also, studies of amphetamines and cocaine—drugs known to prevent reuptake of these transmitters—indicated that these drugs were not useful in the treatment of severe depression. And, finally, it was observed that the antidepressants blocked reuptake or raised the level of the transmitters in the synaptic cleft within minutes or hours of a single dose, and yet the therapeutic response to these drugs took more than two to three weeks to manifest itself. There were holes in the theory.

Perhaps it was a change not just in the absolute number or levels of these neurotransmitters that led to depression or mania, but in the capacity for them to be received and act at receptor sites across the synaptic cleft. The simplistic notion of "too few" or "too many" neurotransmitter molecules did not explain the problem and began to give way to the more complex idea of a finely tuned system of checks and balances—a dynamic interaction of receptor responsiveness, release and firing rate. The focus of inquiry began to encompass yet another level of organization.

Recently researchers have been looking at changes in *receptor sensitivity* as an important factor in the therapeutic effects of antidepressants. With repeated antidepressant treatment, two types of receptor binding sites that accept the norepinephrine molecule appear to become less sensitive or less abundant: a percentage of the alpha 2 and beta receptors seem to sink back into the cell membrane and become temporarily inaccessible to the neurotransmitters. It has been proposed that these changes—which occur only after several days to weeks—parallel the clinical actions of antidepressants, whose therapeutic effects are typically delayed for two or more weeks. By determining through animal studies the number of receptor sites available to a given neurotransmitter, one can deduce whether "supersensitivity" (usually reflected in an increased number of receptor binding sites) or "subsensitivity" (usually reflected in a decreased number of binding sites) occurs after treatment with medications. This so-called downregulation effect, where the binding sites become less abundant, has been reported after treatment with almost all antidepressant drugs tested as well as with electroconvulsive therapy (ECT). This change in alpha 2 receptors is thought to contribute to a compensatory release of norepinephrine in the nerve terminals that employ this neurotransmitter.

If these changes that occur in receptor sensitivity are specifically related to the depressive state, what leads to these changes? Researchers have explored animal models that come close to reproducing the behavioral changes that occur in human depression, while at the same time measuring the effects on the sensitivity of the receptors within selective areas of the brain. While many would debate the validity of extrapolating from animal models, if aspects of human depression can be reliably reproduced in animals, and changes in brain function found to correspond with the depressed state, we may better understand the biochemical mechanisms and develop more specific antidepressant treatments.

One of the animal models that has been explored is an attempt to look at the link between stressful events and biological changes. This model was developed in the late 1960s when Dr. Martin Seligman observed that dogs who were first exposed to inescapable shocks had more difficulty learning to avoid an *escapable* shock than did dogs who had never before been exposed. (Unstressed animals figured out how to escape and did so easily.) The model was called "learned helplessness" because the researchers felt that the previously exposed dogs had learned that they had no control over the situation.

Dr. Seligman found that the helpless animals exhibited behaviors that were similar to those seen in human depression. For example, they began to have difficulty sleeping and eating, they stopped grooming themselves and taking care of themselves, and they showed signs of psychomotor retardation.

When Dr. Fritz Henn and his colleagues at Yale induced depressive behavior in rats using the Seligman model of learned helplessness, some provocative findings emerged. The sensitivity of the beta receptors in their brains was markedly altered in two discrete areas: the receptors were "upregulated," or more sensitive, in the hippocampus and "downregulated," or less sensitive, in the hypothalamus. When Dr. Henn then treated another group of rats with antidepressants, the helpless "depressed" rats regained their capacity to escape the uncontrolled shock. They readily made the effort to push a lever that stopped the shock. Furthermore, this change developed within several weeks—the time frame that would be expected for a typical clinical response to antidepressant treatment. Moreover, the alterations in hippocampal and hypothalamic beta receptors observed during the period of learned helplessness had been reversed by the antidepressant treatment. In a fascinating extension of this study, Dr. Henn and his colleagues induced depression in another group of rats but treated them without medication. They made a behavioral intervention and "taught" the rats how to escape the shock. Actually, a medical student working in the lab knit the depressed rats little sweaters with long sleeves over their front paws. Strings were attached to the sleeves and the researchers could pull the rats' paws up, marionette-like, and train them to push the lever that would stop the shock. With the rats no longer helpless, their symptoms of depression abated, and the beta receptor sites returned to their previous state. Dr. Henn and others have concluded from these studies that just as neurochemistry affects behavior, behavior affects neurochemistry.

Complementary findings have been found in the treatment of human depression. A brief psychotherapeutic treatment called *cognitive therapy* focuses on the thought processes of a depressed person, in particular the hopeless and helpless thinking, and by changing the negative thought patterns has proved to be as effective as the antidepressant imipramine in treating the depression (see pages 151–52 for a description of cognitive therapy).

To summarize: neurotransmitters in the limbic-diencephalic system may play a critical role in the regulation of mood. A change in neurotransmitter activity, through a deficiency or excess of norepinephrine or serotonin, is associated with depression or mania, respectively. However, it is unlikely that changes in the metabolism of these neurotransmitters *alone* can account for the disturbed behaviors seen in depression and mania.

HORMONAL DYSFUNCTION IN DEPRESSION

For many years the neurotransmitters were the focus of attention. More recently, the scope of investigations has widened to include changes in a number of important hormones. Most endocrine systems are controlled by the biogenic amines: norepinephrine, serotonin and dopamine all play a part in the timing and regulation of release of hormones, and the hormones themselves modulate the nerve cell activity of these neurotransmitters. Studies have shown that hormone secretion is influenced by neurotransmitters that are in *limbic centers* and, conversely, that alterations in neurotransmitter function affect hormone secretion. Just recently it has been learned that some hormones and neurotransmitters can occupy the same nerve cells and both transmit messages across the same synapse.

Mood changes occur in association with endocrine disorders. Clinicians have often noticed that people who suffer from diseases of the thyroid and adrenal glands have many symptoms similar to those seen in depressed and manic states. In some instances the behavioral manifestations are indistinguishable. Hyperthyroidism (increased thyroid function) can produce a syndrome that, on first examination, is similar to mania, including hyperactivity, pressured speech, sleeplessness and so on. Hypothyroidism (decreased thyroid function) can present many of the features of major depression: fatigue, lethargy and disrupted sleep cycles. In both cases, however, the functioning of the thyroid gland is abnormal and there are physical changes indicative of the gland's malfunction that do not occur in depression or mania. Both the physical and behavioral symptoms can be alleviated by correcting the hormonal imbalance.

Another hormonal disorder, Cushing's syndrome, is characterized by excessive cortisol secretion and can produce symptoms such as fatigue, change in appetite and insomnia. These are all common symptoms of depression and are associated with a disturbance of the *hypothalamic-pituitary-adrenal axis.* The hypothalamic-pituitary-adrenal (HPA) axis is the endocrine system most extensively studied in affective illness. Is it possible that some vulnerability in this system predisposes a person to developing depressive or manic symptoms?

The HPA axis first came under scrutiny about fifty years ago when Dr. Walter Cannon demonstrated that the neurotransmitter epinephrine was released in response to stress. He made this finding the basis of his hypothesis that this substance mobilized the organism for "fight or flight." Some years later, Dr. Hans Selye called attention to the response to stress of the adrenocortical hormone cortisol. While he was concerned chiefly with responses to physical stress, his observation that *psychological* stress could also stimulate cortisol secretion prompted a great deal of subsequent research.

The neuroendocrine system that regulates the release of cortisol helps the body remain flexible so that it can respond appropriately to changing environmental conditions—whether it be alterations in the day-night cycle, seasonal changes, stressful life events or a sudden threat to survival. This system works to establish an intricate moment-to-moment balance by a series of feedback functions that are orchestrated through the hypothalamus, the central relay system for the endocrine and nervous systems. For example, if a person encounters a man with a knife in a darkened hallway, the eyes relay the threat to the brain, and the brain registers fear or anger. The fearful event is translated into chemical signals that move through a complex pathway that leads through the limbic system and its connection by various neurotransmitters to the hypothalamus. Thus, this emotional response to a stressful or dangerous event provokes a cascade of specific neurochemical responses. The hypothalamus sends a message to the front lobe of the pituitary. This message is relayed by the release of *corticotropin-releasing factor* (CRF). The hypothalamus sends the CRF to the pituitary by the private blood supply that connects them. When the pituitary receives the CRF messenger, it pours out *adrenocorticotropic hormone* (ACTH) into the bloodstream. ACTH, in turn, releases cortisol into the bloodstream.

Within seconds, the ACTH molecule travels to the adrenal ("near the kidney") glands. Stimulated by the ACTH alarm, the adrenal glands pour out cortisol, which converts norepinephrine into epinephrine, and both hormone and neurotransmitter are released into the bloodstream. These substances ready the body for the "fight or flight" response: the heart pumps dramatically harder and faster, the lungs take in more oxygen, the liver releases sugar to provide more available energy, the muscles tense, the pupils of the eyes dilate, and the body begins to sweat so that it can cool itself in the event of violent activity.

This specific neurochemical cascade is clearly of evolutionary value. Even anticipation of threatening or novel events was found to stimulate the release of cortisol. Early animal experiments proved that psychological stress was a powerful stimulant of cortisol secretion, and attention soon turned to its effects in humans. Cortisol levels were measured in normal subjects exposed to experimental psychological stress, as well as in people whose real-life circumstances involved extreme emotional stress. It was discovered that anticipation of any frightening or complicated task, including parachute jumping, hospitalization or landing an airplane, is a potent stimulant of cortisol. The degree of control that the individual could

The Hypothalamic-Pituitary-Adrenal Axis
("The Stress Response")

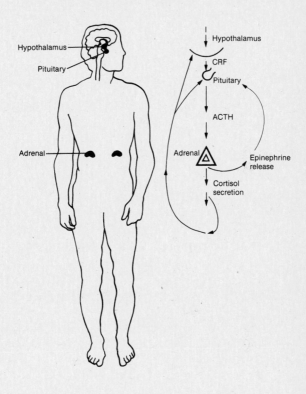

exert over the situation and the personal meaning of the challenge appeared to be important variables in determining the degree of response. (Recall the learned helplessness in rats.)

Things become somewhat more complicated because cortisol is not secreted only during stressful situations; it is also secreted episodically in a series of timed bursts throughout the day. These bursts of cortisol are synchronized with the twenty-four-hour sleep-wake cycle and have both periodic (ultradian) and daily (circadian) variations. The sleep-wake alternation in humans is an example of a circadian rhythm, which requires about twenty-four hours to complete (circa = about, dia = a day). In most people, there is very little secretion of cortisol during the late evening. However, after about two A.M., a rapid rise occurs, with peak excretion between five and nine in the morning.

In the 1970s, Dr. Edward Sacher, working at Columbia Presbyterian Hospital in conjunction with Dr. Elliot Weitzman of the Albert Einstein College of Medicine in New York, began to look at the twenty-four-hour profile of cortisol secretion. Their findings revealed two striking differences between depressed patients and non-depressed, healthy volunteers. In the depressed patients the number of daily episodes was increased, and the level of cortisol in the blood—both at the beginning and the end of the secretory episode—was much higher. Furthermore, in these depressed patients cortisol secretion continued unabated throughout both day and night. The ordinary boundaries of its daily rhythm were lost.

Following these discoveries, other abnormalities of the hypothalamic-pituitary-adrenal axis were reported. Researchers such as Dr. Bernard Carrol have been testing the functioning of the HPA axis by administering a synthetic cortisol, dexamethasone. Normally, the appearance of the increased level of the hormone in the bloodstream causes the hypothalamus to tell the pituitary that the level of cortisol is adequate, and does not need to be replenished. However, in 40 to 60 percent of severely depressed patients, the feedback system does not function correctly: the message to stop sending out cortisol is not sent out, and an oversupply of cortisol is maintained in the bloodstream. Both elevated blood cortisol levels and the dexamethasone suppression test (DST) become normal following recovery from an episode of depression.

More recently, several research groups have developed and employed a "CRF stimulation test" to further examine the HPA axis in affective disorders. They have reported that the ACTH response to CRF was blunted in depressed patients as compared to people who were not depressed. These studies are significant in that they point to a possible key role of CRF in the dysregulation phenomenon that is observed in major depression.

While the effects of CRF on important physiological functions have only recently begun to be explored, this releasing factor has an interesting effect on the locus coeruleus—the area of the brain where norepinephrine cells originate. CRF, when applied directly to the locus coeruleus of animals, causes a rapid increase in the firing rate of cells. This sends waves of norepinephrine release throughout the central nervous system and induces a state of heightened arousal and hypervigilance—a state commonly seen in human anxiety disorders and panic states. Both syndromes are increasingly found in association with major depression and are reported to occur more frequently in families of patients who have an affective disorder. This is another significant clue pointing to the delicate balance between neurotransmitters whose functions are known to be altered during depression and the hormones that regulate the stress response.

All of these findings suggest hyperactivity of the HPA axis in many patients with major depression. This is of more than passing interest since we know that this system modulates our capacity to respond to stress.

SEPARATION AND LOSS: PRECIPITANTS OF DEPRESSION?

Stressful events such as loss or separation have long been implicated as possible precipitants of or antecedents to depression. Indeed, the grief experienced during bereavement in many ways resembles major depression. Researchers have sought to define the relationship of separation events to the development of clinical depression. In these studies separation events are anything a person may experience as a "loss," whether it be the death of a loved one, separation by divorce, the loss of a job or one's status in the community, the loss of some goal or even a promotion. While the studies are not unanimous, the majority suggest that for certain predisposed individuals, loss may be a trigger for depression.

The British psychoanalyst René Spitz was the first to describe the responses of institutionalized children who had suffered recent separations from their mothers (most of the mothers had been killed in the bombings of London during World War II). In response to the separation, these infants went through an initial stage of protest, becoming extremely restless, presumably attempting to attract attention and the return of the parent. This was followed by a period of despair, with weeping and diminished activity, and finally by a detachment phase in which the infants became severely withdrawn. Spitz labeled this entire reaction pattern *anaclitic depression.* (Anaclitic means "leaning on" and is a psychoanalytic term describing the infant's dependency on the mother for a sense of well-being.)

A very similar separation response has been observed in nonhuman primates. Infant monkeys respond to maternal separation by an initial stage of protest characterized by agitation, sleeplessness, distress calls and screaming, followed after one or two days by evident despair, accompanied by a decrease in general activity, feeding, play, grooming and social interaction and by the assumption of a hunched posture and "sad" facial expression.

Studies of the HPA axis activity in such separated monkeys found separation to be accompanied by a rise of cortisol in the blood during the protest stage. The magnitude of the elevation has been found to predict the intensity of depressive responses during the despair phase. As was found in human depression, some separated monkeys also failed to suppress blood cortisol concentrations in response to dexamethasone.

Again we see a hormonal dysregulation in the HPA axis that is seen with the depressive response, this time associated with separation or loss. Whether the evident overactivity of the HPA axis and the high outputs of cortisol in major depression are manifestations of an abnormal state, or are merely attempts to restore homeostasis *after the fact*—for example, after some stressful event—still remains an open question.

To summarize again: The limbic structures, particularly the hypothalamus, are the site for neurochemical events that orchestrate the stress response. In turn, changes in the balance of neurotransmitters in the hypothalamus alter the release of important hormones. Ultimately these hormones feed back upon the brain itself to influence neurotransmitters like serotonin, norepinephrine and acetylcholine. The disturbing signs and symptoms of depression and mania may reflect an imbalance in this complex system.

The information discussed thus far has focused on cellular and regional areas within the central nervous system: the synapse and the pre- and postsynaptic membranes of the neuron, the connections between hormone-secreting cells in the HPA axis and their importance in the regulation of the emotional response to stress and, more directly, their relationship to neurotransmitters implicated in depression and mania. Simply knowing the map, however, does not necessarily provide us with full knowledge of the territory. Moreover, large parts of the map still remain to be charted.

CIRCADIAN RHYTHMS: TIME INSIDE OF SPACE

The timing of events within the central nervous system may be as important as spatial arrangements. Neurotransmitters must not only lock into their corresponding receptor keyhole, but they must also act with appropriate *timing*—in relationship to each other and to events occurring in the environment. The apparently stable functions of the brain and body are poised on the paradox of continuous but well-regulated change. Temperature, blood pressure, hormonal secretions, blood sugar and dozens of other aspects of bodily activity continuously wax and wane according to varying schedules. These schedules occur approximately every twenty-four hours and are called *circadian rhythms*. Many of these rhythms are molded by the daily changes of the light-dark cycle.

All human beings have established sleep and activity cycles, as well as periods of hunger and satiety, but many other regular cycles take place below the level of conscious awareness, most notably the secretions of the endocrine system—hormones such as CRF, ACTH, cortisol, growth hormone and melatonin. Interestingly, there are also regular, daily variations in the production of many neurotransmitters, including serotonin and norepinephrine, and possibly also in the numbers of receptor sites that receive these substances. There are times of day, of month and of year from which a given biological activity is either necessarily restricted or in which it is most appropriately undertaken.

Why are scientists looking at chronobiological systems? For several reasons. If you examine the course of a mood disorder, you may find that each person has a pattern of recurrence: the cycles come and go, sometimes at the same time each year. For some, there appears to be a rhythmic, possibly seasonal process going on. Then there are variations in the symptoms that people with unipolar or bipolar disorders note during different times of the day. Many people suffering depression feel worse in the morning and find their spirits and energy lifting in the afternoon; others report feeling worse as the day goes on. Furthermore, the sleep cycles of people with mood disorders are disturbed. The syndrome of early-morning awakening—the person complains of waking early in the morning and being unable to go back to sleep—is one of the classic symptoms of depression. Also, some people complain of sleeping too much, or, in cases of mania, there is suddenly almost no need for sleep. All of these disturbances are rhythmic and point to the possibility that mood disorders are temporal disorders in which the timing of biological rhythms is temporarily—but pathologically—altered.

The metaphor of alarm clocks hidden in the body, programming bodily processes to switch on and off, and then perhaps losing their function, is worth examining. For example, a look at the architecture of the normal sleep pattern and what happens to sleep rhythms when someone is depressed may make this idea clearer.

Normally, throughout the night a person experiences two kinds of sleep that alternate rhythmically. One is called rapid eye movement (REM) sleep, during which most dreaming takes place; the other (not too surprisingly) is called *non-REM.*

Non-REM sleep has a four-stage development plan as revealed by electroencephalogram (EEG) studies. Stage I is the light sleep that begins the night and from which a sleeper may be easily awakened. The brain waves are small and fast. After about half an hour, the sleeper slips deeper into sleep as Stages II, III and IV of non-REM sleep progress. EEGs of Stage III reveal larger and slower brain waves. Stage IV brain waves are large, slow and regular. This is the deepest period of sleep.

After approximately ninety minutes have passed, a brief period of REM sleep appears (the eyeballs can be observed moving rapidly beneath the eyelids), only to be followed by one of the non-REM stages. A pattern develops in which the REM and non-REM sleep phases alternate with each other, cycling back and forth in a remarkably periodic ebb and flow. Later on in the night, REM sleep asserts itself for longer periods of time. Apparently the sleep cycle oscillates on a ninety-minute time frame, an example of another fundamental biological rhythm (an *ultradian* cycle that occurs more than once a day). For instance, the first ninety-minute cycle might consist of eighty-five minutes of non-REM sleep and five minutes of

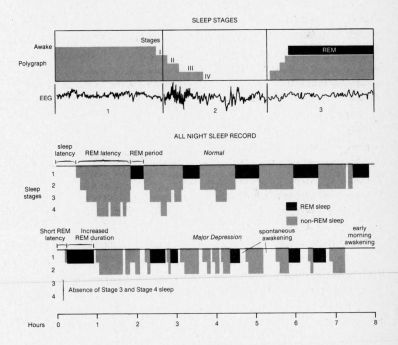

The top chart illustrates the four stages of sleep and the percentages of REM and non-REM sleep throughout the sleep cycle. The two charts beneath that compare the all-night sleep records of an individual with a normal sleep cycle with that of a patient with major depression. Note the depressed patient's shortened REM latency, the increased REM duration and the spontaneous and early-morning awakening.

REM; by the time the fourth cycle rolls around, it might consist of sixty minutes of non-REM and thirty minutes of REM. This time cycle implies that sleep is controlled by a biological clock with a ninety-minute period.

All-night EEG studies of depressed patients reveal several abnormalities. There is a marked absence of slow-wave sleep (Stages III and IV), an increased difficulty in falling asleep and an increased number of spontaneous awakenings after sleep has been achieved. It is not difficult to arouse the depressed person from sleep. But perhaps most striking, depressed people go into their first period of REM sleep sooner than nondepressed people. There is a shortened period between the beginning of sleep and the first dreaming period. This is referred to as *REM latency*. It seems that people who are depressed have more REM sleep in the first third of the night and less REM sleep in the last third of the night than nondepressed individuals.

It has been discovered that the human circadian system is controlled by at least two coupled clocks or pacemakers: a strong one controlling body temperature, REM sleep and cortisol secretion, and a weak one controlling the sleep-wake cycle and sleep-related hormone secretion. It is the relationship of one to the other and to outside time cues such as light or temperature that serves to establish a pattern of temporal order within the body.

Circadian clocks have been likened to cheap wristwatches that run consistently fast or slow and so must be reset frequently (ordinarily, daily environmental cues such as the appearance of dawn and dusk mold these clocks to the ever-changing periods of light and dark). The pacemaker that controls the sleep-wake cycle is inherently flexible in order to adjust to the constantly changing length of the daily light period, determined by the position of the sun relative to the earth. A healthy individual who lives in a normal environment, with regular light or time cues to indicate the time of day, can adhere to the twenty-four-hour day and adjust easily to the slow seasonal changes in the light-dark cycle. However, a number of studies that have examined circadian rhythms have noted that the rest-activity and temperature cycles of patients with affective disorders tended to desynchronize even though they were living lives with typical and regular daily schedules. Indeed, several current theories suggest that some form of circadian rhythm desynchronization may be responsible for the symptoms seen in mood disorders.

Let's look at this problem more closely. One of the "pacemakers" that drives a number of rhythms known to be impaired in states of depression and mania is localized in an area of the hypothalamus. It is called the *suprachiasmatic nucleus* (SCN), and it is a pair of small eggshaped clusters of nerve cells that seem to be responsible for the periodic drinking, eating and activity rhythms in animals (see the illustration on the next page).

The SCN acts like a central relay station exquisitely responsive to day-night changes. During the transition from twilight to dusk, nerve cells in the SCN increase their firing rate dramatically and stimulate the pineal gland to begin the transformation of serotonin to melatonin. The levels of this hormone show a marked circadian variation, rising at night and falling during the day.

A study by Dr. Lars Wetterberg found that depressed patients had a disturbance in the melatonin circadian pattern along with an abnormality of cortisol secretion. Dr. Julien Mendlewicz found that the normal nighttime increase in melatonin secretion was absent in three of four depressed patients studied, and that in patients with bipolar disorder the melatonin rhythm was desynchronized. That this altered pattern persisted beyond the episode of illness has led to the speculation that the pattern of melatonin secretion may be a stable biological "trait" marker for bipolar disorder. Again, these findings have not achieved the status of fact and require further study.

More than one hundred laboratories around the world are now investigating melatonin. Seasonal variations in human melatonin levels have been found with peaks in January and July and troughs in April and October. These findings have led some researchers to suggest a link between the seasonal variation in melatonin and the increased incidence of depression in spring and autumn.

A relationship between the change of seasons and alteration of mood has been observed since ancient times, and modern epidemiological studies show a seasonal variation in both depression and mania. Most studies agree that peak times for depression are in the spring and fall and that an excess of mania occurs most frequently

The Nerve Pathway From
the Eye to the Pineal Gland

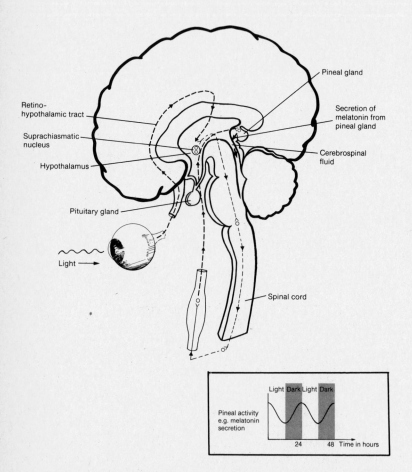

This drawing schematically illustrates the nerve pathways that transmit information about the levels of illumination in the daily light-dark cycle. The information travels from the retina through the retino-hypothalamic pathway to the suprachiasmatic nucleus (SCN), which then connects to the pineal gland via a circuitous pathway. The inset chart demonstrates the normal twenty-four-hour pattern of melatonin secretion from the pineal gland and its relationship to the light-dark cycle.

in the spring, late summer and early fall. The chart below illustrates the dramatic seasonal fluctuation in suicide deaths with peaks in May and October:

Seasonal Fluctuations in Suicide Deaths
Taken from Northern New England Data

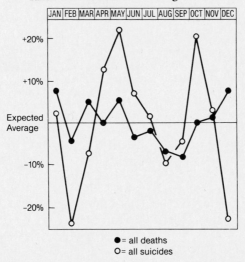

●= all deaths
O= all suicides

Reprinted with permission from *Mood Disorders: Toward a New Psychobiology* by Peter C. Whybrow, M.D., Hagop S. Akiskal, M.D., and William T. McKinney, Jr., M.D. (New York: Plenum Press, 1984).

Dr. Daniel Kripke of the University of California at San Diego has proposed that seasonal patterns of mania and depression might be expressions of vestigial seasonal behavioral rhythms—for example, breeding cycles. These behavioral rhythms are controlled by the neuroendocrine system, with the pineal gland and its hormone, melatonin, playing a key role. Desynchronization of biological rhythms around the spring and autumn equinox may be related to a seasonal susceptibility to affective illness.

Recently, scientists have begun to explore whether circadian rhythms can be shifted using brief pulses of light. Human circadian rhythms were once thought to be insensitive to light. Scientists felt that synchronization to the twenty-four-hour day was accomplished either through periodic social cues and/or the sleep-wake cycle.

However investigators have found that bright artificial light can suppress human melatonin production. Sunlight, which is twenty to two hundred times brighter than ordinary indoor light, also suppresses melatonin production. The demonstration of this intensity-dependent hormonal response has led to a renewed consideration of light as a possible synchronizer of the human circadian pacemaker. In a laboratory study Dr. Charles Czeisler and his colleagues at Harvard University monitored the output of the circadian pacemaker of an elderly woman before and after exposure to four hours of bright light for seven consecutive evenings. The exposure to bright light in the evening delayed by six hours the rhythms of body temperature and cortisol secretion.

The findings of this study imply that exposure to bright light can reset the circadian pacemaker and that bright artificial light can indeed be used to manipulate biological rhythms in humans.

Researchers at the National Institute of Mental Health in Bethesda, Maryland, have found that manipulating biological rhythms using morning or evening bright light exposure appears to be an effective treatment for a subtype of mood disorders. (This form of treatment is discussed in detail on pages 119–22.)

Recently, a research team at the Harvard Mailman Research Center began to look at the twenty-four-hour circadian activity rhythms in elderly patients with major depression. These patients wore monitors on their wrists that counted the rate of activity, and it was found that during the depressed state there was an unexpected difference: the time of daily peak activity was significantly delayed by comparison to normal, age-matched subjects. Also, the activity level in these patients was significantly higher than in nondepressed elderly subjects. Following antidepressant treatment and clinical recovery these alterations returned to normal, suggesting that depressed elderly patients may have a pronounced chronobiological disturbance in activity level and rhythm and possibly other circadian processes.

To summarize, recent studies have raised the possibility that some diseases may be temporal disorders in which the timing of biological rhythms is pathologically altered. The disruption of timing functions within the central nervous system may contribute to or accompany—or perhaps even cause—mood disorders. Patients with manic-depression and depression have been shown to suffer from a variety of abnormal rhythm disturbances. Rhythms of activity, temperature, REM sleep, cortisol and melatonin have been described. Thus, it is possible that manic and depressive symptoms arise from a lack of coordination between two or more circadian pacemakers and the rhythms that they control.

A chronobiological theory of affective illness, while by no means proven, is intriguing. As a model, it allows us to integrate the clinical symptoms of depression and mania, such as early morning awakening, diurnal variation in mood and disturbances in activity, as well as features such as seasonality and cyclicity. In addition, it helps explain the abnormalities in the timing of secretion of various hormones, such as cortisol and melatonin. Research stemming from this theory may increase our understanding of the causes of affective disorders, and perhaps lead to new treatment approaches.

Our present information suggests some plausible hypotheses pointing to the operation of relatively specific social, psychological, biological and environmental processes in the development of major mood disorders. The paragraphs below summarize the findings and hypotheses noted in this chapter:

- The limbic-diencephalic system near the center of the brain is the area that regulates information of an emotional nature and governs the "fight or flight" mechanism. The hypothalamus, which contains the suprachiasmatic nuclei (SCN), is a critical part of this system.
- Two neurotransmitters have been most often implicated in depression and mania: norepinephrine and serotonin. These two neurotransmitter systems reach many parts of the brain that are responsible for a variety of functions disturbed in depression and mania.
- It is thought that antidepressants may change the level of receptor sensitivity to these neurotransmitters.
- Animals who were physically stressed by uncontrollable shocks developed "learned helplessness" and were unable to learn to escape controllable shocks. They exhibited behaviors similar to those seen in human depression (they began to have difficulty sleeping and eating, they stopped grooming and tak-

ing care of themselves and so on). The sensitivity of norepi-nephrine receptors in their brains was markedly altered in the hypothalamus and the hippocampus. When other animals who had such induced "learned helplessness" were treated with antidepressants, they regained their ability to escape the shock. The alterations in the receptor sensitivity were observed after the period of "learned helplessness" to have been completely reversed by the antidepressant, as well as by behavioral inter-ventions. Just as neurochemistry affects behavior, behavior af-fects neurochemistry.

- Hormone secretion is influenced by neurotransmitters in limbic centers, and conversely, alterations in neurotrans-mitter function affect hormone secretion. The hypothalamic-pituitary-adrenal (HPA) axis controls the release of cortisol. Cortisol readies the body for "fight or flight." Depressed pa-tients secrete more cortisol than nondepressed people. The HPA feedback system does not appear to be functioning cor-rectly in depression, and an oversupply of cortisol is main-tained in the bloodstream. Both elevated blood cortisol levels and the dexamethasone suppression test (DST) become normal following recovery from an episode of depression. All of these findings suggest hyperactivity of the HPA axis in depression.

- Stressful events such as a loss or separation have long been implicated as possible precipitants of or antecedents to depression. The British psychoanalyst René Spitz described "anaclitic depression" in which children separated from their mothers in World War II went through an initial stage of protest in which they became extremely restless. This was followed by a period of despair, and finally by a detachment phase in which they became severely withdrawn. A very similar sepa-ration response has been observed in nonhuman primates. Studies of the HPA axis in such separated monkeys found sep-aration to be accompanied by a rise of cortisol in the blood during the protest stage. The magnitude of the elevation has been found to predict the intensity of depressive responses during the despair stage. As was found in human depression, some separated monkeys also failed to suppress blood cortisol concentrations in response to the dexamethasone suppression test. Again we see a hormonal dysregulation in the HPA axis with the depressive response associated with separation or loss.

- Temperature, blood pressure, hormonal secretions, blood sugar and dozens of other aspects of bodily activity wax and wane according to varying schedules. These schedules occur approximately every twenty-four hours and are called circadian rhythms. Many of these rhythms are molded by the daily changes of the light-dark cycle. It may be that mood disorders are temporal disorders in which the timing of biological rhythms is temporarily—but pathologically—altered.

- People who are depressed go into their first period of REM sleep sooner than people who are not depressed. The sleep architecture of depressed patients is different from that of nondepressed people.

    The human circadian system is controlled by at least two coupled clocks or pacemakers: a strong one controlling body temperature, REM sleep and cortisol secretion; and a weak one controlling the sleep-wake cycle and sleep-related hormone secretion. It is the relationship of one to the other and to outside time cues such as light or temperature that serves to establish a pattern of temporal order within the body. Is it possible that these two pacemakers are disassociating—beating out of phase with each other—and producing the symptoms we know as mania or depression?

- A number of studies that have examined circadian rhythms such as rest-activity cycles have noted that the circadian rhythms of patients with affective disorders tend to drift even though they are not isolated from light and time cues. Could these patients lack the capacity to process time and light cues?

- The suprachiasmatic nucleus (SCN) is localized in an area of the hypothalamus. It is one of the pacemakers, and it stimulates the pineal gland to transform serotonin into the hormone melatonin. Patients with affective disorders have a disturbance in the melatonin circadian secretion pattern. Dr. Julien Mendlewicz found that the normal nighttime increase of melatonin was absent in three of four depressed patients studied, and that in patients with bipolar disorder the melatonin rhythm was desynchronized. That this altered pattern persisted beyond the episode of illness has led to the speculation that the pattern of melatonin secretion may be a stable biological "trait" marker for bipolar disorder.

It is still a mystery how these different aspects of the illness combine with a genetic vulnerability to produce the common symptoms of mania and depression. But it is encouraging to remember that much of the information presented in this chapter was unknown even ten years ago. Judging from this perspective, there is every reason to hope that the next ten years will see an exponential increase in the understanding of the causes, and perhaps in improving the treatment, of the major affective disorders.

TWO

ABOUT THE TREATMENT

5

THE SOMATIC THERAPIES: MEDICATIONS AND ECT

In ancient Phoenicia, the mentally ill were boarded on ships—the "ships of fools"—and set adrift to roam the seas in search of more hospitable harbors. In the Middle Ages, exorcists coaxed the "demons" from the bodies of those who acted strangely. Shock treatments were administered to eighteenth-century patients by twirling them on stools until their ears bled, and by dropping them through trap doors into icy lakes.

More humane treatments were developed in the nineteenth century, but effective medical treatments still did not exist. In 1937 Sigmund Freud wrote: "The future may teach us how to exercise a direct influence, by means of particular chemical substances, upon the amount of energy and its distribution in the apparatus of the mind. It may be that there are other undreamed of possibilities of therapy."

Freud would have been fascinated with what happened. When he died in 1939, only electroconvulsive shock treatments were effective for serious depression. Ten years later, John Cade discovered the true value of the salt lithium. In 1952 the French psychiatrists Jean Delay and Pierre Deniker tested chlorpromazine for calming psychotic agitation. Not long afterward the antidepressant drugs were added to the new-found psychiatric armamentarium.

The effectiveness of these new drugs is now firmly established through research studies. Mood swings are prevented or become less severe; lives are returned to more normal paces. In fourteen studies of bipolar disorder, the percentage of patients having a recurrent episode of either mania or depression during one year after the start of treatment was significantly reduced by lithium maintenance in contrast to placebo. In most of these studies the number of recurrences was reduced by 50 percent compared with placebo, and the recurrences were less severe.

Other controlled studies have shown that treatment with lithium or antidepressants can substantially prevent the recurrence of unipolar depression. In most patients, lithium and tricyclic antidepressants decrease the frequency and/or intensity of recurrences. Dr. Jan Fawcett wrote that when he started his practice, families of patients who required hospitalization anxiously asked him if they would ever come out of the hospital. In the 1970s families of patients began asking him why they were not out and well in two weeks!

A new deal? Yes. A cure-all? Not quite. While some people respond to the medications completely and do not suffer side effects, a smaller population responds only partially or finds the side effects uncomfortable or intolerable. The drugs do not cure the illnesses; they *control* them. For now they're the best we have, and the effect they have on the quality of life is impressive.

LITHIUM THERAPY

Forty years ago, when I was ten, my mother was taken away to an asylum because she was "mad." Eventually, and because nothing could calm the turbulence in her mind, she was given a lobotomy. She never came home from the hospital, and all these years of custodial care depleted the huge trust fund that her father had provided. Last year we had to transfer her to a less expensive hospital.

When my brother began to act strangely, everyone thought he had a bit of the family taint. He continued to have periods of illness and became intrusive and even frightening at times. One day he took a flight to England, next we heard from him in Switzerland, and then the family got a call from the Australian Consulate in Sydney reporting that he was found on the beach, alone, and screaming bizarrely at the sky.

We managed to get him home and, like my mother before him, he was hospitalized. Only, this time it was different. The doctor who saw him took a careful look at the symptoms, enquired about the family history, and treated him with lithium. Four weeks later, he left the hospital and began to put his life back together.

Because we now know my brother's diagnosis, I finally realize—after so many years—that my mother was not "mad" or schizophrenic, or that it wasn't just something peculiar to our family. She had manic-depression, and it is now very treatable. If she had become ill today, she would have come home to her family. My beautiful, elegant mother was born too soon.

Lithium is the drug of choice in mania, and when it is used preventively, it protects a person by reducing the possibility of future episodes of mania and depression. This medication, most of it mined in the state of North Carolina, literally makes the difference between lives of chaos and disruption and lives of stability and productivity.

Trace amounts of lithium exist in the human body, in plants and in mineral rocks. It was inserted into the chemists' periodic table as the lightest of the alkali metals when it was described in 1817 by a young Swedish chemist, August Arfwedson. He christened his new element lithium, from the Greek word "lithos," stone.

Interesting intuitions about lithium go way back. About 1,800 years ago the Greek physician Galen formulated a treatment for mania by bathing patients in alkaline springs and by having them "take" (drink) the waters. There was probably lithium in those springs. The medicinal connection began in earnest in the 1840s when it was thought that lithium, combined with carbonate or citrate—it then forms a salt—was a good treatment for gout. It wasn't, but for some reason known only to history lithium was touted as a cure for epilepsy, diabetes, cancer, even sleeplessness. This cure-all was never proven all that effective, but something about this drug led it to turn up constantly in new incarnations.

In the late 1940s lithium chloride was tried as a salt substitute for patients with kidney or heart disease who required low-sodium diets. Later it was learned that lithium is particularly dangerous for people on low-sodium diets, and for those with congestive heart failure or kidney failure, because lithium exchanges for sodium. If a person is salt-depleted, lithium enters the brain cells, occupies the sites normally taken up by sodium and soon rises to toxic levels. Some people suffered poisoning; a few people died.

Meanwhile, in 1949, in a primitive laboratory in Australia, an unknown psychiatrist named John Cade discovered the true value of lithium. What a quirk in timing. After a century of misapplication,

Cade got on the right track just as alarming stories about lithium poisonings spread throughout America.

Dr. Cade began with a hunch that uric acid caused manic behavior. He intended to inject guinea pigs with uric acid, but he needed to control its potency by keeping it in soluble form. And what solution did he use? Lithium salts.

The guinea pigs became calm and unexcitable. Cade could put them on their backs and they would lie there, unresponsive to any poking or prodding. Dr. Cade reasoned that the lithium might have the same calming effect on people with mania, and he switched the drug to human test subjects: ten manic patients, six schizophrenics and three "melancholics." In the *Medical Journal of Australia* for September 3, 1949, Cade reported:

> W. B., a male, aged fifty-one years, had been in a state of chronic manic excitement for five years, restless, dirty, destructive, mischievous, and interfering, had long been regarded as the most troublesome patient in the ward. His response was highly gratifying. From the start of treatment on March 29, 1948, with lithium citrate he steadily settled down and was enjoying the unaccustomed surroundings of the convalescent ward. . . . He remained perfectly well and left hospital on July 9, 1948 on indefinite leave with instructions to take a maintenance dose of lithium carbonate, five grains twice a day. . . . He was soon back working happily at his job. However, he became lackadaisical about his medicine and finally ceased taking it. His relatives reported that he had not had any for at least six weeks prior to readmission on January 30, 1949, and was becoming steadily more irritable and erratic. He ceased work just before Christmas. On readmission to hospital he was at once started on lithium carbonate, ten grains three times a day, and in a fortnight had again settled down to normal. . . . He is now (February 28, 1949) ready to return to home and work.

Ten case histories of lithium's profound effects on manic patients were reported in this landmark article, but its argument failed to galvanize the medical community. The lithium poisonings in America closed people's minds to the subject.

Danish psychiatrist Mogens Schou, the world expert on the use of lithium in psychiatry, was determined to bring lithium to world attention. He began his campaign in 1957. By the 1960s, lithium was being used in quite a few countries, but the U.S. Food and Drug Administration (FDA) restricted its use to small experiments.

Many scientific papers later, the FDA partially lifted the ban and allowed physicians to prescribe lithium for the treatment of acute manic-depressive illness, but it wasn't until 1974 that the FDA permitted doctors to prescribe lithium in order to prevent future episodes. Today hundreds of thousands of people are living normal lives because of it.

Determining Dosages

Before a patient can be started on lithium therapy, he or she needs a medical evaluation including a medical history, physical examination and simple laboratory tests of blood and urine. Because lithium is almost entirely eliminated from the body by the kidneys, laboratory tests of kidney functions are done before starting the lithium, and at regular intervals thereafter. Tests of thyroid function are also advised since lithium can occasionally cause goiter (a harmless, treatable enlargement of the thyroid gland) or a mild decrease in thyroid function (hypothyroidism). A blood test of the level of thyroid hormones is usually done at regular intervals.

In order for lithium to be effective, its concentration in the blood must be held at the proper level. But although too little is ineffective, too much can be toxic—and there is not much leeway between what is necessary and what is dangerously overdoing it. Therefore, the person who takes lithium must have blood tests in order to determine the exact lithium concentration in the blood. At the start of treatment, blood levels are usually monitored every few days. The blood sample must be drawn twelve hours after the last evening dose and before the patient takes the morning dose. A blood test taken more than thirty minutes before or after the twelve hours have elapsed is not accurate. Patients should carefully plan the timing of blood tests.

A lab report is sent to the physician and he or she will look to see that the level remains in the area of 0.6–0.8 for outpatients and 0.75–1.25 for someone experiencing an acute manic episode. These measurements are in milliequivalents of lithium per liter of blood. Once the level of the drug has stabilized in the bloodstream, monitoring is needed only at one- to three-month intervals. Lithium treatment takes ten days to two weeks to become effective.

Several preparations of lithium are now available. Most are 300-milligram, immediate-release lithium carbonate tablets or capsules. The least expensive preparation is lithium carbonate tablets, which have the added advantage of being scored so that they can be broken in half and the dosage adjusted by 150-milligram increments. Capsules are sometimes preferred because they may be easier to swallow and because tablets may have an unpleasant taste. A liquid form of lithium citrate is also available.

When a person takes any of these forms of lithium, the drug is immediately absorbed and, as a result, produces relatively high peak blood levels. For this reason, a divided dosage regimen is prescribed—often three or four times a day. A conventional release formulation produces a peak blood level from one-half to three hours after the patient takes the medication. Several pharmaceutical companies now produce different forms of release designed to minimize the swings in drug levels. One of these is a slow-release form (Lithobid). This preparation releases the lithium slowly so that the peak blood levels are flattened—the blood level peak is approximately four hours. There are reports that the slow-release form reduces side effects. Another of these release designs is called sustained-release (Eskalith CR). The lithium is embedded in a nondigestible carrier that delays absorption even longer (as much as twelve hours after administration). This allows the drug to be given less frequently, perhaps only twice a day. (It should be noted that some patients complain of lower abdominal cramps or diarrhea with these preparations, perhaps because of their delayed absorption in the gut.)

Slow-release and sustained-release preparations are more expensive. Individual preference, cost and side-effect considerations will initiate a choice or change in lithium preparations.

A patient might find it useful to purchase a clear plastic box with divided compartments for lithium storage. (Most health food and vitamin stores and pharmacies sell them.) Each compartment can be labeled with a day of the week and filled with the daily dosage, and a glance will tell a patient whether or not it has been taken. A routine, such as taking the dose at a meal time or at the hour of sleep can be established so that forgetfulness is not a problem.

TYPICAL COSTS OF LITHIUM PREPARATIONS

A patient taking 1,200 mg a day of lithium would spend the following for a one-month supply of any of these formulations:

Generic name	Trade name	Formulations	Cost of one-month supply*
lithium carbonate	Eskalith	300 mg tablets or capsules	$12.00
	Lithane	300 mg tablets	12.00
	Lithotabs	300 mg tablets	12.00
	Eskalith CR (sustained release)	450 mg tablets	22.00
	Lithobid (slow release)	300 mg tablets	17.00
lithium citrate	Cibalith-S	8 mEq/5 ml (480 ml bottles)	24.00/bottle

* Based on 1986 New York City prices for 120 tablets or capsules.

Should a person forget a dose of lithium, he or she should *not* double the next. If, for example, the patient is taking 300 milligrams, three times a day—at nine A.M., one P.M. and five P.M.—and he realizes at noon that he forgot the morning dose, the physician may advise him to take 450 milligrams at one P.M. and 450 milligrams at five P.M. Naturally, each person has an individual dosage and preparation calibrated to his needs. Don't guess—call the doctor.

Lithium is taken by mouth, rapidly and fully absorbed into the bloodstream and carried to all body and brain tissues. It is excreted almost entirely by the kidneys. Sodium is also excreted by the kidneys in a way that affects lithium secretion, so a normal sodium balance is important to ensure a proper lithium balance. The less sodium in the body, the less lithium is excreted, and the greater chance of lithium buildup and possible toxicity. Diuretics that cause the kidneys to excrete sodium and low-salt diets top the list of things to avoid. But patients should also be aware that any loss of fluids and salts (such as those caused by fevers, vomiting and diarrhea) causes the lithium level to rise in the bloodstream. If any one of these conditions exists, the patient will most likely be instructed to get a lithium level assay and to lower the daily dose of lithium.

A woman who is contemplating pregnancy or who is already pregnant will probably be taken off lithium; there is some question as to whether it is harmful to the developing fetus. This issue will be discussed more completely in Chapter 6.

How Does Lithium Work?

Researchers and physicians have unequivocal data that proves the effectiveness of lithium therapy, but no one is sure how it works, especially why it works in both mania and depression. Some theories propose that lithium works because it decreases the release of the neurotransmitters norepinephrine and dopamine, or because it decreases the chemical actions of alpha receptors on nerve cell membranes.

Although we can't, at this time, draw any definite conclusions as to how lithium works, it's good to keep in mind that the vaccination for smallpox was working effectively for one hundred years before scientists figured out the whys and wherefores.

Side Effects

Lithium is nonsedating and nonaddictive. It is safe at appropriate dosages, although when taken in excess it can produce intoxication and potentially dangerous side effects.

Most of the common side effects are both harmless and easily dealt with. Stopping treatment is rarely necessary.

Early Side Effects The following early side effects occur in perhaps 40 percent of those taking lithium and usually subside in several days:

- Gastrointestinal symptoms: nausea, vomiting, diarrhea, stomach ache. These side effects can usually be alleviated through adjustments of dosage and timing of administration. Simple changes, such as taking a few tablets or capsules at a time, taking them on a full stomach or taking them with a glass of milk, are often effective.

- Fine tremor of the hands at rest, which may cause a change in handwriting
- Thirst and frequent urination
- Fatigue, a dazed feeling, muscle weakness

Persistent or Later-Beginning Side Effects   The side effects that are most likely to persist or begin later in lithium treatment are:

- Hand tremor. An individual inconvenienced by continued tremors beyond the first weeks of treatment should speak with his doctor. After ensuring that the hand tremor is not an indication of early toxicity, the doctor may choose to vary the dosage schedule, change to a slow-release preparation or lower the dose. If all of these options fail and this side effect interferes with the patient's livelihood (for example, the patient is a jeweler or a teacher who must write on a blackboard), then the doctor may prescribe small doses of propranolol (Inderal) to steady the hand tremor.
- Severe thirst and frequent urination, which may be reversed by lowering the dose of lithium, or by careful use of a thiazide diuretic (water pill) such as hydrochlorothiazide

Other Side Effects

- Increase in weight. It is not clear why some patients tend to gain weight on lithium, but a few theories have been proposed, including an altered fat and carbohydrate metabolism, improved appetite after the resolution of an affective episode, increased fluid intake and retention and diminished thyroid function. It seems that people who are overweight before starting lithium therapy are more likely to gain weight. At any rate, a recent study showed that weight gain was one of the major factors in lithium noncompliance. Therefore, in order to avoid the distress of weight gain, patients should drink noncaloric beverages to quench their thirst and watch their calorie consumption. Many people in support groups reported that they increased their weekly exercise routines in order to combat the problem and found this to be effective.

- Hypothyroidism. A small percentage of patients (mostly women) on lithium develop hypothyroidism—the thyroid gland becomes underactive and enlarges in size. The following symptoms may appear: tiredness, slow reactions or slow thinking, feeling cold, dry puffy skin, unusual weight gain, hair loss, muscle aches or menstrual changes. These symptoms should be reported to the doctor, who will evaluate the thyroid gland by ordering thyroid function studies. If there is a problem, it can be easily and effectively treated with L-Thyroxine (Synthroid or Levothroid), a synthetic thyroid hormone replacement.

Less Common Side Effects

- Metallic or bad taste in the mouth, a worsening of acne or psoriasis, skin rashes, hair loss and short-term memory loss. Hair loss (alopecia) has been occasionally reported by patients taking lithium. One summary of seven cases of hair loss revealed that six of the seven were women, two had abnormal thyroid function (hair loss can be a symptom of this), and three had hair regrowth even though they continued taking lithium. There appears to be no explanation for the hair loss, which is really more of an increased shedding or thinning. It can appear as early as five months into treatment and as late as fifty-four months. Should this side effect occur, thyroid functioning should be checked before any decisions about reducing or discontinuing lithium are made.

  There are mixed reports concerning short-term memory loss. Patients have occasionally complained of it, but several memory tests have failed to reveal lithium-induced memory disfunction. Dr. Mogens Schou and his research team made an attempt to address the issue some years ago. They took lithium experimentally for periods of one to six weeks and noted that though they felt no mental side effects at normal preventative doses, they did experience some difficulty concentrating and memorizing at higher doses. Patients who experience this side effect should be assured that lithium effects on mental functioning are reversible and disappear when lithium is discontinued.

Signs of Trouble

High levels of lithium in the blood can be damaging or even fatal. Therefore, patients and their families should take careful note of the signs of an impending problem:

SIGNS OF IMPENDING LITHIUM TOXICITY

Fatigue	Coarse hand tremor
Sleepiness	Unsteady gait
Confusion	Tremor of the lower jaw
Muscle weakness	Muscle twitches
Heaviness of the limbs	Nausea, stomach ache, diarrhea
Slurred speech	Tinnitus (ringing in the ears)

Some of these symptoms could be caused by a number of other illnesses. No matter what the underlying cause, the patient should call the doctor and report the symptoms. An immediate blood test to check the lithium blood level will give firm evidence of the problem, and if necessary, the dosage can be adjusted.

Can You Drink Alcohol or Take Other Medications While on Lithium?

Patients often ask if they can drink while taking lithium. While one or two drinks will probably do no harm, alcohol can interact with lithium and cause excessive sedation and confusion. Moderation is the key here.

Several antibiotics, most notably tetracycline and the medication known as Flagyl, as well as anti-inflammatory agents such as ibuprofen (Motrin, Rufen, Advil and Nuprin) and mefanamic acid (Ponstel), can lead to an increase in the plasma lithium level. Therefore, patients should speak to their psychiatrists before taking any prescription or over-the-counter drugs.

How Long Should One Remain on Lithium?

Whether a person should remain on long-term lithium therapy after an episode has ended depends on many individual factors, and it is a decision requiring close cooperation and discussion among the patient, the doctor and the family. Treating someone for a mild illness or one that is not likely to recur for many years, if ever, unnecessarily exposes him to all the potential risks and expenses that come with prolonged use of any drug. Unfortunately, it is rarely possible to predict what the course of illness will be. The pattern of recurrence, the severity and the duration of each episode, help govern the decision. If episodes are minor and are widely separated in time, long-term medication may not be necessary, although it is usually best to continue treatment for at least four to six months after recovery from an acute episode. Other patients, who experience more severe and frequent episodes, may need to take lithium indefinitely. Dr. Robert Prien of the National Institute of Mental Health reviewed the world literature on the issue of who should receive long-term lithium therapy. He summarized the general consensus of studies that investigated the issue. In either of the following situations, the doctor, patient and family members should seriously consider long-term lithium therapy:

1. A patient who has two or more episodes within a five-year period
2. A patient whose second episode was life-threatening or profoundly disruptive to the patient's and family members' lives

But is it safe to take lithium indefinitely? Well, one of John Cade's patients (one of the ten who were first treated with lithium) died of an unrelated illness in June 1980 after thirty-two years of lithium therapy. He held and still holds the world record for length of recorded lithium treatment.

According to the report on this patient, "B. D.," he had no known episodes of lithium intoxication, and the severity of his mood swings was attenuated. His kidneys were normal for his age. The 1984 Consensus Development Conference at the National Institute of Mental Health concluded that, with the exception of possible thyroid problems, there are few significant permanent risks from long-term lithium therapy. Earlier fears of irreversible kidney damage now seem unwarranted. Physicians remain cautious as to the length of time someone should take maintenance lithium; still, these reports are encouraging.

But when all is said and done, how do the patients themselves feel about lithium? We asked this on the questionnaire we used in researching this book and received responses such as these:

"To finally be off that roller coaster is great."

"A necessary evil and yet a blessing."

"Lithium has literally saved my life. Without it, I know I would have committed suicide."

"I think it's great, except for the weight gain. However, I decided it's better to be fat and sane than skinny and crazy."

"It is necessary and it works, but I hope for better medications with less side effects in the future."

"Fine stuff!"

ANTIPSYCHOTIC MEDICATIONS

Patients who suffer from severe mania, psychotic depression and schizoaffective illness may also suffer delusions and hallucinations and may also hear "voices." The antipsychotic (or neuroleptic) drugs such as Thorazine and Haldol—the same class of drugs that calm and reduce the symptoms plaguing a schizophrenic patient—calm and stabilize the patient experiencing acute mania and psychotic depression. While lithium would prevent states like this from occurring in the future, lithium takes ten days to two weeks to become effective. Meanwhile, in order to make the patient more comfortable and ensure his or her safety during a particularly vulnerable period, an antipsychotic drug might be used during the first week or two. As the lithium takes hold, the antipsychotic is discontinued slowly.

Antipsychotic medications have another use in treating some patients. There are a certain number of people for whom lithium by itself does not work. In such cases, a supplementary drug such as an antipsychotic or an anticonvulsant (discussed on pages 103–4) is sometimes added to the medication regimen.

Antipsychotic drugs were originally used for their antihistaminic quality in surgery. French physician Henri Laborit quickly noticed that patients who were given an antihistaminic became remarkably calm. In one of the great understatements in history, Dr. Laborit commented to his colleagues, "It must have an application in psychiatry."

He began to talk to the French psychiatric establishment about his findings, but he failed to arouse much enthusiasm. "Psychiatrists didn't believe that chemical molecules could have an effect on the human brain, especially when it came to human pathology," he recalled in an interview with Richard Restak for *The Brain*. One surgeon who attended a conference given by Laborit went home and told his psychiatrist brother-in-law, Pierre Deniker, about the Laborit findings with the antihistaminic chlorpromazine. By 1952 Pierre Deniker and another psychiatrist, Jean Delay, completed their first clinical trials with chlorpromazine and reported its enormous potential. The drug diminished delusional thought and hallucinations. Before long, this new psychiatric drug was being used all over the world.

The chart on the next page lists the seven different chemical classes of antipsychotic drugs, their generic names and their trade names. (Generic refers to the official name for the chemical compound; trade names are the brand names used by drug companies for marketing purposes. For example, Thorazine is the trade name of the generic chemical chlorpromazine.)

Because there is a tremendous difference in the milligram potency (the amount of antipsychotic effect in a single milligram) of each drug, there is a correspondingly large variance in the prescribed doses. For instance, because haloperidol (Haldol) is approximately fifty times as potent as chlorpromazine (Thorazine), a patient given 800 milligrams of chlorpromazine would be receiving approximately the same amount of antipsychotic benefit as a patient given 40 milligrams of haloperidol.

Generally the antipsychotic medications are prescribed in tablet or liquid form, and they are usually taken once or twice a day. Many of these drugs can be given as a short-acting intramuscular injection. Fluphenazine decanoate (Prolixin) can be given as a long-acting injection that lasts from two to four weeks. Haldol decanoate, which came on the market in 1986, also lasts from two to four weeks.

Some patients may respond well to one antipsychotic medication but not as well to another. The physician would then try another drug from another class. For instance, a patient who does not respond to Prolixin should not be switched to Stelazine but perhaps should be switched to Thorazine or Haldol.

COMMON TYPES OF ANTIPSYCHOTIC MEDICATIONS

Type	Generic name	Trade name
aliphatic phenothiazines	chlorpromazine	Thorazine Chlorprom Largactil
	promazine	Sparine
piperidine phenothiazines	thioridazine	Mellaril
	mesoridazine	Serentil
piperazine phenothiazines	fluphenazine	Prolixin Permitil
	trifluoperazine	Stelazine Pentazine
	perphenazine	Trilafon Phenazine
thioxanthines	thiothixene	Navane
	chlorprothixene	Taractan
butyrophenones	haloperidol	Haldol
	droperidol	Inapsine
dibenzepines	loxipine	Loxitane
dihydroindolones	molindone	Moban Lindone

Side Effects

Among the most common side effects of an antipsychotic drug are constipation, blurring of vision, drowsiness and dry mouth, but these often diminish or disappear as a person becomes accustomed to the medication.

Also common (but extremely frightening to a patient who has not been warned of them) are the side effects that involve movement and posture: dystonic reactions, akinesia and akathisia. These are transient, treatable and reversible and are defined as follows:

- Dystonic reactions. These are involuntary muscle contractions that cause bizarre and uncontrolled movements of the face, neck, tongue and back and an uncontrolled rolling of the eyes (counteracted in minutes by the antiparkinson agents such as Artane or Cogentin).

- Akinesia. This is characterized by stiffness and diminished spontaneity of gestures, physical movement and speech (counteracted by Artane or Cogentin).

- Akathisia. This is a feeling of internal restlessness—inability to sit still, as well as a subjective sensation of discomfort often described as anxiety, and often mistaken for agitation rather than a side effect of the antipsychotic drug (counteracted by propranolol [Inderal]).

These movement disorders can be dealt with by lowering the dose of the antipsychotic medication, adding an antiparkinson drug or switching to another class of neuroleptic. Generally, the more sedating the neuroleptic, the less likely it is to cause movement disorders. A physician might want to select a low-potency, more sedating drug such as a thioridazine (Mellaril) or chlorpromazine (Thorazine) to minimize the likelihood of movement abnormalities for the patient.

Antipsychotic drugs can cause menstrual changes in women, breast discharge in both sexes and a diminished sex drive. They can also cause sexual dysfunction in men, for example, retrograde ejaculation (ejaculation occurs but the seminal fluid passes backward into the bladder), anorgasmia (the inability to have an orgasm) or impotence.

There may be a tendency to gain a great deal of weight on an antipsychotic medication. The reasons why this occurs have not been conclusively determined, but it could become a serious problem and should be watched carefully.

Another side effect (especially common with low-potency neuroleptics) is the development of a sensitivity to the sun (called photosensitivity). Patients who have it may burn very easily. Exposure to the sun should be very limited, and sun-screen lotions with a high sun-protection factor should be used.

Tardive Dyskinesia

Perhaps the most publicized side effect of antipsychotic drugs is tardive dyskinesia, "late appearing movement disorder." It is characterized by involuntary facial grimacing, lip smacking, chewing and sucking movements, cheek puffing and worm-like movements of the tongue. Writhing movements of the body, or jerky, purposeless movements of the arms and legs, complete this disfiguring but unpainful picture. Tardive dyskinesia may not reverse itself, and the peak risk for the patient occurs when he or she has been on a neuroleptic for one to two years.

There are ways to minimize the risk. A person should be put on the lowest dose necessary to control the psychotic symptoms, and the doctor should regularly attempt to reduce the dose. Frequent monitoring by the physician will reveal early symptoms of tardive dyskinesia and the medication can be discontinued.

Before the FDA approved the use of lithium for manic-depressive illness, neuroleptics were the only drugs that could control some of the psychotic symptoms of a manic phase. Today the use of lithium and perhaps some anticonvulsants prevents manic or psychotic depressive episodes to a degree that alleviates the need for long-term use of neuroleptics at high doses. As stated earlier, if an antipsychotic drug is needed, it is usually for only a short period of time, or if it is part of a drug regimen, it can usually be prescribed at low doses. The specter of tardive dyskinesia, while still a possibility, is not now the threat it once was for people with manic-depressive disorders.

OTHER ANTIMANIC MEDICATIONS

Lithium has gained worldwide acceptance for the treatment of affective disorders, and approximately 70 to 80 percent of bipolar patients respond to it and are not troubled by serious side effects. But where does that leave the 20 to 30 percent who either don't respond or respond only partially, who can't tolerate the side effects or who, for medical reasons, can't take lithium at all? Especially difficult to stabilize are the group of patients known as "rapid cyclers." These are people who have four or more episodes of illness in a one-year period, and their response to lithium is often partial—they still have breakthroughs of mania or depression. If these patients become depressed, the doctor can treat them with an antidepressant, but at a risk of reinducing mania. And so the cycles begin again.

Fortunately things are looking up. There are alternative treatments for these groups of patients. Studies completed within the last few years in Japan and the United States show that two drugs introduced for temporal lobe epilepsy, carbamazepine (Tegretol) and valproic acid (Depakene), can be very effective treatments for acute mania, perhaps have antidepressant properties (but may not induce a manic swing) and work to prevent future episodes of bipolar illness. These drugs are not associated with movement disorders or tardive dyskinesia.

A number of patients who failed to respond to lithium and then failed to respond to carbamazepine have responded well to a combination of the two. There is speculation that the two have a synergistic effect.

These drugs are not without their side effects and hazards, however. The most common side effects are dizziness, drowsiness, nausea and some mental confusion, although many of these were considered generally mild. Women on birth control pills should understand that carbamazepine interferes with the contraceptive capability of the pill.

There have been some reports of bone marrow suppression (aplastic anemia) with carbamazepine. While rare, this is a life-threatening condition. Therefore, it is good practice for the patient to have a blood cell count weekly at first, and once a month thereafter. Photosensitivity—the skin's extreme sensitivity to sunlight—and easy bruising may be early symptoms of this potentially lethal development.

Another anticonvulsant drug, clonazepam (Klonopin), has been found to control a number of manic symptoms. Clonazepam is a member of the benzodiazepine family (as is Valium) and, unlike the antipsychotic drugs, produces no movement or anticholinergic side effects (see pages 101–3). It works more rapidly than lithium in acute mania and is highly sedating.

While clonazepam controls manic features such as pressured speech, racing thoughts and hyperactivity, it has not been demonstrated to be as effective for psychotic symptoms such as delusions and hallucinations. In mania with these features, a combination of clonazepam and a low-dose antipsychotic medication may be beneficial.

MEDICATIONS FOR DEPRESSION

A psychiatrist or physician can treat a person suffering from depression in a number of ways: with tricyclic antidepressants, with monoamine oxidase inhibitors (MAOIs) and with electroconvulsive therapy (ECT). If there is a history of recurrent depression, the patient may be treated with lithium and an antidepressant—either a tricyclic or an MAOI—during the acute depressive episode, and remain on the lithium alone thereafter in order to prevent future episodes. We'll discuss the tricyclic antidepressants first because they are the first line of treatment and are most often prescribed.

Antidepressants

Tricyclic antidepressants were discovered in the 1950s when the Swiss pharmaceutical firm Geigy tested a compound that resembled chlorpromazine's chemical structure. The animal data looked good, so they gave the new compound, imipramine, to psychiatrist Roland Kuhn. Dr. Kuhn began trials with schizophrenic patients, but imipramine did little to help the delusions and hallucinations. It did, however, have remarkable effects on depressed patients, as it elevated mood and activated behavior.

Dr. Kuhn reported his results with the drug in a paper given at the Second International Congress of Psychiatry at Zurich in 1957, but only about twelve people attended the session. Fortunately the news spread rapidly thereafter. A new class of drug was added to the psychiatric armamentarium, and many, many patients were helped. The other pharmaceutical houses in Europe and America rushed to produce their slightly altered versions (the "me too's") of tricyclic antidepressants.

Tricyclic antidepressants (named with a nod to their three-ring chemical structure) were just the beginning. Today there are antidepressants with a four-ring structure (Ludiomil), and an atypical antidepressant called trazodone (Desyrel) that doesn't resemble the tricyclics or the tetracyclics. Newer antidepressants are available or are soon to be introduced.

Typically, a psychiatrist may start a patient on 25 to 50 milligrams of an antidepressant and increase the dosage each day until the effective daily dosage is reached. Patients should not expect to feel better immediately. For reasons the researchers are still puzzling out, it often takes three to four weeks for a person to experience relief from depression (see page 64 for a possible explanation). Some patients, after a few weeks of the treatment, feel their depression lift almost overnight. They simply wake up feeling good. Others report that their symptoms improve slowly over a period of days to weeks.

Although all patients have individual response patterns, the usual sequence of events that occurs when a person is treated with a tricyclic antidepressant is as follows:

1. The patient notices an improvement in his sleep disturbance within the first few days of therapy.
2. Other people note the changes, although the patient may not feel greatly improved.
3. Within two to three weeks the patient finds him or herself more interested in people, in surroundings and in activities.
4. The patient feels better as the symptoms recede or disappear.

Side Effects

Each of the antidepressants can cause varying degrees of side effects, which fall into the following three categories:

- Sedation (drowsiness or sleepiness)
- Anticholinergic effects (dry mouth, blurred vision, constipation, difficulty urinating, increased heart rate)
- Orthostatic hypotension (light-headedness or dizziness when rising quickly from a sitting or lying position)

The more infrequently reported side effects of tricyclic antidepressants are:

- Skin rash
- Sweating
- Tremor
- Altered orgasmic function
- Weight gain

In the best of all possible worlds, the drugs that doctors prescribe would affect only target symptoms—the ones the doctors seek to relieve. This, unfortunately, is not the case, especially with the tricyclic antidepressants. On their way to interacting with the chemical substances norepinephrine or serotonin, the tricyclics block the acetylcholine receptors at the junctions between nerve fibers and internal organs. The blockade at the salivary glands is responsible for dry mouth; the blockade at the iris of the eye causes blurred vision. Constipation can occur because these drugs affect the system that regulates the contractions of the intestines. These side effects are called anticholinergic, and they are usually more annoying than worrisome.

If a drug is said to have low anticholinergic activity, the blockade is less complete and the side effects are less noticeable. High anticholinergic activity means a patient can usually expect more of the dry mouth, blurred vision, constipation and so on. However, it is important to keep in mind that many patients respond well to the antidepressants with higher anticholinergic activity.

There are several ways to minimize the three categories of side effects caused by antidepressants. The symptoms of dry mouth can be alleviated partially by stimulating the saliva by sucking on *sugarless* candies or chewing *sugarless* gum. When a patient is particularly troubled by the symptom, a doctor may prescribe a saliva-stimulating medication like pilocarpine. Because a lack of sufficient saliva may indirectly lead to tooth decay and gum problems, it is very important that the patient pay attention to oral hygiene.

While constipation is indeed a possible side effect of a tricyclic antidepressant, it is associated frequently with the depressive syndrome itself and may actually stop being a problem as the antidepressant begins to have an effect. If constipation does occur as a side effect of the antidepressant treatment, the patient should increase his intake of fruits, vegetables and other sources of fiber and ensure that his fluid intake is adequate. If these measures fail, the psychiatrist may prescribe a stool softener or a laxative or switch the patient to an antidepressant with fewer anticholinergic side effects.

The light-headedness caused by orthostatic hypotension can be minimized by rising to a sitting position slowly, and sitting for a few seconds before standing.

Some people are helped by the sedating side effects of some of the antidepressants: they begin to sleep better, and they are less troubled by anxiety and agitation. But there are those who find the sedation troubling and would like to get up in the morning feeling less groggy. Then, too, some people have to drive or operate machinery and cannot afford to feel sedated or drowsy. There is always the possibility of switching to another, less sedating antidepressant.

The chart below outlines the range of dosages and the side effects of the commonly prescribed antidepressants.

COMMON ANTIDEPRESSANT MEDICINES

Generic name	Trade name	Usual daily starting* dose (mg)	Usual effective daily dose* (mg)	Relative sedative effects	Relative anticholinergic effects	Relative hypotensive effects
Tricyclic antidepressants						
amitriptyline	Endep Elavil Amitid	75	150–300	high	high	more
amoxapine	Asendin	50 three times daily	150–400	medium	low	less
desipramine	Norpramin Pertofrane	50	100–300	low	low	more
doxepin	Adapin Sinequan	75	75–300	high	medium	more
imipramine	Janimine SK-Pramine Tofranil	75	150–300	medium	medium	more
nortriptyline	Aventyl Pamelor	50	50–150	low	medium	less
protriptyline	Vivactil	5 three times daily	15–60	low	high	more
trimipramine	Surmontil	75	50–200	high	medium	more
Other antidepressants						
maprotiline	Ludiomil	75	125–225	medium	low	less
trazodone	Desyrel	50 three times daily	150–400	high	low	less

* Lower doses (often ⅓ to ½ of the usual dose) are used with older patients.

Reprinted with permission from *Depression and Its Treatment* by John H. Greist, M.D., and James W. Jefferson, M.D. (Washington, DC: American Psychiatric Press, Inc., 1984).

Some patients require a higher dose of an antidepressant than others. One of the reasons for an incomplete response is the failure on the part of some doctors to prescribe adequate doses of antidepressants. (Many patients who are referred to affective disorders clinics because they do not respond to treatment are found to have been treated with inadequate doses of the medications. They subsequently recover when the dosage is raised.) A depression not treated aggressively is demoralizing and dangerous to a patient. Therapeutic blood levels have been established for several of the tricyclic antidepressants, most notably imipramine and nortriptyline. To ensure that the dosage of medication is adequate, the physician may order blood tests to determine the antidepressant level.

Caveats

It's ironic that the very drugs that treat depression and stave off suicidal impulses can be used to express them. An acute overdose of ten to fifteen times the usual therapeutic dose can cause convulsions or even death in adults as well as in children. For this reason, a doctor faced with a potentially suicidal patient may choose to administer the treatment in a hospital setting, or to limit each prescription to a one-week supply and to monitor the blood levels to ensure that the patient is not saving up a supply.

A psychiatrist would rarely give an antidepressant to a person with cardiovascular disease, cardiac arrhythmia, thrombophlebitis, hyperthyroidism, a history of narrow-angle glaucoma or increased intraocular pressure. Therefore, it is good medical practice for the patient to have a complete physical examination, electrocardiogram and routine blood tests before an antidepressant is prescribed.

Bipolar patients should be aware that treatment of depressive episodes with tricyclic antidepressants (or the monoamine oxidase inhibitors described in the next section) may induce a rapid switch into hypomania and even mania or increase the frequency of cycles of illness. For these reasons, antidepressants without lithium maintenance therapy are not indicated for long-term use in bipolar patients.

Patients who wear soft contact lenses and take antidepressants may have some special problems. The anticholinergic side effect of decreased tearing may lead to excessive deposits of thick mucoid secretions on the contact lenses, and this may cause an itching, gritty sensation under the lenses. A patient should be sure to mention the use of contact lenses to his or her physician. Should a problem occur, the doctor can prescribe a different antidepressant, or reduce the dosage or prescribe the use of artificial tears.

Older patients often need a lower dosage of antidepressants with the lowest level of anticholinergic side effects (see chart, page 133).

How Long Should One Remain on an Antidepressant?

Studies show that 70 percent of the people who stopped taking an antidepressant five weeks or less after they became symptom-free relapsed; 42 percent of the people who discontinued treatment eleven to twenty weeks after becoming symptom-free relapsed; the number fell to 14 percent among those who had been symptom-free for over five months before discontinuing treatment. The amount of time a person stayed on an antidepressant was directly related to the rate of relapse.

Therefore, many psychiatrists prescribe the medication for six months to a year. Afterward, there is a carefully supervised discontinuation process in which the dosage is reduced gradually over a period of several weeks or longer. Abruptly discontinuing the medication may precipitate withdrawal symptoms such as restlessness, anxiety and akathisia—a feeling of internal restlessness and the inability to sit still.

The Matter of MAOIs

At about the time that tricyclic antidepressants made their debut, doctors in Europe noticed that an antibiotic, iproniazid—a monoamine oxidase inhibitor used for the treatment of tuberculosis—was producing a euphoric effect in the patients taking it. Because the patients felt too good to take proper precautions with their illness, the physicians switched them to another medication, and the antibiotic retreated to the drug company's shelf inventory.

Two American psychiatrists, George Crane and Nathan Kline, reported favorably on its mood improvement characteristics and helped resurrect the drug. Within one year, approximately four hundred thousand people were given iproniazid.

Many were helped, but unfortunately the rose hid thorns: several people who took the drug developed problems ranging in seriousness from headaches to jaundice to cerebral hemorrhage. The FDA recommended iproniazid's removal from the market, and the drug company complied.

Today, there are three classes of monoamine oxidase inhibitors (MAOIs as they are called) used in this country. Although doctors are concerned that they can cause dangerously high blood pressure if patients are not careful about what they eat and that there can be adverse reactions when they are taken with certain other drugs, the MAOIs are increasingly recognized as a useful treatment in depression. The drugs lack the severe anticholinergic side effects of the tricyclic antidepressants, and they can be used by patients with heart disease. Moreover, these drugs often work when all others fail, and seem to be increasingly useful for patients with so-called atypical depression (those who eat excessively, sleep for irregularly long periods of time, are lethargic, feel worse later in the day, experience extreme anxiety or fear or who are hypochondriacal). For certain patients who do not respond to tricyclic antidepressants, or who will not opt for electroconvulsive therapy, the MAOIs just might make the difference and return the patient to health.

The three MAOIs available in the United States are: isocarboxazid (Marplan), phenelzine (Nardil) and tranylcypromine (Parnate).

MONOAMINE OXIDASE INHIBITORS

Generic name	Trade name	Usual daily therapeutic dose*
isocarboxazid	Marplan	30–50 mg
phenelzine sulfate	Nardil	60–90 mg
tranylcypromine sulfate	Parnate	30–50 mg

* All the dosages noted above are approximate. Some patients respond to lower dosages than those listed; others may require higher dosages.

The side effect profile of MAOIs can include: insomnia, inability to have an orgasm (anorgasmia) and low blood pressure (hypotension).

Restrictions When Using MAOIs

The dietary prohibitions for patients taking MAOIs need some explaining. The body has within it a marvelous mechanism for halting neurotransmitter activity. The monoamines norepinephrine, dopamine and serotonin are "retired from service" by an enzyme circulating in the synapses called monoamine oxidase. It breaks down the monoamines through a metabolic process. But since depression is thought to be caused by a lack of norepinephrine or serotonin, the inhibition or blockade of the monoamine oxidase grants the "stay of execution" to the norepinephrine and serotonin, thus increasing the amount available for transmission.

Certain foods contain the amine tyramine. Normally tyramine is metabolized by monoamine oxidase in the gut and liver, but a person taking an MAOI cannot metabolize it efficiently, and the tyramine enters the general circulation in abnormally high concentrations. Once there, it can stimulate the release of norepinephrine and so cause a sudden, sometimes dangerous increase in blood pressure. Such a hypertensive reaction can cause symptoms ranging from throbbing headaches, nausea and vomiting to serious rupture of blood vessels in the brain—stroke. Therefore, although an MAOI definitely combats the problems of depression, its use is safe only in the absence of the foods, drinks and medications that in combination with an MAOI would be dangerous for the patient. They are listed on the next page.

In addition, a person taking an MAOI must not use nose drops or cold remedies such as Contac or Nyquil—anything that shrinks the mucous membranes. These cold medications are pharmacologically similar to norepinephrine and thus can't be metabolized when an MAOI is in the picture. They'll concentrate in the blood and also provoke increases in blood pressure.

The signs of elevated blood pressure are: a headache at the back of the neck, a stiff neck, a pounding heart, nausea and vomiting. If a patient feels any of these symptoms, he or she should stop taking the MAOI and go immediately to the doctor's office or a hospital emergency room. The patient should explain the type of medication he is taking and ask to have his blood pressure taken. If it is elevated, the medical personnel will probably prescribe a blood pressure lowering agent such as phentolamine (Regitine).

And while we're pounding away at the precautionary notes . . . A patient on an MAOI should take no other medications unless they've been cleared by the physician prescribing the MAOI—especially no

FOODS AND BEVERAGES TO BE AVOIDED WITH
MONOAMINE OXIDASE INHIBITORS

The following foods should be avoided definitely:
Aged cheeses of any kind and foods prepared with them, such as pizza and
  fondue (cottage cheese, cream cheese and farmer's cheese are allowed)
Yogurt
Liver of all kinds (pâté)
Fermented sausages (bologna, pepperoni, salami, summer sausage)
Pastrami
Corned beef
Salted or smoked fish (lox or nova, etc.)
Caviar
Snails (preserved)
Pickles
Pickled fish (herring, etc.)
Fava beans, lima beans, Italian beans or Chinese pea pods
Yeast products (Bovril, Oxo, Marmite, dietary supplements containing brewer's
  yeast). *Note:* Baked goods made with yeast are allowed.
Avocado (especially overripe; guacamole)
Figs (overripe, canned or spoiled)
Bananas (overripe)
Chianti

*The following foods and beverages may cause problems in large amounts, but
are less troublesome in small quantities:*
Alcohol
Sour cream
Chocolate
Caffeinated beverages (coffee, tea, cola, cocoa)
Sauerkraut
Raisins

Note: Rare reactions have been associated with the ingestion of soy sauce, cyclamate sweeteners
and overripe fruits. Patients should check with their physicians about the use of these products.

barbiturates or opiates. Demerol, in particular, is potentially lethal
due to a central nervous system reaction of unknown basis. Patients
who need surgery and require a surgical anesthetic should be taken
off the MAOI several days prior to the operation.

So who is a candidate for the value MAOIs have to offer? Ob-
viously someone with a good memory, someone with the ability to
look at a piece of pizza and think, "cheese," and someone with the
desire to sacrifice and stick to the dietary prohibitions in order to
recover health. They're tricky, without a doubt. They also work. And
sometimes when nothing else does.

Combined Antidepressant and Lithium Treatment for Depression

Studies from the NIMH Collaborative Project on the Psychobiology of Depression indicate that approximately 25 percent of patients with severe depressions show little or no improvement despite adequate antidepressant trials. Another group of patients who have depressive symptoms that remit for only brief periods of time relapse even with intensive treatment. These patients are referred to as "treatment resistant," and lately much attention has been focused on these conditions. (It should be noted, however, that many patients described as "treatment resistant" have not been treated with an adequate dosage of a traditional antidepressant or have not been treated with the medication for a long enough period of time—for instance, five to six weeks.)

Several prominent research groups have reported that many patients with true treatment-resistant depressions have improved considerably when they were given a combination of a standard antidepressant (either a tricyclic antidepressant or an MAOI) *and* lithium. In one study, 31 percent of previously unresponsive patients had a complete remission of symptoms while 25 percent improved significantly.

Xanax and Other Benzodiazepines

One other drug with an antidepressant effect needs to be mentioned here: alprazolam (Xanax). Alprazolam is an antianxiety medication, a benzodiazepine ten times more potent than Valium. While it is approved for the treatment of anxiety symptoms and panic disorder, several studies found it to have an antidepressant effect on patients with mild to moderate depression.

Like other benzodiazepines, alprazolam can be somewhat sedating. Because of its potency and short half-life, alprazolam may be difficult to discontinue without a prolonged tapering period. Some cases require that Valium be substituted for alprazolam in the final phase of this tapering process in order to minimize symptoms of withdrawal.

Patients should note that none of the other benzodiazepines are appropriate as the principal treatment for major depression. While there is perhaps a place for their use in combination with an anti-depressant medication, surveys in this country show that nonpsy-chiatrist physicians tend to inappropriately prescribe antianxiety drugs alone. Very often the diagnosis of major depression is not made, and the doctor treats some of the symptoms—for instance, the anxiety and sleep disturbance—with the antianxiety drugs. This practice is detrimental as it can lead to prolongation of the depression and/or drug dependence.

ELECTROCONVULSIVE THERAPY (ECT)

During the writing of this book, we reviewed a videotape that had been made to teach medical students at the Albert Einstein College of Medicine how to administer electroconvulsive therapy—ECT. The tape began with an interview with a woman suffering from severe depression. She had been unresponsive to medications, had been depressed for eight months and sat hunched in a chair. She refused to look at the doctor conducting the interview, and she gave short, irritable and hopeless-sounding answers to the questions asked of her. When the ECT treatment was described to her, she didn't seem to feel it (or anything else) could help.

Toward the end of the tape, and after three treatments of ECT, the viewer sees this woman sitting in the same chair, in the same room, but now she's dressed up and not only looking directly at the doctor, but also laughing and teasing him about something he's said. The woman, at the end of the video, actually tells the doctor that she would recommend the treatment to other people in her situation. The before-after differences in the woman are so marked that it occurred to us that a person viewing this tape and unfamiliar with ECT would strongly suspect that the talents of an actress had been employed to convince people that ECT wasn't really so bad.

This year marks the fiftieth year that ECT has been an option in the treatment of depression (and intractable mania), and there's been a resurgence of interest because it has evolved into a safe option, one that works. But for a public influenced by Ken Kesey's *One Flew Over the Cuckoo's Nest,* whose associations with electric shock start with the electric chair and move on to lightning bolts, electric eels and third rails, it makes for queasy conversation. For all of us. Let's replace a few of the myths with facts.

The idea that electrical stimulus can be a therapeutic agent goes back to before A.D. 43 when the torpedo fish was used to shock people to treat headaches. Physicians in the twentieth century (erroneously) thought that schizophrenia was rare among epileptics and decided that seizures might prevent the schizophrenia. Somewhere in the 1930s Dr. Ladislas Meduna injected patients with the stimulating drug metrazol, induced a seizure and found that 70 percent of his depressed patients got well. At about the same time, Dr. Manfred Sakel used injections of insulin to produce coma and noted that there was improved functioning after the treatment. Two physicians in Italy, Drs. Ugo Cerletti and Luigi Bini, began to look at the data on this chemical convulsive treatment and thought that they could achieve a desired neural discharge by applying an electric current to the temples of a human being. They gave the treatment the distressing label l'elettroshock.

Before we describe the procedure, let us state that ECT has a higher success rate for severe depression than any other form of treatment. It can be life-saving and produce dramatic results. It is particularly useful for people who suffer from psychotic depressions or intractable mania, people who cannot take antidepressants due to problems of health or lack of response and pregnant women who suffer from depression or mania. A patient who is very intent on suicide, and who would not wait three weeks for an antidepressant to work, would be a good candidate for ECT because it works more rapidly. In fact, suicide attempts are relatively rare after a course of treatment has started.

ECT is usually given three times a week. A patient may require as few as three or four treatments or as many as twelve to fifteen. Once the family and patient consider that the patient is more or less back to his normal level of functioning, it is usual for the patient to have one or two additional treatments in order to prevent relapse. Today the method is painless, and with modifications in technique it bears little relationship to the unmodified treatments of the 1940s.

The patient is put to sleep with a very short-acting barbiturate, and then the drug succinylcholine is administered. This medicine temporarily paralyzes the muscles so that they do not contract during the treatment and cause fractures. Then an electrode is placed above the temple of the nondominant side of the brain, and a second is placed in the middle of the forehead (this is called unilateral ECT); or one electrode is placed above each temple (this is called bilateral ECT). A very small current of electricity is passed through the brain, activating it and producing a seizure. Because the patient is anesthetized and his body is totally relaxed by the succinylcholine, he sleeps peacefully while an electroencephalogram (EEG) monitors the seizure activity and an electrocardiogram (EKG) monitors the heart rhythm. The current is applied for one second or less, and the patient breathes pure oxygen through a mask. The duration of a clinically effective seizure ranges from thirty seconds to sometimes longer than a minute, and the patient wakes up ten to fifteen minutes later.

Upon awakening, a patient may experience a brief period of confusion, headache or muscle stiffness, but these symptoms typically ease in a matter of twenty to sixty minutes.

The setting and composition of the treatment team are important factors in reducing the risks associated with ECT. During the few seconds following the ECT stimulus there may be a temporary drop in blood pressure. This may be followed by a marked increase in heart rate, which may then lead to a rise in blood pressure. Heart rhythm disturbances, not unusual during this period of time, generally subside without complications. For this reason, however, and because there is always a risk (although very small) associated with short-acting anesthetics, a hospital setting with a treatment team composed of a psychiatrist, an anesthesiologist and nursing personnel trained in ECT procedures and recovery would decrease the risk of complications. A patient with a history of high blood pressure or other cardiovascular problems should have a cardiology consultation prior to treatment.

Because as many as 20 to 50 percent of the people who respond well to a course of ECT relapse within six months of the treatment, a maintenance treatment of antidepressants, lithium or one treatment of ECT at monthly or six-week intervals might be advisable.

Short-term memory loss has always been a concern to patients who receive ECT and the doctors who administer it, but several studies conclude that patients who received unilateral ECT performed better on attention/memory tests than those who received bilateral ECT. However, there is a question as to whether unilateral is as effective. Experts agree that changes in memory function do occur and persist for a few days following treatment, but that patients return to normal within a month. A 1985 Consensus Conference convened at the National Institute of Mental Health concluded that while some memory loss is frequent after ECT, it is estimated that less than one-half of 1 percent of ECT patients suffer severe memory loss. Memory problems resulting from ECT usually clear up within seven months of the treatment, although there may be a persistent memory deficit for the period immediately surrounding the ECT treatment.

How Does ECT Work?

Animal research shows that ECT enhances dopamine sensitivity, reduces the reuptake of serotonin and activates the systems in the brain that use norepinephrine. It also increases the amount of the major inhibitory neurotransmitter, GABA, yet much remains unclear about its mechanism of action.

How Distressing Is ECT to Patients?

While there are certainly patients who perceive the treatment as terrifying and shameful, and some who report distress about persistent memory loss, many—like the woman in the video—speak positively of the benefits. An article entitled "Are Patients Shocked by ECT?" reported on interviews with seventy-two consecutive patients treated with electroconvulsive therapy. The patients were asked whether they were frightened or angered by the experience, how they looked back at the treatment, and whether they would do it again. Of the patients interviewed, 54 percent considered a trip to the dentist more distressing, many praised the treatment, and 81 percent said they would agree to have ECT again. Those are comforting statistics about a treatment that has an ugly name and ugly connotations but sometimes beautiful and even life-saving results.

6

SPECIAL ASPECTS OF THE DISORDERS: SEASONAL AFFECTIVE DISORDERS, MOOD DISORDERS IN CHILDREN AND THE ELDERLY, MOOD DISORDERS AND PREGNANCY

IN THE RIGHT LIGHT: SEASONAL AFFECTIVE DISORDER

Seasonal affective disorder (SADs) is a newly described syndrome, characterized by recurrent depressions that occur every year at the same time. When the days grow shorter in the fall, these patients experience depression, extreme sluggishness, irritability and anxiety. They begin to sleep for longer and longer periods of time, and to withdraw from social activities. In effect, they hibernate for the winter. But in marked contrast to depressed patients who stop eating and lose significant amounts of weight, they binge on carbohydrates and often gain between ten to twenty pounds throughout the winter months. Once spring comes and the photoperiod lengthens, people with SADs experience new energy, shed the gained pounds and find their mood returning to normal or slightly elevated levels.

This depressive syndrome, defined by Dr. Norman Rosenthal and his colleagues at the National Institute of Mental Health, received much media attention because of the unusual treatment devised for it: patients who met the criteria for SADs were seated in front of a bank of high-intensity, full-spectrum lights for three hours before dawn and three hours after dusk. By recreating the photoperiod of a summer day, almost all the patients experienced partial or complete remission of their depressive symptoms. When the light treatments were stopped, a number of the patients relapsed.

In order to understand the causes of these seasonal depressions and why this form of light treatment was effective, researchers are focusing attention on the pineal gland—a small reddish-gray structure that sits near the center of the brain. Its name is derived from the Latin word for "pine cone" because early viewers glimpsed a resemblance.

All vertebrates possess a pineal gland, and in certain reptiles and birds the gland is situated close enough to the top of the skull to monitor the intensity of sunlight. This "third eye" appears to help the animal adjust to changes in the day-night cycles of the yearly seasons. Although the seventeenth-century philosopher René Descartes thought the human pineal to be the seat of the rational soul and the second-century physician Galen believed it to be the valve that regulated the flow of thoughts out of storage in the brain, modern scientists until recently felt that the buried-down-under human pineal had been abandoned by the roadside of human evolution. No longer a third eye, it had no present function.

Not so. In the mid-sixties, researchers discovered that the pineal gland secretes an important hormone called melatonin. It is now clear that information about light is brought by special nerve pathways to the pineal gland where it affects the secretion of melatonin (see the illustration on page 78). And it is the secretion of melatonin that may provide a link to depression. There are several reasons for this. First, the neurotransmitter serotonin (believed to be associated with depression) is a precursor of melatonin. Also, melatonin is a sleep-inducing hormone, produced in the dark, which appears to depress both mood and mental agility; its secretion is at its highest levels in winter. To build the case further, studies by Dr. Alfred Lewy found that, compared to others, bipolar patients had a supersensitivity to light as evidenced by a markedly increased suppression of melatonin on exposure to bright light. Melatonin is also thought to have a part in the synchronization of circadian (daily) rhythms.

Today scientists accept that a kind of biological clock in the human organism establishes a fundamental daily rhythm for bodily functions such as body temperature, the release of cortisol, rest/activity levels and the secretion of melatonin. But nature has built some flexibility into the organism so that the body can adjust and synchronize to the ever-changing environmental rhythms—such as longer and shorter photoperiods in summer and winter.

Apparently some people do not adjust so easily. Dr. Lewy hypothesized that certain depressed people have a desynchronization in their twenty-four-hour internal clock rhythms. For instance, their sleep, temperature and cortisol cycles may be in synchrony with each other, but be out of step with other twenty-four-hour rhythms, thus causing their internal clocks to run a few hours behind or ahead of schedule. They either start and stop releasing melatonin earlier than usual (leading to evening sleepiness and early morning awakening), or start and stop releasing melatonin later than usual (leading to difficulty sleeping at night as well as difficulty getting up in the morning). In 1980 Dr. Lewy was able to determine that bright light inhibited the level of melatonin secreted. By exposing the first group of patients—those who experienced evening sleepiness and early morning awakening—to bright light for three hours in the evening, he delayed the release of melatonin, and the symptoms of depression improved; by exposing the second group—those who had trouble sleeping at night and couldn't get up in the morning—to bright light in the early morning, he phase-advanced the patients by shutting off the melatonin levels at a more normal time. Again the symptoms of depression improved. The twenty-four-hour rhythms seemed to resynchronize.

Dr. Daniel Kripke and his research group in San Diego are exploring the impact of light and the secretion of melatonin from the perspective of the hibernation response. Melatonin triggers hibernation and mating cycles in animals. Perhaps the depression of seasonal affective disorders in humans is a vestigial hibernation response. Dr. Kripke's group looked at the hibernation cycle in hamsters and discovered that it was triggered by a lack of light during a specific period in the early morning. Conversely, if there was exposure to light during that critical period, the hibernation response was inhibited. Kripke and his colleagues wondered if there isn't such a point in the human circadian cycle, possibly occurring right after awakening. Perhaps depressed patients are reaching this critical point earlier than normal people—while they are still sleeping and cannot be exposed to the light. Researchers find that circadian cycles occur earlier in some depressed patients.

Hoping to reset or phase-advance the cycle, Kripke called reveille for the depressed patients two hours before their normal waking time and exposed them to bright light for one hour. The results were mixed. It should be noted, however, that Dr. Kripke's patients had depression but not SADs. Dr. Rosenthal's patients met the criteria for seasonal affective disorder and had a more robust response to the light therapy.

Without doubt, this noninvasive treatment for depression has great appeal. Following the publicity, quite a few psychiatrists reported a flurry of phone calls from depressed people inquiring where they might buy the light banks. Self-treatment is not advised as the phototherapy must be precisely timed and the brightness calibrated for effect and safety. Moreover, this form of treatment might be applicable to only a small subgroup of patients. The mechanism of the effect of bright light treatment is unknown, and the studies, still in early stages, require further validation.

Still, these new looks at the relationship between circadian and seasonal cycles and sunlight and depressive disorders are important. Future reports could help to further define and document the physiology of depression.

MOOD DISORDERS IN CHILDREN AND ADOLESCENTS

Until the early 1960s depression in children was rarely (if ever) diagnosed. It was almost never mentioned in textbooks on child psychiatry. Psychoanalytic theory held that a classical depressive syndrome could not occur in prepubertal children. Others felt that what might be regarded as depressive symptoms are merely transitory developmental phenomena that would disappear over time. The debate continued as different factions argued that children do suffer depression but that they have different symptoms than those seen in adults. In 1980 the DSM–III stated that the criteria for depression in children is the same as that for adults, but that the form of expression may be different and related to the developmental level of the child. Although much still remains unclear, there are researchers who feel that depression is an underdiagnosed condition in childhood.

A wide range of depressive symptoms may be noticed by the parents or teachers of a child. These can include an appearance of sadness or loneliness and decreased energy. The child may have difficulty sleeping at night or want to do nothing but sleep. He or she may fail to make expected weight gains, or there may be an unusual change in appetite. Teachers often notice that the child daydreams or has little ability to concentrate, and it is not uncommon for a depressed child to resist going to school, and even to refuse altogether. Any interest in after school or social activities vanishes.

Sometimes children don't say they feel sad, but express feelings of being ugly, stupid or dumb and useless. They may feel inordinately guilty about things. Their behavior may change, with irritability and temper tantrums becoming more frequent. Children can also begin to act aggressively. If the depression becomes severe, the child may experience delusions and hallucinations as well as entertain suicidal thoughts. It is imperative that the parents intervene and have the child evaluated by professionals.

Who Should Diagnose and Treat Children and Adolescents?

Ideally, a child psychiatrist should diagnose and treat psychiatric disorders in children and adolescents. The doctor needs to elicit the information necessary for a diagnosis and must be trained to speak with a child in a way the child can understand, utilize play therapy and then treat the child in the context of the family unit.

A child psychiatrist is a medical doctor who has completed one year of internship, two or three years of an adult psychiatric residency and two additional years of a child psychiatry fellowship program.

The best way to go about locating a good child psychiatrist is to talk to the family pediatrician or family practitioner. Also, a school psychologist or guidance counselor might be able to make a referral. If these avenues fail to locate someone competent, the department of child psychiatry at a major teaching hospital would be a very likely resource.

Locating a child psychiatrist in such states as Alaska, Arkansas, Mississippi, Nevada, Washington, West Virginia or Wyoming presents a real problem. In 1980 these states each had fewer than ten practicing child psychiatrists. In the event that a child psychiatrist is not available, an adult psychiatrist with an interest in and a history of treating children would be the likely alternative. A call to one of the patient or family support groups listed in the appendices of this book would no doubt shorten the search, as the people you contact there could use their networks to help.

The Treatment of Depression in Children

The doctor evaluates the child's symptoms and behavior and gathers additional information through psychological testing and from the parents and teachers. Very often, therapy, support and parental counseling that could result in a change in the home life or in communication patterns in the home are enough to counteract the depression. Sometimes, however, when the child manifests symptoms of a major depressive syndrome, the physician considers treating the child with an antidepressant medication since the child's discomforting feelings may so undermine his or her confidence and outreaching ability as to seriously impair future undertakings and relationships.

Before any pharmacological treatment begins, the physician orders a complete exam. Blood tests, urinalysis and an electrocardiogram (EKG) will be done. Since imipramine (Tofranil) is the most studied antidepressant for young children, the chances are great that this will be the antidepressant prescribed. The drug is started at low doses (for example, 25 milligrams per day) and increased by 25-milligram increments every few days until the symptoms begin to clear. The dosage is calibrated according to the weight of the child because cardiac functioning may be affected at higher levels. While the child is on the drug, the blood pressure, pulse rate and heart rhythm should be monitored.

Typically a child takes the medication for three to six months. Daily medications should *always* be dispensed by a parent or responsible adult as overdoses can and do happen. In the event of an overdose, rush the child to the nearest hospital. The cardiac functioning will be monitored for at least twenty-four hours, and physostigmine salicylate can be administered as an antidote.

Side Effects of Antidepressants

Children experience the same spectrum of side effects of antidepressants as adults, but less frequently. Many suffer no side effects, while others report dryness of mouth, insomnia, gastric upsets, nausea and vomiting, tremulousness, dizziness and headache. This list sometimes expands to low blood pressure (hypotension), high blood pressure (hypertension), weight gain or loss, irritability, skin rash and fatigue. Most of these common side effects, should they occur, abate within the first weeks of treatment. If not, the doctor should lower the dosage the child is receiving.

Suicide

It is particularly poignant and distressing to think about children suffering with depression, but it is harrowing to think that children attempt suicide and are frequently successful in their attempts. Clinical reports show that children as young as five and six years old have made attempts to kill themselves. Dr. Cynthia Pfeffer of Cornell University Medical College has reported that her studies of children reveal that approximately 75 percent of the children who are psychiatrically hospitalized are suicidal, while about 33 percent of those treated outside the hospital are suicidal. It is estimated that about half of all suicide victims suffer from depressive illness.

The burgeoning statistics on adolescent suicides are shocking. It is estimated that five thousand adolescents kill themselves in the United States each year, and that at least four hundred thousand youngsters make unsuccessful attempts annually. Suicide is the third leading cause of death in adolescents. Dr. Pfeffer feels that adolescents are particularly at risk for suicide attempts because they progress through a variety of rapid developmental stages. "Besides those that are physiological," she writes, "the youngster may also be biologically vulnerable to psychiatric illnesses such as depression." She adds:

Although the incidence of major affective disorder in preadolescents is relatively low, it increases greatly in adolescents. These young people are in the process of psychologically "leaving home," and the relationship to their family changes as peer relationships become more important. The development of a firm sense of identity is a critically important issue. When this process is hampered or inhibited, adolescents may be especially prone to suicidal behavior.

There are certain signs and symptoms that may warn of an impending suicide attempt in an adolescent. They are:

- Depressed mood
- Changes in sleep and/or appetite patterns
- Decline in school performance
- Increased social withdrawal
- Loss of interest and pleasure in previously enjoyable activities
- Changes in appearance—for instance, no longer caring about one's clothing or hair
- Preoccupation with themes of death—the youngster may begin to read books with themes of death and dying
- Increased irritability and behavior problems
- Giving away important possessions
- Use of drugs and alcohol
- History of a previous attempt
- History of abuse and neglect
- History of learning disabilities and a sense of failure
- Frequent somatic complaints
- Verbal expression about self-death—for instance, a youngster who actually says, "I wish I were dead"
- No longer concerned about making plans for the future

An adolescent who is potentially suicidal may make an attempt following a variety of events. These may include the breakup of a romantic relationship, disciplinary problems with parents, difficulty with school or work or an injury to self-esteem such as the failure to win an important award or position. The loss of an important person in the child's life may also serve as a precipitant.

Should a parent, a teacher or other adult suspect that a child is suicidal, the matter should be discussed immediately. Too often people avoid introducing the subject because they think it will "plant ideas." "To the contrary," says child psychiatrist Dr. Rosalie Greenberg, "asking a young person about self destructive wishes can help make him or her feel more understood and less trapped. Ignoring suicidal thoughts or behavior is a way of making suicide more likely to happen."

Once it becomes clear that an adolescent is at risk for suicide, it is crucial that he or she be seen immediately by a psychiatrist (ideally by a psychiatrist familiar with the treatment of adolescents). This doctor can then assess the risk of suicide and decide whether protective hospitalization is necessary, what kind of therapy the child needs and whether or not medications are indicated. The family will need information and support at this time also, and the psychiatrist should work closely with family members and possibly the personnel at the child's school.

Suicide rates among young people have tripled in the past thirty years, yet much remains unclear as to its causes and the most effective interventions. In order to address the subject and assess and consolidate current information, the Secretarial Task Force on Youth Suicide was established by Margaret M. Heckler while she was Secretary of Health and Human Services. A two-volume report that will identify risk factors, assess current interventions and make recommendations for improving understanding and helping direct research efforts is to be published by the winter of 1987. This report is available to the public from the Superintendent of Documents, U.S. Government Printing Office, Washington, DC 20402.

Manic-Depression in Children and Adolescents

Manic episodes can begin early in life. A look back at the histories of adults with bipolar symptoms often shows that mood swings began around puberty, but there are even case reports of manic symptoms seen in prepubertal children.

Some of the most common manic symptoms in children are increased psychomotor activity (hyperactivity, distractibility), a push of speech, sleep disturbances and a low frustration tolerance and outbursts of rage. Older children may have racing thoughts and flights of ideas, as well as grandiose thinking.

Manic-depressive illness is not easy to diagnose in children as many of the symptoms overlap with attention deficit disorder (ADD). Symptoms of ADD include easy distractibility and inattention and impulsive and hyperactive behavior, and the picture can resemble aspects of a manic episode. A differential diagnosis must be made between ADD and manic-depressive disorder.

The following is a case history of manic-depressive illness in a young boy:

> Milo, a thirteen-year-old boy, had a family history of bipolar illness. His paternal grandfather reportedly had been "explosive and temperamental," and two cousins had been hospitalized for manic episodes. Milo's paternal grandmother had had four hospitalizations for manic or depressive episodes and was receiving lithium maintenance.
>
> The father had had two depressive episodes that were treated with tricyclic medication. Milo's sixteen-year-old brother had dysphoric moods, and a fourteen-year-old sister had had a learning disability since age seven.
>
> Milo was referred by the school because of poor academic achievement, lack of concentration, and distractibility. He had a history of extreme separation anxiety in infancy, phobias, tantrums, bed-wetting, hypersensitivity to noise, and "thoughtless behavior" (e.g., destructiveness). His parents reported that he had a low frustration tolerance and that his moods varied from "ecstasy to black despair."
>
> Milo was treated for two years with psychotherapy. The school reported increasing numbers of incidents such as unprovoked school fights, vandalism, and minor theft. A violent attack on a schoolmate led to Milo's expulsion. Lithium carbonate was begun and there were no further reports of uncontrolled explosive aggression.
>
> A follow-up study revealed excellent academic achievement and improved social skills until Milo stopped taking the lithium when he was sixteen. Impulsive behavior, drug abuse, running away, and brief psychotic episodes were reported before psychotherapy and lithium carbonate were restarted, with good results.

Although lithium worked very well in this case, much about the long-term effects of the drug on children and adolescents remains unclear. The FDA does not recommend its use in children under twelve since there is a lack of information regarding its safety and efficacy, but it appears that young people tolerate lithium very well. In fact, due to the efficiency of the kidneys and the speed with which lithium is excreted by children and adolescents, they often need doses similar to those prescribed for adult patients to maintain adequate blood levels of the drug for maintenance therapy (between 0.75 and 1.00 mEq/liter).

Dr. Gabrielle Carlson, in a chapter of the book *Affective Disorders in Childhood and Adolescence,* explains one point of view urging the use of lithium in young people when appropriate:

> Even in the case of mild episodes of depression and mania, if they occur with any frequency (at least two per year), the youngster may have a less stormy adolescence on medication and will be better able to cope with the other age-appropriate demands of making relationships, finishing school, and identifying himself as other than flagrantly psychiatrically ill.

(See Chapter 5 for a complete discussion of lithium and antidepressant drugs.)

MOOD DISORDERS IN THE ELDERLY

As attention has turned to the treatment of affective disorders in children and adolescents, so it has turned to the large population of the elderly. There are nearly thirty million people sixty-five years of age or older in the United States, and it is estimated that 15 to 20 percent of them, or about five million people, suffer from depression.

Some of the precipitants may be social or psychological. The elderly sustain many losses: their work with its meaningfulness, income and structured routine, their friends and loved ones and their physical strength. Depression is common after retirement, and it is easy in this society for an aging person to feel superfluous, isolated and alone. The burden of these adjustments could perhaps be lightened with the help of a psychotherapist or counselor.

Other precipitants of depression may be medical illnesses or the drugs used to treat them. Elderly patients more commonly have diseases that may appear as depression: hypothyroidism, hyperthyroidism, Cushing's disease, Parkinson's disease, cardiovascular and pulmonary disorders, vitamin B12 and folic acid deficiencies, carcinoma and stroke. Many of the drugs that the elderly consume can induce depression in vulnerable individuals.

The following medications are sometimes associated with depression:

Antihypertensives (for controlling blood pressure)

clonidine (Catapres)
hydralazine (Apresoline Hydrochloride)
methyldopa (Aldomet)
propranolol (Inderal)
reserpine (Serpasil, Ser-Ap-Es, Sandril)

Antiparkinsonism Agents

levodopa (Dopar, Larodopa)
levodopa and carbidopa (Sinemet)
bromocriptine

Hormones

estrogen
progesterone
cortisone
prednisone

It is vitally important that the diagnosing physician know, and better yet see, the bottles of prescription and nonprescription drugs that the patient is taking. This may provide a clue to one of the contributing factors of the depression.

But in order for an accurate diagnosis to be made, the doctor needs to spend time talking with and examining the patient. Depression in an older patient may manifest different symptoms than in a younger adult. The aging person often reports less change in mood and attitude and more of the somatic complaints such as constipation, headaches and fatigue. Moreover, the elderly depressed patient may appear confused, have memory loss and be agitated, and the deficits in mental functioning may be ascribed too quickly to dementia. Because doctors expect to see dementia in this age group, there is a tendency to overdiagnose it. In fact, approximately 12 percent of the elderly diagnosed as suffering from a dementia are thought actually to have a false dementia arising from untreated depression. The failure to diagnose depression results tragically in unnecessary suffering, suicide attempts, antisocial behavior, premature retirement, overuse of social and medical services, unnecessary hospital and nursing home admissions and alienation of family and friends.

It takes a highly trained and sensitive physician to determine whether the problem is dementia, depression mimicking dementia or depression existing alongside dementia. Tests are needed to help rule out dementia, and the patient will be given a series of radiological and laboratory tests, including an electroencephalogram (EEG), a computerized axial tomogram of the brain (CAT scan), thyroid function studies and blood tests.

If the results of these tests indicate that there is no other underlying cause for the mood changes the patient is experiencing and the state of confusion the patient is in, then the doctor should suspect that the patient is suffering from depression masquerading as dementia. A previous history of depression or a family history of mood disorders would further implicate depression as the problem.

One such case was a sixty-year-old man who was admitted to the hospital complaining of fatigue, loss of appetite, difficulty sleeping and confusion, symptoms he had had for a month. When interviewed by the psychiatrist, the patient was disoriented—he could not remember the date or time of year, nor could he remember events from day to day. His mood shifted rapidly from tearfulness to irritability. The family members were extremely disturbed and afraid that he had Alzheimer's disease.

A close examination of the patient's history revealed that he had suffered two previous depressions: one at age twenty-two, the other at age forty. The first depression lifted after seven treatments of ECT, and the second was successfully treated with a tricyclic antidepressant, desipramine. Further neurological and neuropsychological examination revealed no evidence of dementia, and the man was again treated with desipramine. Two and a half weeks later his mood was normal and the confusion and memory disturbance were gone. He was discharged home to his family.

Treatment

If the treating physician decides that the problem is a depression that could benefit from drug therapy, he or she has a complicated prescription task to confront. The side effects of tricyclic medications can be more serious and pose more problems in this age group. An older patient experiencing the dizziness of orthostatic hypotension (see page 106) is more likely to fracture bones in the event of a fall. Also, because an elderly person's heart is more sensitive to the cardiovascular challenge of these medications, there is increased risk of heart attack and stroke. For these reasons, a doctor would want to prescribe a drug that produces less sedation, and fewer effects on the heart and blood pressure (desipramine and nortriptyline are often prescribed).

There is another consideration when prescribing medications for an older patient. The dosage of medication that would be well tolerated by a young person might be toxic to someone older. Psychiatric drugs remain in the elderly patient's body longer, and exert stronger and more prolonged effects for several reasons.

Chemicals circulating through the body are metabolized by the liver and excreted by the kidneys. Because these organs are less proficient as a person ages, it takes longer for a drug to pass through these "breakdown stations." Also, an increase in body fat relative to lean muscle comes with age. Psychiatric drugs can be stored in fat, and often these drugs are sequestered there and released only slowly. This sustained release can cause a buildup in the body. Toxicity is a considerable problem.

Therefore, elderly patients receive lower doses of medication than are normally prescribed to young adults. But before any medications are dispensed, the doctor requests that the patient have a complete physical exam, including a pretreatment electrocardiogram (EKG). Also, because other prescription and nonprescription drugs can interact poorly with the psychiatric drugs prescribed, the physician asks for a complete list of all medications, including such common household remedies as milk of magnesia, Kaopectate, sodium carbonate, analgesics (Motrin, Advil or Nuprin), antacids and Dilantin. A discussion of alcohol and coffee consumption is important also.

The chart below demonstrates the differing doses prescribed for the average adult and the elderly patient:

DOSE RANGE OF ANTIDEPRESSANTS

Drug	Dose (mg daily)	
	Average adult	Elderly
doxepin (Adapin, Sinequan)	75–250	30–150
imipramine (Tofranil)	75–300	20–150
trazodone (Desyrel)	150–400	25–200
desipramine (Norpramin, Pertofrane)	75–300	20–75
nortriptyline (Aventyl, Pamelor)	50–150	10–100
protriptyline (Vivactil)	20–40	20–30
amoxapine (Asendin)	150–300	50–150
maprotiline (Ludiomil)	75–250	25–150

The common side effects of antidepressants are sedation, dry mouth, constipation, urinary hesitancy or retention, precipitation of narrow-angle glaucoma, weight gain, increase in heart rate and the orthostatic hypotension mentioned above.

The patient should tell the doctor if he or she has previously responded to a certain antidepressant (chances are that it will work again), or if a relative has had a particularly good response to an antidepressant medication (a possible genetic link may render it effective in the patient also).

During the course of treatment with an antidepressant, the elderly patient should have his or her blood pressure and urine output monitored periodically. An electrocardiogram should be done weekly until a therapeutic level has been achieved.

In the case of an agitated depression (the patient is extremely anxious, paces around and can't sit still) or if there are psychotic symptoms, it is not uncommon for a psychiatrist to prescribe an antipsychotic medication along with an antidepressant. However, the antipsychotic drug is prescribed in low doses because the elderly experience more muscle stiffness and rigidity (see pages 101–3 for a discussion of the antipsychotic side effects).

Patients who have serious cardiovascular problems may be

treated more safely with ECT. It has fewer and less dangerous adverse effects than the antidepressant medications, and it usually works well in severe depression (see pages 115–18).

Lithium Use in the Elderly

The use of lithium in the elderly is quite common, but here again, special precautions are taken. Many older patients are on a salt-restricted diet or take diuretics, leading to increased reabsorption of lithium from the kidneys with higher and more dangerous lithium blood levels. The patient is at greater risk for developing lithium toxicity. Therefore, the blood levels are increased cautiously to usual adult levels, and heart, kidney and thyroid functioning, as well as lithium blood levels, are checked regularly. It may be best to use a slow-release formula of lithium such as Lithobid in order to flatten peak blood levels (see page 92).

Symptoms of lithium toxicity may include nausea, vomiting, restlessness, tremor, confusion, disorientation, fear and agitation. Should any of these occur, the patient should take no more medication, and he or the family should call the physician immediately.

THE QUESTION OF PREGNANCY

A thirty-one-year-old woman from Maine who had a bipolar disorder wrote: "I started looking around for material on lithium and pregnancy and found literally nothing! I called my obstetrician and found out that he would allow no lithium the whole term of pregnancy, and not just the first three months. That gave me something to think about seriously."

This young woman faced the dilemma that all women who take medications for mood disorders face when they decide to have children: can one get through the nine-month period of pregnancy without the protection of lithium or other antimanic or antidepressant drugs, and what happens if an episode of mania or depression develops?

Any kind of medication exposes the developing fetus to possible risk, but evidence suggests that the risk of heart malformation is especially high with lithium (about thirteen times higher than that of the general population). A birth defect called Epstein's anomaly, in which the tricuspid valve of the heart is malformed, occurs approximately once in every twenty thousand live births. The Langley-Porter Lithium Registry in San Francisco kept track of babies born to women treated with lithium during pregnancy, and found that out of 166 cases, eighteen children had malformations, twelve involving the heart and great vessels, and four of the twelve had Epstein's anomaly. Because this syndrome is so rare in the general population, its high incidence among lithium-treated pregnancies is worrisome. Even though a significant percentage of women treated with lithium in the first trimester had normal babies, these reports encourage a conservative approach and suggest that lithium should not be prescribed during the first months of pregnancy when the fetal organs are being formed. Because one-third to two-thirds of the first trimester passes before the diagnosis of pregnancy is made, a drug-free period of one month is advisable before attempting conception.

Lithium used at the end of a pregnancy can be a problem also. Fetal distress can occur: the babies may be born lethargic and listless with decreased suck response and Moro reflex (the startle response of newborns). They may have decreased oxygenation and appear bluish.

The mother has a greater risk of lithium toxicity after the delivery. Increased kidney function during pregnancy results in more lithium's being excreted, so higher doses may have to be prescribed. However, during and after delivery kidney function returns to normal, and there are major alterations in fluid and electrolyte metabolism. More lithium may be retained in the body, leading to a too-high blood level. Therefore, the lithium dose should be reduced by 50 percent or more in the last week of the pregnancy and stopped completely with the onset of labor. Once the fluids return to normal (approximately three to four days after birth), lithium therapy can be reinstated. Breast feeding is not a good idea because breast milk lithium concentration is about 30 to 50 percent of the mother's blood level. A newborn does not have well-developed systems of excretion, and there have been reports of insufficient oxygenation of the blood (cyanosis) and poor muscle tone in infants breast fed by mothers on lithium.

There is less information about the problems of antidepressant drugs used during pregnancy or in nursing mothers. These drugs do pass the placental barrier and can be excreted in low levels in breast milk, and there are rare reports of neonatal distress in infants born to mothers given these medications. Some of the babies suffered muscle spasms, an unusually fast heart rate (tachycardia), congestive heart failure and respiratory distress.

Antipsychotic drugs can be a problem also. There continue to be disturbing reports on neurological and behavioral abnormalities in neonatal rats born to rat mothers exposed to these medications. Therefore, their use should be limited in pregnancy if possible, but if they are necessary, a relatively potent antipsychotic such as haloperidol (Haldol) or fluphenazine (Prolixin) should be prescribed in small, divided doses.

Sedatives, benzodiazepines such as Valium or Klonopin and anticonvulsants such as Tegretol and Depakene should be avoided also.

Undoubtedly the safest and most effective way to treat a pregnant woman experiencing a manic or depressive episode is with electroconvulsive therapy (ECT). This treatment option can be used during any stage of the pregnancy and is thoroughly described on pages 115–18. An obstetrician should be a part of the ECT treatment team, and external fetal monitoring should be done before the treatment and for several hours afterward. In the event that the woman is carrying more than one baby, or has high blood pressure, diabetes, a history of premature labor or heart or kidney disease, ECT may not be the right treatment as there may be some concern about premature labor.

All of the above speaks in favor of exercising extreme caution when planning a pregnancy. A close-working team of psychiatrist, obstetrician and patient is critical. A woman should understand the risks of medications, particularly in the first trimester and right around the period of delivery, and decide which options might be preferable.

It goes without saying that pregnancy produces a host of physical and psychological changes in a woman, and there is some debate as to whether the hormonal shifts of pregnancy stress the woman with a mood disorder or whether they have a protective effect. There is, however, agreement that the period immediately following childbirth is a time of increased vulnerability to depression and (in those who are bipolar) mania. Forearmed with this knowledge, a woman should stay in close contact with her psychiatrist who, if necessary, can prescribe medications to stabilize her mood.

We wanted to convey what's known or suspected in the medical arena regarding pregnancy, but the human experience of what a woman faces is virtually absent in the scientific literature. The young woman who couldn't find information when she planned her pregnancy told her story with informative detail:

After I had been stable for about a year, I decided that I should try getting pregnant. On December 31, 1984, I stopped taking all medications. I told my psychiatrist that my obstetrician advised no lithium. If worse came to worst, I could always have electroshock therapy. I just hoped nothing would happen.

I was very, very lucky to become pregnant in one month. When I found out I was pregnant, I began to worry, of course, that I would lose my mind by the end of the week, that I would have to have shock treatments, etc., etc. I remember getting up in the morning, looking in the mirror and thinking: "Well, will you lose it this morning?" After a few weeks (probably about ten weeks) I began to have more confidence that I would not have my ups and downs. Of course I was very moody from the hormones of pregnancy. This is quite common, and most everyone goes through it, but I thought with each mood that "this was it" and I would really have trouble.

I was very fortunate, because I never did have serious mood swings while I was pregnant. I know now that if I would have had trouble, both my obstetrician and psychiatrist would have worked together to make sure both the baby and I were okay. I also know that in my case, somehow, the hormones of pregnancy "insulate" me from serious mood swing. This is not a medical fact, just something I know. I know that other avenues of treatment are available for me (I plan on having more children) although no methods are as effective as lithium. I am simply willing to take the chance.

Probably the most important things are to communicate with your spouse at all times as to how you are feeling, keep in touch with the psychiatrist as often as is necessary, and make sure to inform the obstetrician that you are a lithium-medicated patient and are considering pregnancy. The obstetrician will also have to know if you are treated *at all* during the pregnancy.

I am now the proud parent of a three-month-old baby girl named Alice. She and I have survived colic and a very serious post-partum depression for me. I think that it took me almost five weeks to recover from the birth (I had a C-section, as Alice was breech). A difficult part of the post-partum weeks is the depression and moodiness that go along with losing all those hormones. I was sure I was going to have to take medication again. However, one day I started feeling better, and although I have moods just like other people do, I am essentially without serious mood swings.

I am attending college again. I have changed my major from business administration to nursing and I'm trying to survive my first chemistry course.

I would certainly encourage women who are on lithium to at least give pregnancy serious consideration. But, lithium during the first trimester is very dangerous for the baby, so anyone considering pregnancy should be very careful regarding their method of birth control. I know of a woman who wanted to be pregnant, started "forgetting" her birth control pills, and remained on lithium. The child was born with serious heart defects, and the mother, of course, was devastated. It's certainly nothing to play "forgetful" and "I hope" games with.

7

WORKING THROUGH: DENIAL, ACCEPTANCE AND THE PSYCHOTHERAPIES

Prior to the availability and widespread use of lithium and antidepressants, individuals in this country who had mood disorders were treated with psychotherapy. This involved the therapist and the patient in a dialogue intended to reveal unconscious causes or determinants of the symptoms. Today, thanks to ever-expanding knowledge about the nervous system and the medicines that affect it, and a more refined system of diagnosis, treatment practice has moved in a different direction—these disorders are viewed primarily as medical disorders. In the rush to spread the good word about the new drug treatments, psychotherapy was dismissed by some or viewed as unnecessary.

This was short-sighted. Simply relegating these disorders to the realm of physiological disturbances that require only medical treatment is a serious clinical oversight and a gross scientific presumption, similar to those of the earlier psychological oversimplifications and prejudices. These disorders affect mood, thinking and behavior, and vitally influence a person's view of himself and his relationships with others. The problem—as well as its solution—now rests firmly in the realms of medicine *and* psychology.

AN INTEGRATED TREATMENT APPROACH

A widely accepted strategy in a commonsense treatment plan is to relieve painful symptoms by the appropriate medication while educating the patient and his family members about the nature and course of the disorder, as well as expected effects and course of treatment. Medications can indeed relieve the symptoms of depres-

139

sion and mania for most people, but the alleviation of symptoms is not the whole story, especially for those who suffer recurrent episodes. The advent of a recurring or chronic illness such as an affective disorder represents a significant loss for an individual. There is a loss of function and a loss of confidence and security. Questions—Why me? What did I do to deserve this? Will I be able to accomplish my life goals? What will happen to my relationships? Can I have a family?—will loom large for an individual. Each person will deal with the questions and the answers in his or her own way, but make no mistake: there will be an emotional response to the illness. All will have to come to terms with feelings of anger, sadness and shame. (These issues become even more complicated if parents, siblings or other relatives have the illness—not an uncommon occurrence with a disorder that is heavily familial.) These feelings and questions need to be addressed, but that can happen only in the context of an integrated treatment plan where the therapist and patient talk about more than symptoms and prescriptions. An adjunctive psychotherapy is recommended.

In the most fundamental sense of the word, psychotherapy is a dialogue between two people where the patient has the respectful attention of a professional trained to elicit information. The professional, through clarification and interpretation, helps the person see things about him or herself in a realistic light—one not clouded by a lingering sense of worthlessness or victimization. In the treatment of a recurrent affective disorder this can mean many things. Psychotherapy can strengthen the capacity to cope, help the person to understand and come to terms with the vulnerability and develop an adaptive way of coping with interpersonal problems that emerge or are magnified as a result of the illness.

This respectful dialogue between patient and therapist may at first focus on the acceptance of the need to take medication. The taking of any medicine, and especially a psychotropic drug, can raise highly charged psychological issues. The medicine may become a concrete symbol of a chronic illness, a nagging reminder that something within is not working as it should. For anyone, a deficit— something that makes one more vulnerable in relation to others— has the potential for decreasing one's sense of self-worth. This deficit may be experienced as a slight that is reinforced daily by the taking of medications. There may be a wish to deny the illness, and this may lead to a person's discontinuing the prescribed drugs.

Many people feel: "I've been well for a while; I've beaten this. I don't need the drugs anymore." It is not uncommon for patients to go off the medications a number of times, testing their limitations. This often (but not always) results in further episodes. Unless there is an early recognition of the symptoms of an impending swing and a treatment intervention, there will again be disruptions in family life, work and social relationships. This returns the patient to square one and further disturbs his sense of self-worth.

Some patients are very upset by the idea that it is not their own will but a medication that is responsible for preserving control over their behavior, mood or judgment. They may view the lack of psychological control as a weakness. These feelings can lead to a rather negative attitude about the taking of medication and may complicate or prevent accepting the disorder and its medical treatment and entering into a collaborative relationship with the doctor.

An illness that changes mood and affects thought processes makes it extremely difficult for the person experiencing the changes to sort out which feelings are valid and should be acted upon and which are symptoms of an impending swing. Often, a person with recurrent mania or depression will need to learn to distinguish between normal human mood changes and episodes of illness. One young man in California complained that he felt disenfranchised from his feelings. If he was elated, he worried that it was the beginning of a hypomanic period, and if he was blue, that it was the beginning of a descent into a hellish depression. He spoke about his worries and doubts with his psychiatrist, and after noticing on repeated occasions that the mood change did not progress to extremes, he was better able to accept his normal expression of emotion.

This sort of working through, discussion and learning about oneself is a critical element in the treatment of affective disorders. If an individual can learn to recognize the symptoms of an impending mood swing, he can help short-circuit it by talking to the doctor. The physician, alerted early, is then in a position to adjust the medication and hopefully prevent relapse.

Furthermore, if a person can recognize changes in behavior, alterations in thinking and changes in the pattern of relationship with others early during periods of mood swing, he may be able to temper his behavior and thus save himself potential embarrassment. One twenty-four-year-old man said that when he becomes slightly hypomanic, he presents his employer with all kinds of ideas. Sometimes he is given the go-ahead to implement a project, and then finds himself out of the hypomanic period and out of steam—thus risking his credibility. He has learned to wait and consider things carefully before racing ahead. A woman who begins manic cycles with buying sprees has decided to divest herself of credit cards in order to protect against financial ruin. Self-awareness and the capacity for control can be enhanced. On the other hand, a person mustn't stifle and inhibit his ambition and creative drive; a balance must be achieved. These complicated issues are fruitful areas for discussion and clarification with an informed therapist.

How else can psychotherapy be useful? An ongoing dialogue that examines fears and behavior can help one relinquish the defenses and coping strategies that were marshalled during episodes of illness but which may no longer be adaptive or necessary once maintenance medication has stabilized the mood swings. Some people have become overly dependent on family members; others have withdrawn from all social situations. When asked to name the most enduring and painful aspect of having this disorder, one woman said, "I personally hesitate to be in any kind of a group for fear that I'll do something embarrassing that I'll later regret." This fear and inhibition about being with other people is a persisting problem for many who suffer mood disorders, even years after they have been stabilized on a medication. Others never lose the painful sense of humiliation about what they did during a manic episode and how people reacted toward them afterward. The shame of one's behavior during a manic episode can linger long after the symptoms of the episode have disappeared.

Bipolar patients suffer another kind of humiliation during the recovery period. During the manic episode they may have felt more creative and intelligent, more able to accomplish things they never thought possible. These feelings of great exaltation, self-importance and power are difficult to give up. Once out of the manic phase, however, the patient needs to face himself and assess his natural limitations and the realities of his life. The insult to the patient's self-respect can be enormous when he realizes that he not only had a false sense of his abilities, but must also now deal with the fact that he has a psychiatric disorder.

A woman with a bipolar disorder elegantly summed up the need for an integrated treatment combining medications and psychotherapy when she wrote:

> I cannot imagine leading a normal life without lithium. From startings and stoppings of it, I now know it is an essential part of my sanity. Lithium prevents my seductive but disastrous highs, diminishes my depressions, clears out the webbing of my disordered thinking, slows me, gentles me out, keeps me in relationships, in my career, out of a hospital, and in psychotherapy. But psychotherapy heals, it makes some sense of the confusion, it reins in the terrifying thoughts and feelings, it brings back hope, and the possibility of learning from it all. Pills cannot, do not, ease one back into reality. They bring you back headlong, careening, and faster than can be endured at times. Psychotherapy is a sanctuary, it is a battleground, it is where I have come to believe that I someday may be able to contend with all this. No pill can help me deal with the problem of not wanting to take pills, but no amount of therapy can prevent my manias and depressions. I need both.

All of the above helps build the case for a treatment approach that combines psychopharmacological management and psychotherapeutic dialogue. The following list illustrates the principal elements of a combined treatment approach that integrates medical, psychological and educational aspects:

Principal Elements of an Integrated Treatment Approach

Medical

- The physician establishes the proper medication regimen for the treatment of the acute episode.
- The physician develops a record of retrospective and prospective cycle frequency.

- The physician and the patient determine the need for long-term maintenance medications.
- The physician reviews periodically the effectiveness of the medications.
- If the patient is on lithium, the physician monitors levels on a monthly basis and assesses thyroid and kidney functioning every six to twelve months.

Educational

- The patient and family learn about the disorder: course, symptoms, medications and their side effects.
- The patient and family learn about individual symptom patterns of the illness (early signs and symptoms of an episode, seasonality, yearly patterns).
- The patient learns to differentiate normal mood variations from episodes of illness.

Psychological

- The patient engages in a collaborative and trusting relationship with the therapist.
- The patient and the therapist explore the psychological meaning of taking the medications for the treatment of the disorder.
- The patient and the therapist review past episodes and examine their effect on self-esteem, life goals and relationships.
- The patient and the therapist assess defenses and coping strategies—adaptive or maladaptive.
- The patient confronts the stigmas associated with the diagnosis, symptoms and treatment and learns how to deal with the limitations imposed by the illness.
- The patient accepts the disorder.

EDUCATING THE FAMILY

Ironically, because of the efficacy of lithium and antidepressant treatment, and because individuals with these disorders experience periods of well-being, there has been a tendency to underestimate the disruptive fallout these illnesses can cause the patient and his family. In many cases a profound rupture in familial ties persists long after the episodes of illness end. Children of a mother who was severely depressed who no longer trust her love and nurturing capacity need help in understanding what she was experiencing in order to reestablish the bond; a father who perceives his daughter as a tramp following a hypomanic episode needs the opportunity, through education, to see that her excessive sexuality was yet another manifestation of the illness.

Families could be a tremendous support to the patient if they were given information and an active role in the treatment. Every person we interviewed felt that family involvement and education made a critical difference in the posthospitalization period and beyond.

A model program to educate patients and family members was developed at the Albert Einstein College of Medicine. It is based on the psychoeducational work of Drs. Carol Anderson, Gerald Hogarty and Douglas Reiss with schizophrenic patients and their families in Baltimore and Pittsburgh. The approach is a practical one that goes far, in a short amount of time, toward clearing up the myths surrounding the illness. It seeks to increase the stability of the family environment by decreasing the family members' anxiety about the patient and increasing their self-confidence and knowledge about the disorder. It improves the family's capacity to react constructively to the patient during episodes of illness. The approach typically requires five to ten patient and family meetings.

If the first of these sessions takes place following an initial episode, or if the family has not been involved in previous episodes, it is often the case that each member has a theory about the disorder. The goal of the first meeting, then, is to understand the family members' theories. Family members are then asked to entertain the new standard medical hypotheses about the possible causes of the disorders and are given a copy of the pamphlet *Primary Affective Disorders* (written by Demitri F. Papolos, M.D., and published by The National Alliance for the Mentally Ill), which describes in a question-and-answer format the nature, symptoms and course of major affective disorders.

The provision of information usually sparks a lively discussion between the family members and the therapist at the second session.

There are often emotional responses to the idea that the illness has a biological basis and is familial. Questions about medication efficacy, side effects and criteria for long-term maintenance are discussed also. In the meetings that follow, the patient is encouraged to describe his or her subjective experience of the symptoms and the limitations they impose, and the family members begin to pinpoint how they each responded to the loss of the ill member during episodes of depression or mania. How did each person try to rouse the patient from his illness during episodes of depression? How did each family member attempt to set limits for the patient during episodes of mania? What feelings were aroused when these attempts failed?

During the final sessions, the therapist and the family review what has been learned: the nature, course and treatment of the disorder, the effects on the relationship system and the strategies developed to avoid the conflicts that arose as a consequence of the patient's change in behavior during an acute episode of illness.

In summary, the goals of the psychoeducational approach are:

- To enable the patient and family to accept the idea that the patient has a medical disorder that may be recurrent and produces symptoms that affect mood, self-esteem, thinking, speech, activity, sleep, appetite and social and sexual behavior
- To identify and label the specific symptoms that occur at the onset of an episode
- To allow family members to acknowledge that the most recent and/or past episodes have had an impact on the way they view the patient and to identify and describe any change in their attitudes toward the patient and in the pattern of their relationship with the patient during and after an episode of either mania or depression
- To examine the changes that occur in the usual caretaking roles during an acute episode
- To teach that major affective disorders are familial disorders and may therefore affect others in the family
- To aid in an understanding of the potential advantages and risks of preventive treatment, as well as of no treatment, from the time the acute episode is under control
- To teach the importance of long-term monitoring, including

laboratory tests, and of the family's sharing in the decision to initiate maintenance treatment

- To distinguish medication side effects from the symptoms of illness (for example, fatigue as a side effect of lithium may be misconstrued as a depressive symptom)

If all goes well, the conflict between family members is decreased, healthy coping skills are attained, and the family becomes more supportive of the patient.

The following case demonstrates how a psychoeducational approach worked for a patient and for her family members:

Joanne Summers is a young single woman. As a teenager she had her first episode of hypomania, in which she became uncharacteristically and excessively sexual, propositioning family friends and strangers. She also had symptoms of insomnia and pressured speech and felt euphoric. This first episode ushered in a period of promiscuity and drug abuse.

Thinking that she was a "bad girl" who had disgraced the family, Joanne's father reacted violently, beating her for her sexual indiscretions. She became more and more agitated and eventually required hospitalization. At the hospital she was diagnosed as having schizophrenia, treated with haloperidol, an antipsychotic drug, and discharged several weeks after admission when her agitation subsided.

Joanne continued to suffer periodic exacerbations of her illness over the next several years. During the hypomanic episodes her behavior bewildered her family since they assumed she had received appropriate treatment and they did not attribute her excessive sexuality and argumentativeness to a disorder. Her father continued to lose his temper, to confine her to home and to beat her severely.

Following a second hospitalization, the diagnosis of bipolar affective disorder was established, and she responded well to a trial of lithium. Relations with her parents eased somewhat, but they never fully understood the periodic nature of her disorder. The threat of physical violence loomed over the household, yet Mr. and Mrs. Summers feared that any confrontation or stress might trigger another episode.

A few months later Joanne's lithium level fell below the

therapeutic range. She felt herself becoming ill and her boyfriend drove her to the hospital where she requested voluntary admission. She told the resident in the emergency room that she hadn't slept for a week, had racing thoughts and increased sexual feelings. Her speech was pressured and she was hypertalkative on admission. The dosage of lithium was increased and within a week she was free of symptoms.

Joanne's psychiatrist felt that the Summers family could benefit from the psychoeducational approach, and the social worker invited the family to participate in the five-session family therapy.

In the first family meeting it became apparent that Joanne had a profound fear of her father as a consequence of the beatings she had suffered. Mr. Summers expressed a desire to learn more about his daughter's illness, although initially he did not read the pamphlet *Primary Affective Disorders* that was given to him. When asked about his response to Joanne's illness, he reported that he would typically stop talking to her when she appeared agitated, lest he set her off again. He felt that the only solution to the problem was for his daughter to move out of the house.

During the family sessions, Mr. Summers reported how very guilty he felt over the way he had treated his daughter. He admitted that the guilt and the outrage at his daughter's behavior left him feeling helpless.

During the sessions the nature of Joanne's periodic disorder was explained to the family. The social worker clarified that Joanne's hypersexual behavior was a symptom of the illness and not the volitional act of a "bad child." This led the family to the realization that she had been punished and shunned for behavior that was out of her control. Mr. Summers apologized for the years of physical abuse, and the family elected to continue in family treatment to further work through their responses to Joanne's illness.

Recently Dr. David Kupfer and Dr. Ellen Frank of the Western Psychiatric Institute and Clinic in Pittsburgh underscored the value of the psychoeducational approach when treating patients with recurrent unipolar depression. They found a significantly reduced relapse rate following the acute episode and a markedly increased compliance to treatment in those patients exposed to the combination of imipramine, psychotherapy and family psychoeducation. They stated that the overall clinic approach that offers this psychoeducational workshop fosters a climate of clinician–patient–family member alliance that leads to a collaborative participation in the treatment.

MARITAL THERAPY

The person most intimately involved with the individual suffering a depression—the spouse—often responds to a partner's loss of interest, withdrawal, diminished sexual arousal and hopelessness in a very personal way. One woman described the year prior to her husband's receiving treatment for depression as one in which she felt inadequate, guilty and angry. She began to feel detached from him and to think of separation and divorce.

During her husband's depressive episode, he experienced an extreme loss of interest in her and in their children. He felt worthless and guilty, and, in the worst moments, told her over and over again how anguished he was that he no longer loved them. His wife, not understanding this outpouring of feelings in the context of his major depression, felt confused and shaken. She knew that there was something terribly wrong but continued, as he did, to find cause for their problems within their immediate situation. Later she learned that these expressions of guilt were no more than an outgrowth of his general loss of interest in the world around him.

The effects of an illness that alters mood, thinking and behavior will clearly have an impact on the way one sees oneself and, in turn, the way one relates to and feels about others. Interpersonal problems, especially in the marital arena, can lead to serious and painful repercussions when not understood as part of a medical condition. This is no less true for episodes of mania or hypomania.

Individuals experiencing hypomania or mania are often driven to impulsive acts. Sexual indiscretions, perhaps uncharacteristic during well periods, are common. The experience of infidelity can scar a marriage and easily abrogate basic trust. It is a tragic fact that, while time-limited, episodes of affective illness can persist for months to years if undiagnosed and untreated. Since individuals experiencing hypomania frequently do not come to psychiatric attention, the episodes—and their impact on a marriage—may continue indefinitely until either a severe depression intervenes or the hypomania escalates to mania.

The relationship between marital problems and depression has been examined in a number of clinical studies, most notably those involving women with depression. Drs. Myrna Weissman and E. S. Paykel found that marital relationships were the most impaired areas of social functioning in acutely depressed women and that the impairments were slow to resolve and persisted long after the symptoms of the illness resolved.

In a study of seventy-six depressed women treated for eight months with individual psychotherapy and/or antidepressant drugs, Drs. Bruce Rounsaville, Brigitte Prusoff and Myrna Weissman found that, by comparison, those women who came into treatment complaining of marital disputes experienced less improvement in their symptoms and had a greater tendency to relapse than those women who had no marital disputes at the onset of treatment.

These studies stress the need for couple's therapy in conjunction with the pharmacological treatment of the acute episode. Clearly, educating both patient and spouse about the course and nature of an affective disorder can go a long way toward reducing the interpersonal conflicts that commonly develop between partners in a relationship where one member has the disorder. Once treatment has stabilized the acute symptoms, a retrospective review of the relationship and the course of illness is helpful for both parties, as the origin and intensity of current marital disputes often can be traced back to the onset and evolution of the depressive or manic symptoms.

SHORT-TERM THERAPIES SPECIFICALLY FORMULATED FOR DEPRESSION

We can't close this chapter without mentioning two short-term therapies designed specifically for depression. These therapies are especially worth discussing because in May 1986 a six-year $10 million study funded by the National Institute of Mental Health concluded that *cognitive therapy* and *interpersonal psychotherapy* were as effective as imipramine in reducing the symptoms of depression and improving the functioning of patients.

The study was conducted at three sites—the University of Pittsburgh, George Washington University and the University of Oklahoma—and involved 240 moderately or severely depressed patients and twenty-eight therapists. The patients were divided randomly into three groups: the first and second groups received sixteen weeks of either cognitive or interpersonal psychotherapy and the third group received the tricyclic antidepressant imipramine. A control group was given a placebo plus some verbal support and encouragement by psychiatrists.

Initially there was a faster response to imipramine, but after three months the talking therapies caught up. At the conclusion of sixteen weeks, all three treatments had eliminated serious depressive symptoms in more than half the patients.

Questions as to the long-term effect or relapse rate have yet to be answered, but this landmark project intends to test patients after six, twelve and eighteen months, and will furnish a report with these results in December 1986.

Following is a brief description of cognitive and interpersonal therapy (IPT) as well as an indication of their availability in this country at present.

Cognitive therapy, developed by Dr. Aaron Beck, is a time-limited, structured approach based on the proposition that an individual's affect—his moods and emotions—is determined by his thoughts and ideas. Therefore, by modifying the ideas, one modifies the moods and emotions.

According to the theory, depressed patients consistently distort their interpretation of events so as to maintain negative views of themselves, their environment and their future. This predisposition stems from the development of early negative assumptions or "schemas." For example, a child may develop the schema that nothing he or she will ever do will be good enough. This assumption may be unconscious until a life event, such as being fired from a job, activates it. Once the schema springs to life again, the patient processes the experience so as to maintain the failure schema. The distortions in thinking magnify until depression and hopelessness set in and take over.

Cognitive therapy seeks to change this type of depressive thinking and thus alter the depressed mood. The therapist and patient achieve this by examining and modifying depressive ideas that the patient maintains about himself. The patient is asked to do "homework" assignments between sessions and is instructed to keep a journal. The sessions are aimed at overcoming hopelessness, identifying problems, setting priorities, demonstrating the relationship between cognition and emotion and labeling errors in thinking. The patient learns to question his negative assumptions and put them "to the test" by examining evidence and trying graded tasks. By the end of the therapy patients begin to view themselves and their problems more realistically, change their maladaptive behavioral patterns and feel better.

Should you wish to find out if cognitive therapy is available in your area, call or write the Center for Cognitive Therapy at 133 South 36th Street, Room 519, Philadelphia, PA 19104, (215) 898-4100. Normally the therapy is conducted over a twelve-week period including fifteen to thirty sessions. There is an evaluation fee, and each session costs approximately $75.

Interpersonal psychotherapy was developed by Drs. Gerald Klerman and Myrna Weissman and the New Haven–Boston Collaborative Depression project. It is similar to cognitive therapy in that it is structured and time-limited, but it emphasizes social bonds and relationships and works to improve a person's self-concept and communication skills. Issues such as grief and social and family role transitions are the focus, as is the patient's ability to form and sustain adequate and nurturing relationships. The interpersonal psychotherapist recognizes the role of genetic, biochemical, developmental and personality factors in causation of and vulnerability to depression.

There are approximately twelve sessions to the treatment, and fees average about $90 per session. There is, however, a great problem in locating a practitioner to administer the treatment outside of research centers. This should change as efforts are being made to train practitioners across the country.

8

HOW TO GET GOOD TREATMENT

The last few chapters indicate the importance of a combined medical and psychological treatment approach to affective disorders, but a patient doesn't usually just fall into an ideal treatment program administered by ideal treatment providers. There is a confusing array of mental health providers out there—psychiatrists, psychologists, social workers and therapists, all with different orientations—and it will take serious investigation on the part of the patient and family members to seek out the treatment best suited to their needs. The quality and amount of treatment a person receives will also be determined by the kind of practitioners available in the area, the type of insurance policy the patient has or the amount of money the patient or family can afford to pay.

The first and most crucial step is the diagnosis. A medical doctor is the only person who can rule out diseases that might be masquerading as an affective disorder (such as multiple sclerosis, hypo- or hyperthyroidism, vitamin B12 deficiency, temporal lobe epilepsy and other brain disorders). Should the problem prove to be an affective disorder, a psychiatrist is the only professional trained to treat these disorders with medications and electroconvulsive therapy and able, if need be, to admit the patient to a psychiatric unit.

WHAT TO LOOK FOR IN A DOCTOR

One survey estimated that 54 percent of adults with psychiatric disorders in the United States are treated by internists or family practitioners, and that there is a resistance to seeking out or receiving treatment from a psychiatrist. (No doubt stigma and limited insurance coverage for mental health services do much to produce this resistance.) In some situations, when the illness is mild and the doctor is knowledgeable about and interested in affective disorders, treatment by a nonpsychiatrist may be sufficient. But in the case of severe depression where there is a possibility of suicide, or where there are bipolar or psychotic symptoms, the patient should be cared for by an experienced psychiatrist.

A patient needs a psychiatrist who has had experience with the full range of affective syndromes, one who is adept in diagnosis and very familiar with the use of such medications as lithium, antidepressants, MAOIs, antipsychotics and anticonvulsants (see Chapter 5). The psychiatrist should be affiliated with a good hospital and be able to deal with patients who may experience psychotic symptoms and require vigorous intervention or protection, sometimes against their will. The doctor should also be able to explain thoroughly what is known and what is not known about the disorder and the medications, and speak frankly with the patient about what he or she may expect.

But a patient should look for more than a diagnostician/pharmacologist. The doctor should have an empathic understanding of a person's experience during a state of depression, hypomania or mania. He or she can then help the patient determine which aspects of behavior, wishes or decision making are induced by the episodic mood swings and which arise out of personality, background or everyday life situations.

Because depressive, hypomanic and manic episodes can dramatically change the way in which a person relates to the people closest to him—a spouse and other family members—and because a family member's misunderstanding of the illness can lead to conflict and estrangement, it might be advantageous to choose a psychiatrist who, if necessary, will involve the family members in the treatment. Some psychiatrists, however, feel that couple or family treatment violates the patient's contract of confidentiality. If it's important that the family have the option of meeting the psychiatrist and discussing their attitudes and feelings with him or her, this should be discussed before treatment commences. (Naturally it is difficult to "doctor shop" during a crisis, and we do not intend to downplay the time element and judgment problems to be considered when someone is in an acute state.)

Patients who had been treated by a number of psychiatrists were very emphatic about what constituted a good doctor. They advise looking for someone who:

". . . has basic qualifications: medical knowledge, pharmacological knowledge, psychological knowledge. I would advise someone to look for honesty. By this I mean a doctor willing to tell the patient the truth. I had a number of doctors who were very evasive for one reason or another."

". . . gives details and talks to you like an intelligent person (doesn't patronize). Someone who lets you know what to expect and what to prepare yourself for, with the illness and the medications."

". . . is not one-track-minded, like a psychopharmacologist. Someone who does not pressure you to hurry what you're saying. Preferably someone who appreciates the benefits of talking therapy."

". . . shows genuine concern for your well-being, is available during emergencies, stays current with new alternative drugs and research, is willing to change medications if necessary and conducts psychotherapy as a useful adjunct."

HOW TO FIND A DOCTOR

There are several avenues to explore in finding the right doctor. Ask your personal physician for a referral. Or, if you live near a university-affiliated teaching hospital, you can call the department of psychiatry and ask to speak to the chief resident or the admissions director or the clinical director, and tell the person with whom you speak that you are looking for the names of psychiatrists who have expertise in the area of mood disorders. It is always a good idea to get two or three names so that you can not only seek a "second opinion," but also decide with whom you feel most comfortable. Trust your instincts.

Another source is the appendices of this book, where you can find the patient or family organization nearest to you. When you call the office listed, tell the person you reach what it is you need. The patients and families who belong to these organizations have had firsthand experience with many of the psychiatrists in your area and they are often in a good position to steer you toward a highly competent physician.

Once you have the referral, make a telephone call. Just give your name, mention the name of the doctor or person who referred you and tell the psychiatrist that you would like to schedule an appointment for a consultation. This is not the time for a long, detailed discussion—all of that will be handled in the consultation session.

THE CONSULTATION

The first meeting is simply a conversation between you and the doctor. The psychiatrist gets a complete picture of the specific symptoms that are troubling you by asking questions about mood, appetite, sleeping and daily activity levels, as well as about relationships at home and at work. Because there is a genetic component to mood disorders, and because other problems can produce the symptoms of a mood disorder, the psychiatrist will ask about your family and medical history. As the doctor begins to get an impression of the current episode or problem, he or she explores the possibility that there may have been episodes of mania, hypomania, depression or mood changes in the past.

Most people are uncomfortable telling a virtual stranger intimate things about themselves, their feelings and behavior, and a sensitive psychiatrist expects and understands this. But since, as we mentioned before, there are no foolproof laboratory tests that can confirm or refute a diagnosis in psychiatry, the symptoms, behavior patterns, history and course of illness are the clues that point to a correct diagnosis.

If the diagnosis of an affective disorder is made, and if the symptoms are now acute, it is likely that the psychiatrist will want to attenuate the symptoms with a medical intervention—one of the medications mentioned in Chapter 5. Before writing and explaining a prescription, however, the doctor should ask the patient to visit his internist for a complete physical examination, including routine blood tests and an electrocardiogram. The psychiatrist looks at the results of the physical exam, considers the course of the disorder and which drugs the person or his family members may have responded to in the past (medication response and side effects can be heritable) and decides on a medication trial. The patient should be informed as to why the drug was chosen, what laboratory tests, if any, will be required while taking it and what short- and long-term side effects might be expected.

Because medications address only certain of the problems caused by a mood disorder, and psychotherapy addresses others, the patient and prescribing physician should talk frankly about the advantages of an adjunctive psychotherapy. This may necessitate a referral to another mental health professional because it is not always the case that the physician provides both the medications and the psychotherapy. And here's where things get confusing—an unfortunate polarization currently exists in the treatment of major affective disorders.

There are so-called "biological" psychiatrists and "psychodynamic" psychiatrists. Biological psychiatrists focus principally on precise diagnosis and medical treatment, and although they pay lip service to the need for the talking therapies, few make use of this body of knowledge in their approach to treatment. (A study by Drs. Frederick Goodwin and Kay Jamison of patients treated with lithium found that 50 percent of the patient group considered psychotherapy to be important in lithium compliance, while only 27 percent of the clinicians regarded psychotherapy as important. This observation may indicate a tendency for physicians to estimate the potency of a drug so highly that they underestimate the psychological aspects of the illness.) Conversely, while many psychiatrists with a psychodynamic or psychoanalytic orientation recognize biological contributions to the treatment of the symptoms, many do not make use of the knowledge in practice, and may believe that psychological treatments alone are adequate or even preferable. These real biases have contributed to a fragmentation in the field and in the care of patients that reflects the training and indoctrination of the psychiatrist rather than the current knowledge of the nature and course of the disorder.

Part of the problem is that there has been such a rapid accumulation of knowledge in the field. Discoveries constantly occur after the formal training of any professional and require the person to update his knowledge constantly through continuing education programs and careful attention to scientific and clinical journals. Because there are still gaps in our understanding of the causes and treatment of these disorders, and because physiological factors may predominate in some cases of depression while psychological factors predominate in others, there has been no uniform standard of treatment.

As a result, a patient is presented with a confusing array of practitioners whose conceptualization of the illness may include:

1. A view of the disorder that focuses on the treatment of some underlying deficit (presumed to be at the level of transmission between nerve cells) with medications. Psychological conflict, stress or interpersonal issues may be seen as arising from the disorder or are considered unimportant.

2. A view of the disorder that focuses on the resolution of psychological conflict as the primary goal of treatment and precludes the conception that there may exist an underlying deficit at the level of neurotransmission. (Neither of these views has been proven.)

3. A view of the disorder that explains the symptoms as a reflection of interpersonal conflict occurring between family members. The focus of the treatment would be to reveal and modify this conflict.

4. Modern, integrated, commonsense approaches, which we support.

During the consultation, patients and family members have every right to inquire about the mental health professional's orientation and clinical views, and such questions as "Do you believe drugs are important in treating the illness?" and "Do you feel psychotherapy is an important supplement to the medical treatment?" will reveal the orientation of the practitioner. The psychiatrist should help a patient decide if an adjunctive psychotherapy is indicated, and if the psychiatrist does not provide it, he or she should make a referral.

COSTS

Beyond the question of the psychiatrist's training and biases is the question of whether or not the patient can afford frequent psychotherapy with that psychiatrist. Many patients who recognize the need to address the psychological aspects of their situation seek out less expensive mental health professionals to conduct the psychotherapy (this may be a psychologist, social worker or nurse practitioner). The psychiatrist, then, manages the medical aspects of the treatment on a less frequent basis.

But a note of caution should be injected here also: if the professional managing the psychotherapeutic aspects of the treatment does not have a solid understanding of the disorder, its course and medical treatment, it is possible that aspects of the patient's behavior, mood and thinking may be misinterpreted. For example, if a patient suddenly begins planning an exotic trip abroad and the therapist assumes that the behavior is motivated only by a wish to avoid the intensity of the therapy or some other unpleasant situation, and does not think to inquire about the presence of other symptoms (such as decreased sleep, changes in libido and appetite, et cetera), the advent of a manic episode could be missed. Teasing apart motivations that arise from personality and background from those propelled by an impending episode of illness can be exceedingly difficult. However, the patient is best served when all things are considered, and this requires a comprehensive view of the person and the disorder that affects him.

How much would treatment with any of these different professionals cost? As this book goes to press, the estimated national fees per session are:

Psychiatrist	$75–125
Clinical psychologist	$45–90
Social worker	$35–75

A follow-up visit to a psychiatrist for medication management may take twenty to thirty minutes and will probably cost about $50–$80. Some social workers or marriage and family counselors see patients for as little as $25–30 a session, and many mental health professionals have a sliding scale for fees based on an individual's ability to pay. At the other end of the spectrum, some psychopharmacologists charge several hundred dollars for an expanded diagnostic consultation.

CLINICS

Anyone scanning the private fees listed above quickly realizes that the long-term medical and psychological treatment of these disorders costs a great deal of money or requires a very comprehensive insurance policy. Fortunately there are other alternatives: in most areas there are clinics that provide treatment based on a patient's income and ability to pay. As with any service, the quality of treatment varies.

In certain areas of the country there are major affective disorders clinics—usually attached to the departments of psychiatry in academic centers—and their interests often include research into the nature of the disorders and their treatment. The medical leadership of such clinics is usually sophisticated in the diagnosis and pharmacological treatment of the disorders, but not all of them assess the psychological and social ramifications of these illnesses with equal vigor and skill, or make patient education one of the primary goals.

Another kind of outpatient setting is the university-affiliated teaching clinic. Here the patient is seen by a resident who may have good training and supervision (although limited experience), but who will be in the clinic for only a limited period of time. The patient has a long-term disorder; the doctor may change every year or less. Should a close collaborative relationship develop, the patient suffers a loss when the resident rotates off the service. Then a new doctor-patient relationship has to be formed, and the new doctor will not have a level of training higher than the last.

More common is the publicly funded community mental health or catchment area clinic that serves a specific locality. Again the quality and level of sophistication varies from clinic to clinic. Affective disorders are not the only psychiatric conditions treated, and funds are limited. Very commonly a patient sees a doctor only for initial evaluation, medication renewal or adjustment or to deal with a crisis. If psychotherapy is offered, it is almost always administered by a nonmedical therapist.

Few, if any, of these kinds of clinics actively involve the family, and this just doesn't make sense. In many instances the family is the only support the patient has during periods of illness and recovery, assuring the patient's adherence to medication and recognizing symptoms early. Moreover, given that there is a genetic vulnerability in families (see page 44), involving family members and educating them about the symptoms, course and available treatments provides a measure of preventative treatment, assisting in the early recognition and treatment of the disorder should it appear in other family members.

THE IDEAL COMPREHENSIVE CLINIC PROGRAM

It is obvious that there are positive aspects as well as pitfalls in the current organization of psychiatric care and other mental health services. So, what constitutes an ideal approach to treatment that could be developed in an outpatient treatment setting? Let us draw a picture of how a good program can effectively address the needs of patients and families. Such a clinic would serve as a diagnostic, medical treatment and education center. It would assess the psychological impact of the illness on both patients and families and offer supportive services for long-term management of the disorder.

In this ideal arrangement, a patient is seen individually by a psychiatrist for several sessions. During these hours, a history of past episodes is spelled out and their frequency and duration documented. The family history is explored, as are previous treatments, their effects and side effects. The doctor then orders a complete medical evaluation, including a physical exam, in order to exclude other medical causes for the symptoms and to guide treatment.

Once the diagnosis has been clearly established, the patient and family are invited to participate in a workshop where the nature, course, possible causes and treatments of the disorder are reviewed. The "psychoeducational" approach described in Chapter 7 is explained, and the family has the option of entering into several sessions of family counseling.

Then a recommendation for follow-up treatment is made. While a psychiatrist follows each patient individually for long-term medical treatment, some patients may also opt for individual psychotherapy, and some families may wish to continue in a family-centered treatment or join a multiple-family group. Attached to the clinic is a manic-depressive and depressive support group run by patients and family members (see pages 237–38).

Research into the nature and possible causes of these disorders is rapidly moving in the direction of identifying a genetic marker that would identify those at risk. These clinics could serve as a resource for this kind of research, perhaps contributing to a better understanding of the disorders and better treatments in the future.

Unfortunately, such a comprehensive program is not commonly available. Nevertheless, institutions responsible for the delivery of medical care in this country are becoming more responsive to consumer needs. If patients and family members come together and work with the leaders of such clinics, they can sensitize them to the services they need and want, and thus forge a better system. A group of people bound by ideas, commitment and strong resolve could have their say and effect change.

THE PATIENT'S ROLE
IN OBTAINING GOOD TREATMENT

Now that we've alerted patients and family members to the possible pitfalls in psychiatric care, we want to close this chapter with a discussion of the patient's role in a good treatment plan. For there are two parts to the equation: a skilled, empathic doctor and a patient who realizes that he or she also shapes the outcome of treatment. Success very much depends on the ability of the patient to take an active part in and make a commitment to the treatment alliance.

First the patient must accept that it is not uncommon for there to be a trial-and-error period of drug selection and adjustment. Some people respond dramatically to lithium and antidepressant treatment and have few, if any, problems; others have a more difficult time of it. Either the response is not a complete one or the side effects are intolerable. Should this be the case, a period of new medication trials is initiated. During this time of uncertainty, which may last months or even a year, the patient is often frustrated, angry and demoralized. A patient who understands the realities and the potential difficulties inherent in treating these conditions may be more willing to give the psychiatrist the time it takes to initiate and assess the medication trials and may feel more comfortable in the time preceding stabilization.

It is important that the patient report the side effects accurately to the physician. If there are considerations about changing the medication or adding a medication to counter the side effects, an open dialogue between the doctor and patient regarding the risks and benefits of alternate courses of action must take place. Naturally, it is the physician's responsibility to inform and educate the patient at each juncture of pharmacological treatment, but because there are these varying alternatives, the patient should expect to be part of the decision-making process.

Even though the psychiatrist and patient may initially concern themselves with the pharmacological treatment, any caretaking relationship rekindles earlier conflicts around dependency, attachment and intimacy. Some patients are fearful of becoming dependent on the psychiatrist and may express these feelings by wanting to control the management of the medications entirely. They may either discontinue the medications or adapt their own regimens without consulting the doctor. Other patients have highly unrealistic expectations of the psychiatrist and can become disappointed and angry when these expectations are not met. These issues, which can interfere with the establishment of a therapeutic alliance, often have less to do with the illness than with specific personality problems. Although these conflicts and issues are foreseeable, they add to the complexity of the medical treatment and could cause the patient to terminate therapy. However, a good psychiatrist recognizes that just as patients respond differently to medications so they have variable responses to their having to take the medications and to the practitioner who prescribes them. These issues can be resolved, but only if the patient stays in treatment, discusses his or her feelings openly and is able to work through the fears, unrealistic wishes and positive and negative feelings toward the psychiatrist/therapist.

THREE

LIVING WITH THE ILLNESS

9

THE FAMILY
AND THE ILLNESS

When a relative experiences recurrent episodes of depression or mania, there is a profoundly disruptive and disorganizing effect on family life. The other members of the family are faced with the challenge of looking after and providing for the needs of their relative while at the same time maintaining their other responsibilities at work and at home—often within an atmosphere of confusion, isolation, embarrassment, anger and guilt. Before long the individual needs of all the family members are ignored as each tries to grapple with the tension and uncertainty that accompany these disorders.

It is probably not possible to calculate the degree of pain and the exhaustion such families feel. With guidance and encouragement, however, families can gain a better perspective and organize themselves so as to expend energy most effectively. There may still be bad feelings and even emotional storms, but the family doesn't have to weather them without the life preservers of knowledge, understanding and practical coping strategies.

There are stages of recognition, adjustment and adaptation to illness, and each family travels through the stages in its own time and in its own fashion. Many factors influence the family's initial response to the onset of the illness: some members need to protect themselves with the cloak of denial; almost all invent theories or take responsibility in an attempt to explain the changes in behavior. When the symptoms are mild, and if they are interspersed with periods of functioning well, it is not difficult to attribute them to external events, personal circumstances or personality quirks. Some families are more able or willing than others to tolerate behavior that deviates from the norm. Sooner or later, though, if the symptoms become more severe and disruptive, the patient and the family members may seek professional advice and find a name for their problem. Then a new period of adjustment and regrouping can take place within the family.

Each family is actually a caretaking system that over time has established rules, expectations and basic assumptions about caring for each other. Illness of any kind has an impact on this caretaking system and necessitates shifts in the interactions among the members. It is vital that all the members seek a common perspective about the nature of the illness, its course, the limitations it imposes on the patient and what they can expect during acute episodes and over the long term in which there may be recurrences of illness and sustained disability.

The first change that confronts the family is the loss of functioning of the ill member. Since he or she is no longer able to fulfill usual responsibilities within the family, someone else must take on the tasks, and time must be devoted to caring for the person who is ill. In the case of a patient who is the principal wage earner and/or organizer of the home, severe disruption of ordinary family life may occur until effective role shifts have taken place.

When the patient is a young person in the family, parents suffer the anguish of watching their child in pain, and fear for the quality of his or her future. Hopes and expectations may have to be modified and mourned, and the child may grow into an adult who needs more attention, caretaking and financial support than had previously been planned for, which sometimes causes anger and guilt.

Many families search for the blame among themselves and feel shame in having their relatives, neighbors or colleagues know that there is mental illness in their home. Sadly, these worries deplete them all the more.

A host of problems and questions arise for each family, and the answers will vary from patient to patient and family to family. There is no typical scenario, but there are common problems and emotions that emerge in every family's attempt to cope with a major mental illness. The following pages examine a few of these.

ONE FAMILY'S RESPONSE TO DEPRESSION

When a person is feeling depressed and helpless, it is common for loved ones to assume that attention, assistance and assurances will restore that person's capacity to respond. Most family members offer this kind of help and provide what seems to be required by the situation. But a person suffering depression usually feels fatigue, lack of energy, loss of appetite and a general loss of ability to care for himself, and may respond negatively to well-wishers the harder they try to motivate him. A vicious cycle develops: the family members who have extended themselves conscientiously, and to no avail, may feel frustrated, resentful, angry or despairing, and this further compounds the sense of isolation, guilt or hopelessness the ill relative already feels.

One family's experience of this cycle began every morning as they tried to rouse their severely depressed mother. All the children would gather at her bedside offering positive statements and encouragement, impressing upon her the need to eat. As the day wore on her mood seemed to brighten somewhat, and in the late afternoon she actually got out of bed, joined the family at the dinner table and shared in one of a string of jokes her son told to ease the tension and entertain her. The children, although exhausted, felt a great sense of relief and pride at night, thinking their efforts had done much to lift her spirits. They fully expected that each day would bring further improvement.

The following morning their mother was again unable to eat and did not want to get out of bed. She was irritable and seemed annoyed by the children's attention to her condition. The family, in turn, felt increasingly ineffectual and irritated with their mother. Their good intentions and best efforts had made no lasting impact and even seemed to make matters worse.

And therein lies the cruel hoax of depression. There is typically a daily variation in the intensity of symptoms called a *diurnal mood variation*. The person may feel awful in the morning, but as the day progresses, the mood brightens. This pattern continues day after day, dashing the hopes and expectations of family members—in some ways mocking their efforts.

The children consulted their mother's psychiatrist, and after informing them that the antidepressant she was taking would take at least two or three weeks to work, the psychiatrist helped them devise a method of coping with the situation. They set up a schedule of two-hour shifts among themselves to ensure that someone was always in the house and nearby, but they stopped pressuring her to make immediate gains. They simply expressed confidence that time would pass and she would recover.

This family coped with the vicious cycle of tremendous effort, fluctuating hopes, exhaustion and resentment by modifying their expectations. While their mother needed to know of their continued concern and support, the children realized that their best efforts would not permanently restore her disposition. In some ways they were doubly burdening her with their wishes for early improvement. She experienced this as an impossible demand with which she was unable to comply and about which she felt increasingly guilty and frustrated.

By modifying their natural tendency to expect immediate results and improvement, the children lessened the demands they placed on themselves and on their ill mother, and they increased their stamina and capacity to endure.

SUICIDAL BEHAVIOR

Few things in life are more threatening than a relative (or patient) who expresses suicidal thoughts or behavior. When a person is overtly suicidal, most families recognize the necessity of immediate professional help. However, suicidal intentions are often expressed in more subtle and ambiguous ways. Most families are not prepared to judge the seriousness of the threat, and the lack of a plan of action or response raises their anxiety level to such a degree that the family is unable to act effectively and in a timely fashion.

If relatives even suspect that the patient is thinking about suicide, they should call the treating psychiatrist immediately and alert him to that fact. Depending on a variety of factors, hospitalization may be indicated. Suicide is often an impulsive act: the patient can be having coffee in the kitchen with someone one minute, retire to the bedroom and leap from an open window. It happens that fast; it happens that unexpectedly. The myth that people who threaten to commit suicide never do so is a dangerous one to subscribe to. People often carry out their threats, particularly if they are ignored.

The family may have to resort to involuntary commitment to prevent the patient from killing him or herself. Family members who have a severely depressed relative should first consult with a psychiatrist. If the patient's condition warrants hospitalization, the family members should discuss with the psychiatrist the procedure for admission to a psychiatric unit. Chapter 10, on hospitalization and commitment, as well as the state laws listed in the appendices of this book should help to clarify this process.

What are the common warning signs of suicidal intention?

- Feelings of worthlessness or hopelessness
- Preoccupation with morbid topics or death
- Withdrawal from previous activities or relationships and estrangement from family and friends
- Increased risk-taking behaviors (for example, driving too fast, drinking heavily, handling knives or guns)
- Sudden brightening of mood or increased activity in someone who has been seriously depressed
- Putting one's affairs in order (for example, writing a will, giving prized possessions away, saying goodbye to people)
- Feelings of anguish or desperation
- Voices that are commanding the patient to hurt himself or other irrational experiences
- Actually thinking about a plan to take one's own life

People with a family history of suicide are at particular risk. Others before them have used suicide as a solution to a problem and they may use that self-destructive act as a model. Moreover, there is evidence to suggest that for some there is a genetic predisposition to suicide. Biological studies conducted ten years ago by Dr. Herman van Praag in Holland and Dr. Marie Asberg in Sweden revealed that certain suicide attempters had a decreased level of the metabolite of the neurotransmitter serotonin in their spinal fluid (5-hydroxyindoleacetic acid or 5-HIAA). Individuals with these lower levels of 5-HIAA were more likely to attempt suicide in an impulsive and violent manner. Some researchers believe that this finding may one day lead to a biochemical test to predict who is at risk for suicide.

In the meantime, once the family suspects the patient's suicidal potential and has located and consulted a psychiatrist, there are some practical steps that the family can take to limit the expression of the impulse:

- Remove access to knives, guns, medications, automobiles and other potentially lethal instruments.
- Monitor the taking of medications, first to ensure that the patient is taking them (thus limiting the time that he suffers with suicidal depression), and also to guard against an overdose. Antidepressants or lithium and some sleeping pills (especially if taken with alcohol) can be fatal if taken in too large a dose.
- Let the patient talk about suicidal thoughts without the family's expressing shock and condemnation. If the family understands that suicidal thoughts and impulses are not unusual in severe depression, and conveys this understanding, the patient may feel less guilty and isolated. The patient is not forced into secrecy, and such open communication may allow both the family and the patient to better judge when protective hospitalization is necessary.

COPING WITH MANIC BEHAVIOR

Coping with a relative who is in a manic state can be exhausting and demoralizing also. A person experiencing depression is usually so fatigued and tentative that, unless he or she is suicidal, there is little likelihood that he or she will make rash and impulsive decisions that would have an impact on other family members. In mania, just the opposite is true. The patient has boundless energy, unshakable drive but little capacity to appraise the consequences of his actions realistically. It is common for individuals in a manic episode to engage in reckless buying sprees. Huge and unreconcilable debts can be incurred, and our legal system often holds families accountable for their relative's financial mismanagement. Judgment and insight can be so impaired in the manic state that patients may flout all authority and become so intrusive and demanding as to harass others and violate social and sexual mores. At the worst, they may become irritable, aggressive or even assaultive, leading to the involvement of the police and legal authorities. The family is often placed in the unenviable position of having to set limits on someone who refuses to acknowledge the family's responsibility and concern or who becomes openly hostile when challenged.

Once an episode has reached a certain pitch and the patient cannot be reasoned with, it is both protective of the patient and expedient to move quickly toward hospitalization. Because the patient's mood can fluctuate—ranging from mild euphoria to extreme irritability—and because the patient may speak logically and coherently for periods of time, it is often difficult for families to know when to force this issue. These lucid intervals can be deceptive, however. Unless the patient is being treated aggressively with antipsychotic or mood-stabilizing medications (and the patient is taking the medication), it is unlikely that the manic episode will end safely without hospitalization. Thus the hospitalization should be viewed as a positive step as it will serve to limit the damage that people in a manic state could do to themselves, their social network and their family.

Therefore, should the family observe the following behaviors and be unable to convince the patient to see his or her psychiatrist and take the necessary medication, arrangements should be made for immediate hospitalization:

- Sleeplessness for several nights with frequent shifts of mood, pacing and agitated behavior and no acknowledgment on the part of the patient that anything is wrong
- Reckless and impulsive decisions or actions that may lead to financial ruin or social ostracism
- Threatening, menacing or assaultive behavior
- The presence of delusions or hallucinations

THREATS AND ASSAULTIVE BEHAVIOR

When someone is experiencing mania or acute psychosis, his or her mood may shift rapidly from excitement to irritability. Some manic patients become exceedingly hostile and angry. The fear that the ill person will lose control and not be able to contain aggressive impulses paralyzes those around the patient. Family members, afraid to anger their relative or inflame an already volatile situation, often step back, trying to placate or mollify their agitated relative. Not knowing what to do or how to act, most families tend to wait it out and hope the mood will shift back to reasonableness and equanimity.

This is rare. Mania in most cases continues long after the family's patience and stamina have been exhausted. It is in no one's interest to tolerate threats and assaultive behavior. When faced with threats, the family should confront them directly. For instance, if a patient tries to intimidate a relative by saying, "I'll get you for doing this to me," the family member can respond by identifying the statement as a personal threat and refusing to accept it. He or she may say something like: "I take what you're saying to be a threat and I can't accept that. This kind of behavior shows me that you are out of control because when you are not ill, we're able to resolve our differences without threatening each other." Often, people experiencing mania are frightened by their loss of control, and a firm stance may help to establish temporary boundaries. They may be dangerous, however, and family members should not place themselves in a situation from which they cannot withdraw easily.

If this is not a first episode, and the patient has a psychiatrist, the family should naturally call and consult with the doctor. The questions most in need of answering are: How dangerous is the situation and how quickly must an intervention be made? The answers to these questions often depend on the answers to the following questions: Has the patient ever been assaultive before? At what point in the episode did this occur, and is he or she approaching that point? Has the patient been taking street drugs or drinking alcohol? Is the patient severely irrational and misperceiving or distorting events?

EMERGENCY INTERVENTION AND ITS AFTERMATH

Delusional thinking and misinterpretation of events can lead to violent or assaultive behavior. Therefore, when an ill relative expresses delusional thinking in the context of a manic episode (when the control of impulses may be lost), it is imperative that the family act

quickly to consult the psychiatrist and initiate commitment procedures. The family may even have to call the police and ask an officer
to take the patient to a hospital for an evaluation. The police are
trained to work with people who are psychiatrically ill and can be
a tremendous help. (See the next chapter for an explanation of the
commitment procedure.)

Families who have been called upon to commit a relative in the
past are sometimes loathe to do it again as they feel the patient has
never fully forgiven them. Something was ruptured in the relationship
and both family and patient harbor fear and resentment. The family
must overcome those feelings sufficiently to act responsibly, even if
that requires involuntary hospitalization. Certainly it takes great
courage to assume this responsibility and to see it through. Despite
the toll that this exacts, there may be some consolation in knowing
that you are protecting someone who is no longer able to judge the
situation accurately.

The aftermath of an acute episode of mania poses another set of
problems. Fearing that the least stress might set off another episode,
the family lives with prolonged uncertainty and apprehension. In
such an atmosphere, the patient's behavior and natural expressions
of emotion—joy or sadness—come under close scrutiny or even
suspicion. The family, in the position of being an "early warning
system" of impending mood swings, can easily slip into the role of
prosecuting attorney: the patient may be faced with seemingly endless
questions and doubts and be asked to provide motives for almost
every act. One woman with a history of mania told us that if she
washed the dishes at midnight, she'd turn around to find her husband
and children standing uneasily in the doorway, checking to see if
this was a sign of sleeplessness or increased activity. They were afraid
of another episode; she just wanted to clean up the kitchen and have
some time to think quietly.

This is a corrosive atmosphere for everyone concerned: the patient's credibility and competence as a person are called into question
by the sometimes unspoken suspicion of his motivations and emotions, and the family is placed under a terrible strain.

Thus, before the patient is discharged from the hospital it would
be to everyone's advantage to meet with the psychiatrist to talk about
the impact the episode has had on everyone and to develop a strategy

for aftercare that is fair to the patient *and* the family. The idea is to help the patient understand what the family members went through in trying to cope with him or her during an episode, and encourage the patient to participate in an agreement that will help reduce the chances of a future hospitalization or establish guidelines if another hospitalization becomes necessary. (It is helpful for families faced with the wrenching situation of having to commit a relative to think back to that meeting and remember the patient's agreement to a future hospitalization.) A formulated plan establishes guidelines, reduces misperceptions and relieves the family members of the onerous task of deciding if and when to hospitalize. An episode can be resolved more swiftly if there is less conflict over this decision.

Some of the questions that need to be worked out include: What behavior will constitute sufficient cause to call the psychiatrist and ask for an emergency intervention? Which family member will make that call? What will be sufficient cause for voluntary hospitalization or for involuntary hospitalization? A family that attempts to deal with these questions beforehand can avoid becoming paralyzed with guilt and indecision when a crisis occurs.

Such a plan worked well for a family with an eighteen-year-old daughter. She had bipolar disorder, and had had two previous manic episodes. The episodes began with her staying out late for several nights, and with her becoming irritable and accusing her mother of not understanding her need to be independent. The daughter viewed her need to be out late at night as a natural part of growing up and being on her own, and saw her mother's protestations of her violation of curfew as an example of rigid parental authority. The parents, not fully understanding the course of the disorder and feeling that there might be some truth to their daughter's accusation, did not press her to see her psychiatrist.

During the next few weeks, her sleeplessness and activity level increased, and she began playing her stereo at full volume late into the night and dancing in the hallway scantily dressed. Her accusations of her parents' rigidity progressed to delusional thoughts that her family was imprisoning her and controlling her behavior. A crisis ensued, requiring a late night call to the police and an involuntary commitment to the hospital.

Several weeks later, when the daughter was stable and about to be discharged from the hospital, the entire family sat down with the psychiatrist. Everyone got a chance to explain his or her response to the onset of the symptoms. The patient's brother revealed how ashamed and embarrassed he felt by his sister's provocative sexual behavior. The mother was also very upset and stated that she thought her daughter had become a loose woman and had been taking drugs with an unsavory group of friends.

The patient described her experience of freedom during the hypomanic part of the episode and remembered that she had thought that others were envious of her and that her mother was "uptight and inhibited." However, after listening to their genuine concern and fears for her, she was more willing to acknowledge that her behavior may have been determined by the illness.

Prior to discharge, the patient and the family members, along with the treatment team at the hospital, worked out a written, step-by-step plan detailing how the family would manage a recurrence of the illness. The plan was as follows:

1. *The patient and family members would identify the specific list of symptoms that precede a manic episode.* For this patient they were: (a) sleeplessness for more than two nights; (b) increased socialization (for example, talking on the telephone excessively, defined as more than forty-five minutes at a time, more than five times a night, for more than three nights); (c) pressured speech—talking so fast that on at least two occasions members of the family did not understand what she was trying to say.

   Irritable mood and accusatory statements to the mother were discussed but purposely excluded from the plan because they were tied to an ongoing conflict over independence and therefore potentially confusing. This issue was something that would be talked about in the daughter's psychotherapy and in the family therapy.

2. *The patient would choose someone in the family to inform her when the signs and symptoms of the disorder started to manifest themselves.* The daughter chose her father because she felt less threatened when he called attention to changes in her behavior and thus would more easily be able to cooperate with the plan.

   If the father did notice the signs of an impending episode, he would ask his daughter to call her psychiatrist and find out if a change should be made in her medication regimen. If the daughter refused to make this contact, the father would make the call and arrange an appointment with the psychiatrist.

If the daughter refused to follow through and the mania spiraled out of control, the following agreement was reached regarding guidelines the family would follow in order to initiate hospitalization:

(a) The parents would ask the daughter to commit herself voluntarily to the hospital.

(b) If the daughter refused voluntary hospitalization, and both parents felt hospitalization was necessary, the police would be called to assist in transporting her to the hospital. The father would sign the family application for commitment.

Parents who bring a newborn home from the hospital and follow the baby through every developmental stage, urging the child on with love and high hopes, never dream they might have to call the police and watch that child be wrestled into restraints and taken away to a psychiatric hospital. Those who have had to do it never forget the experience and the events that led to its necessity. But a few people who had been hospitalized involuntarily looked back on the experience and spoke of it differently. One woman summed up their feelings by saying: "If our families won't look after us and take over when we're out of control, who will?"

HOW THE FAMILY CAN HELP WITH MEDICATIONS

Family members who've been traumatized from a previous episode can be desperate that their relative remain symptom-free by taking the medications. They may start hovering over the patient and pressuring or cajoling him or her on the subject. A clash of wills may ensue.

This is a particular problem when the patient is an adolescent or young adult. Adolescence is a vulnerable time: a person is struggling to achieve independent functioning and move out of the orbit of parental supervision. There are concerns over the need to show oneself as capable, mature and not in need of anyone's help. At this time in life, the idea of having a disability or needing medications to control it may be intolerable, and conflicts over independence may arise, particularly over the subject of medication.

Because of the potentially tragic effects of frequent episodes at this critical period in life, every effort should be made for the family as well as the patient to enter treatment to help the patient and family to separate conflict over issues of independence from the necessity to adhere to a medical regimen. Somehow the family must seek to strike a balance between legitimate concern and overprotectiveness and intrusiveness.

How else can family members help with the subject of medication? One way would be to keep a list of the drugs prescribed, the dosages and the results and side effects. In the event of a relapse, they can give accurate information to the hospital physician and eliminate a lot of guesswork. Also, should the patient and doctor decide on a change in the medication regimen, the family members can act as an "early warning system" and report any symptoms or untoward side effects.

HOW BROTHERS AND SISTERS ARE AFFECTED

People tend to underestimate the effect that one sibling with a mood disorder has on other children in a family. After all, it's reasoned, they're the healthy ones; they're lucky to have escaped such problems.

Yes. But these healthy siblings suffer in subtle, often insidious ways that affect their sense of self-esteem and the quality of their lives. It is crucial that they be given careful consideration and that their needs not be overlooked by family members and professionals working with the family.

A host of conflicting emotions overwhelm the well siblings. Often love and admiration for the brother or sister who is diagnosed with an affective disorder are entwined with guilt and regret. The well brothers or sisters may be secretly triumphant that they escaped the illness and consequently feel anxious or guilty about their good fortune. If the brother or sister with the affective disorder is older, and if he or she begins to founder in life, younger siblings may find it distressing and uncomfortable to surpass their sibling and go on to fulfill ambitions and dreams.

Resentment and jealousy dog the footsteps of many well siblings because so much of the parents' attention and energy goes toward worrying over and solving the problems of the patient and because so much of the family resources are channeled into treatment and support rather than into the education and pleasure of the rest of the family.

Many siblings reported that they were frustrated with the way their parents denied the illness or attempted to deal with it. One sibling said: "Getting together with the family isn't fun anymore. There's always that tension about my brother's mental illness between us. I'm always angry at everyone for not dealing with the problem like I think they should." It is discomfiting for children to see their parents being ineffectual in the face of their sibling's depression or mania.

The well siblings are perhaps angriest that the patient has so disrupted family life and the good times all families should share. They may feel that they've been cheated. They also can become socially isolated. The turmoil and uncertainty that overtake the household often prevent children from inviting their friends home. They don't want others to be frightened by what their brother or sister may do, and begin to worry that others will conclude that they have a "touch of it" also. Children who don't feel proud of their family find it difficult to be confident socially. As one woman wrote: "The feeling that my family was different distanced me from other people."

Years later, the fear of the heritability of the disorder can again hover over the well siblings—this time as they have their own children. They may become apprehensive about any signs of shifting moods in their offspring, and may even question their decision to have children.

Other problems arise as the parents age and urge the well siblings to look after their ill brother or sister. The well children may not wish to be involved as they now have their own families to care for, and they may feel that their lives have already been too influenced by the problems the disorder has thrust their way.

It's not difficult to conclude that siblings suffer loss—the loss of the companionship of their ill brother or sister, the loss of their parents' attention and a unified family life and a loss of expectations. What can ease their burden and help dissolve the anger they feel? Education and understanding. Only by understanding that their brother or sister did not deliberately act to embarrass them or disrupt the family life can some sympathy be gained and some of the rancor be erased. One man described his stages of coming to terms with his sister's disorder thus:

> During the first few years of my sister's mental illness I was totally intolerant and unsympathetic. My reaction to mental illness was representative of the mainstream of our society today. I was embarrassed by my sister's unconventional behavior and style of dress. I was outraged by the disruption that mental illness caused within our family. I often felt angry about the entire situation.
>
> Eventually because of parental prodding I began to educate myself about mental illness. This is the second stage, the stage of learning. . . . I learned that the symptoms of this disease contributed to the malaise that characterized my sister's disposition. I learned the most important lesson of all: that my sister did not choose to lead a life of chaos lacking direction or continuity. I learned that this had all been imposed upon her life in a cruel and arbitrary fashion and that she deserved enormous credit for continuing her life and attempting to improve it.

Recently, the many problems confronting the siblings of people with a psychiatric disorder have begun to be confronted—and by the siblings themselves. In 1983 the National Sibling Network was organized and affiliated with the National Alliance for the Mentally Ill. Its mission is to recognize and build on the special needs of these siblings by encouraging them to develop self-help groups around the country. These groups provide information and peer counseling and are exploring sibling concerns and coping strategies. The Network also publishes a newsletter called *The Sibling Bond*. For further information contact: The National Sibling Network, 5112 15th Avenue, Minneapolis, MN 55417.

MOM AND DAD COUNT TOO

Having read the material in this chapter, the empathic reader will feel for the parents of children with mood disorders, or recognize themselves in the vignettes. Next to the patient, the parents carry the greatest burden. They trained at no special school, they have no experience to guide them, yet they are forced to deal with an illness that they *and* the professionals don't fully understand. If the emotions of the situation don't paralyze them, then the state laws or the cost of psychiatric treatment may. No matter what the parents do or don't do, say or don't say, it is likely that they will feel they're doing it wrong, saying it wrong and that society and the rest of their family are holding them accountable.

Many of these parents begin to pull away from people rather than deal with the odd looks and questions. Sometimes they are just not ready to admit that anything is wrong, and they don't want their friends to recognize and comment on the problem first. Some parents find it agonizing to hear about their friends' healthy children and shut themselves off from the envy and anger by avoiding social situations. If their friends begin to avoid the subject of their child, or seem strained in his or her presence, the friendships will quickly unravel and the parents become all the more isolated.

Marriages are placed under a heavy strain. The exhaustion of trying to deal with the crises leaves a couple little energy for evenings out, and they may wake up to realize that almost every conversation centers around the problems of their ill child. It is difficult for parents to demand and reserve time for themselves and to develop a plan for their own needs and pleasures in life; yet if they don't, they'll have even less energy. As author Maryellen Walsh writes: "Self-sacrificers tend to burn out early; they haven't taken care of themselves. To be effective over the long run, to keep our psychic and physical tanks full, we parents *must* take care of ourselves."

Where can parents go to let off some steam, learn about some better ways to cope and gain the support and sympathy of others who've been through the same ordeal? Two groups come to mind. A manic-depressive support group that offers education, information and emotional support to patients and their families, and any of the more than seven hundred nationwide family support groups affiliated with the National Alliance for the Mentally Ill (some of these family groups may have a majority of members whose child or sibling has schizophrenia, but they have programs that address the problems of families with manic-depression also).

Members of these support groups exchange information on doctors, hospitals, medications and coping strategies and offer each other a sympathetic ear. Furthermore, families can band together to seek changes in commitment laws, lobby for better housing or launch their own halfway houses. These two groups are committed to educating the public about psychiatric disorders, combatting stigma and campaigning for increased research funding. Each family voice swells the ranks and makes a difference.

To locate a family group or manic-depressive support group near you, check the appendices of this book. Because they are multiplying so rapidly, we advise you to call the headquarters of the National Depressive and Manic Depressive Association in Chicago, or the National Alliance for the Mentally Ill in Arlington, Virginia, for an up-to-date listing.

10

COPING WITH HOSPITALIZATION

Hospitalization—even for a happy occasion such as a birth—is attended by feelings of helplessness and fear. But mention a psychiatric hospitalization and you've got an even darker picture: the words conjure images of forgotten back wards with hapless and bizarre inmates subordinated by Miss Ratched-like nurses. Unfortunately, Hollywood and the press have sensationalized isolated stories and depicted fiction so realistically that the patient who needs hospitalization, and the family who must support and sometimes request the hospitalization, suffer immensely from the associations.

We're not trying to suggest that neglect and abuse never happen, but today there are so many advances being made in the treatment of psychiatric illness, so many laws protecting patients' rights and so many quality assurance agencies surveying hospitals on a regular basis that the picture has radically changed. Today's psychiatric hospitalization ranges from an average of two weeks to thirty days. The object is to diagnose, treat and return the individual to family and community as quickly as possible. The doors of a psychiatric ward may lock; they also always open.

The majority of people with even severe mood disorders, if treated appropriately and in time, do not need hospitalization. But for those who do, we want to outline the procedures and introduce the professionals that a patient and family members encounter throughout the period of hospitalization.

WHEN HOSPITALIZATION IS WARRANTED
AND WHAT IT ACCOMPLISHES

There are a variety of reasons for hospitalizing a person with acute symptoms of an affective disorder. A hospital is a protected environment where a team of professionals participate in the diagnosis of the illness, order and administer the medications and treatments and observe any untoward side effects. Since suicidal thoughts and impulses often accompany moderate to severe depression, the patient is far better off in an environment where twenty-four-hour monitoring is available.

The symptoms of depression—social withdrawal, poor concentration, lack of initiative, slowed-down movement, thought and speech, disrupted appetite and sleep cycles—make it difficult or nearly impossible for the person to cope. The depressed person's lack of concentration and hopeless feelings about the future frustrate the family's attempts to help, and the depressed person may feel irritable and may experience shame when he or she cannot respond to the family's efforts. This may touch off a corresponding set of feelings in the family members. A professional staff taking over the caretaking responsibilities at this time eases the tensions for everyone.

The person experiencing an acute manic state has a spectrum of symptoms that may necessitate hospitalization for other reasons. A primary consideration is whether the patient can control his or her impulses. While sometimes the mood of a person who is in a manic state is euphoric, overconfident and optimistic, it may deteriorate rapidly into irritability or anger. He or she may engage impulsively in activities that could be devastating to personal relationships and careers, such as buying sprees, sexual indiscretions, foolish business investments or even violent behavior. Some manic patients suffer delusions that cause them to lose touch with reality.

In this case, hospitalization provides a badly needed brake on the impulsive behavior and checks the tendency to engage in the reckless, possibly ruinous activities that could endanger a livelihood or a life. The medications temper the agitation and impulsiveness, and the staff has the legal authority and physical capability to restrain the person who might do harm in an uncontrolled state.

The hospital is probably the only place where the unusual, often frightening behavior of these patients is tolerated without judgment and recrimination. Hospitalization has another function, however: it takes the individual who has temporarily lost control out of his work and social environment, thereby limiting the damage that could be done. Not only might the ill person scar or sever relationships during an acute episode, he or she often loses credibility and respect. This would very much complicate the person's return to society.

People who have been hospitalized during a depressed or manic episode report feeling in retrospect that the hospitalization was helpful for the following reasons:

"I needed safety from myself and what I might do if depressed or manic."

"It made me realize that I do have a problem, and that I don't have to live with the ups and terrible downs if I am compliant with treatment."

"I was hospitalized following a serious suicide attempt. After recovery I had time to reevaluate life and conclude that there might be a better answer than suicide."

"Isolation from the outside world . . ."

"Being out of your home when you can't function and into a place where you have only yourself to care about."

"Being with people who were having like problems made me feel secure."

"It was a safe place to pull myself together, regulate the medication, have constant supervision and scheduled activities. I didn't feel alone during my recuperation."

GETTING A PERSON INTO A HOSPITAL

Some patients sense their urgent need for more intensive treatment and express the wish to go to the hospital. It is vital that family members heed the cues and begin to act on them. Sometimes the patient can't actually spell out the need for hospitalization, but if family members are firm and positive about it, he or she may not argue and may depend entirely on the relatives' better judgment. In this case, the hospital commitment is by voluntary request. The patient signs into the hospital for a specified number of days and can walk out at any time. Some states, however, require the patient to write a request for release to the director of the hospital. The amount of time that a patient has to wait to be released varies according to state laws. A voluntary commitment can be converted to an involuntary one if the treating psychiatrist, after observing the patient, feels that a release would not be in the better interest of the patient or the community. But he or she would have to initiate legal proceedings to convert the status of the patient.

But what if, as is so often the case, the patient does not recognize the need for treatment? The family and friends may be trying to reason with someone who not only does not grasp their point of view, but who also is rapidly beginning to view them as the enemy. The very mind that needs to be engaged and addressed is, as a result of the illness, misperceiving reality.

So now we enter the sticky but unfortunately necessary world of involuntary commitment with all its attendant legal terms, guilt and furor. The family member who must take the responsibility and press for the hospitalization is in a very uncomfortable position. But this relative is probably the only person who stands between the patient and the dangers that exist during an acute phase of the illness. In fact, many family members tell us that once a patient stabilizes he or she is often grateful to the relative who took a stand.

The purpose of commitment laws is to enable persons who are mentally ill to be put forcibly into hospitals for treatment before they harm themselves or others. Each state enacts its own laws governing commitment (see appendices).

These laws rest on two legal foundations: parens patriae—the right of the state to act as parent and protect the well-being of a citizen who cannot care for him or herself (this concept evolved from English common law, which held that the king was "father" of all his subjects); and the right of the state to protect its citizens from a person who is dangerous. This means that if a person is so disabled that he cannot recognize the need for treatment, cannot provide for his own basic needs or may otherwise be dangerous to himself or to other people, he may be committed to a psychiatric treatment center for a specified period of time.

But since the 1960s, a movement in this country has focused attention on the civil rights of the psychiatrically ill, with the aim to amend the commitment laws. Today it is more difficult to commit a patient to a hospital against his or her will. Dr. Thomas Szasz, a vocal antagonist of involuntary commitment, states that "we should value liberty more highly than mental health no matter how defined" and "no one should be deprived of his freedom for the sake of his mental health." Bruce Ennis of the American Civil Liberties Union feels that the goal "is nothing less than the abolition of involuntary hospitalization."

Their respect for the individual and his or her civil rights is indeed admirable, but our feelings lie closer to those of Dr. Paul Chodoff, who took more into consideration in his article "The Case for Involuntary Hospitalization for the Mentally Ill":

> It is obvious that it is good to be at liberty and that it is good to be free from the consequences of disabling and dehumanizing illness. Sometimes these two values are incompatible, and in the heat of the passions that are often aroused by opposing views of right and wrong, the partisans of each view may tend to minimize the importance of the other. Both sides can present their horror stories. . . .

He concludes rather cogently:

> We are now witnessing a pendulum swing in which the rights of the mentally ill to be treated and protected are being set aside in the rush to give them their freedom at whatever cost. But is freedom defined only by the absence of external constraint? Internal physiological or psychological processes can contribute to the throttling of the spirit that is as painful as any from the outside. Today the civil liberties lawyers are in the ascendancy and the psychiatrists on the defensive to a degree that is harmful to individual needs and the public welfare.

All voices sounding all views maintains a healthy balance, and no doubt the impassioned opponents of involuntary commitment have been responsible for the correction of many abuses, but in some states it is extremely difficult to get people who need treatment into a hospital. This has caused undue suffering for patients and family members and has thwarted psychiatrists who might otherwise treat the patients and protect them and others.

Recently, after almost two decades of restrictions, the pendulum is making a return swing: the national trend is toward making it easier to commit involuntarily patients with psychiatric illnesses. Addressing the issue, the American Psychiatric Association has devised a model commitment law that would allow commitments not only when patients are dangerous to self and others, but also when the patients are suffering and would be likely to deteriorate without treatment; in the presence of a major psychosis that could be treated, provided that treatment is available; and when patients are mentally incapable of deciding for themselves. At present, a few states are in the process of amending their laws and broadening the commitment criteria. (Alaska, Arizona, Hawaii, North Carolina and Washington have recently changed their laws and made it easier to commit patients to a hospital.)

These laws (and the debators who aim to restrict or broaden them) directly affect the person struggling with mental illness *and* his family, and it's vital that everyone keep informed. The *Mental and Physical Disability Law Reporter* will accomplish this. It's published bimonthly by the American Bar Association, 1800 M Street, N.W., Washington, DC 20036. At this writing, the yearly subscription cost is $115.

HOW TO HAVE SOMEONE COMMITTED

As a result of a 1975 U.S. Supreme Court ruling that a state cannot confine a patient who refuses voluntary hospitalization and can manage outside the hospital alone or with the help of family or friends, the states demand proof that a person is mentally disturbed and a danger to him or herself or others. Each state varies somewhat in its wording of its grounds for commitment and the standard of proof required. Some states allow a little flexibility and do not rely strictly on "dangerousness" criteria—the parens patriae rationale we spoke of earlier still plays a part. For instance, the state of South Carolina says that a person can be committed if "he is mentally ill, needs treatment and because of his condition (1) lacks sufficient insight or capacity to make responsible decisions with respect to his treatment, or (2) there is a likelihood of serious harm to himself or others." The chances of getting a commitment in a state like this are greater than in New Hampshire, whose law states starkly that a "person must exhibit dangerousness to self or others."

The standard of proof is another murky area; if someone *says* he'll kill someone, is that admissible evidence proving dangerousness or does he have to injure that someone first? The least stringent level of proof is "clear and convincing evidence," while the "beyond a reasonable doubt" level of proof demanded by California, Kansas, Kentucky, Massachusetts, New Hampshire, Oklahoma and Oregon makes it more difficult to get a commitment. This of course does not take into consideration a judge's interpretation of the law, which is also governed by personal bias and the feelings of the community at a particular time.

It all sounds dry and legal on paper, but living with the law is another matter. Consider the case of one mother in California whose son had a bipolar disorder. He stopped taking his lithium and she began to see signs of mania. When she suggested that he see a doctor and continue with his lithium, he told her she was crazy and stormed out. Because of the stringency of California law, she was powerless to do anything and had to stand by and let the illness run its course. Three days later, after he'd ransacked his apartment and threatened his girlfriend, the police found him wandering the streets and were able to convince him to go to the hospital.

The procedure for initiating a commitment is also dictated by state law, and each state varies somewhat. We'll explain how a person could be committed in the state of New York, and then direct readers how to check the procedure in their area.

Should a family member or responsible adult see that a person is exhibiting conduct that is dangerous to self or others, there are two ways they could try to get the person to the hospital: the police can be called, or the family can go to the State Supreme Court and file a petition for commitment. The patient must have either made a suicide attempt or have acted in a menacing fashion, such as punching people or harboring a weapon such as a knife, or the patient must be dazed or confused and seem unable to take care of him or herself. If the responsible adult calls the police and they don't come to check out the situation (they most often do), the responsible adult must go to the Supreme Court and file a petition, an affidavit with the court, setting forth the reasons why this person needs to be hospitalized and why the person is a danger to self or others.

If the judge is convinced by the argument, he issues a warrant. The police can then find the patient and bring him or her to the emergency room of a hospital for an evaluation. In order for the person to be hospitalized, the evaluating psychiatrist must decide that the person is a danger to self or others. Within seventy-two hours, a second doctor must confirm that opinion or the person is released. If the second doctor does confirm that the person needs hospitalization, the person is held under an emergency commitment status, not to exceed fifteen days. At the end of that period, the person must be released unless the director of the hospital or the family petitions the court for longer-term commitment. In practical terms, this simply means signing commitment papers provided by the hospital with a statement documenting the reasons the family member is requesting commitment. To complete the commitment procedure two psychiatrists are required to evaluate the patient and sign the certification document stating that in their opinion the patient's mental state warrants involuntary commitment. The patient can then be kept in the hospital for a period not to exceed sixty days (if there was an emergency fifteen-day commitment initiated beforehand, the long-term commitment lasts for no longer than forty-five days).

At any time, the patient can go to court and contest the commitment. A Mental Health Information lawyer is available to represent the patient at a hearing held before a judge, usually within chambers in the hospital. The patient, family members and the examining psychiatrist testify at the hearing, where normal judicial rules of evidence and due process apply.

Perhaps it would be easier to go over this in context. The following case happened in and proceeded according to the laws of New York State:

> Jonathan was a twenty-five-year-old man suffering from a bipolar disorder. He lived at home with his mother and two

younger sisters, and was being treated by a psychiatrist. Frequently, however, Jonathan would not comply with treatment and he would refuse to take his medications. This time, two and a half weeks after he stopped the drugs, he stopped sleeping at night. He began pacing around his room and began to see himself as a religious figure destined to save the world.

His mother urged him to see his psychiatrist and go back on his medications, but he responded with irritable anger and outright threats. One afternoon, after a particularly upsetting confrontation, Jonathan reached out and scratched his mother's face.

She then called the psychiatrist he'd been seeing. The doctor questioned her at length to determine the symptoms and agreed to make a house call and talk to Jonathan. At the house, he was able to see that Jonathan was indeed behaving bizarrely and he decided that, at this point, hospitalization was indicated.

The psychiatrist wrote a letter to the local police stating that Jonathan had a well-documented mental illness with recurrent relapses. He went on to describe Jonathan's delusional ideas, the aggressive incident with the mother, and indicated that Jonathan might be a threat to himself or others. The doctor closed the letter with the request that Jonathan be taken to a psychiatric emergency room by the police and that he be evaluated there.

Jonathan's mother took the letter to the police station, and two policemen came to the house and asked to speak to Jonathan. After viewing his unusual and idiosyncratic behavior, the policemen decided to bring him to the emergency room of the city's public hospital.

Once there, Jonathan was evaluated by a staff psychiatrist who noted that he was experiencing auditory hallucinations. Jonathan began to discuss his conversation with Jesus the night before. Jesus told him about the special role that only Jonathan could fulfill. The doctor recommended that he enter the hospital on a voluntary basis, but Jonathan refused and kept stating that his mother just wanted to put him away.

The emergency room psychiatrist decided to pursue an involuntary commitment on an emergency basis. This kind of commitment lasts for fifteen days. Unfortunately, at the end of that period, Jonathan was still delusional, and the staff decided to convert Jonathan's status to a commitment that lasts for sixty days. It requires a three-part petition: two certificates signed by two examining psychiatrists, and a form on which a family member or person living with the patient signs his name and outlines his reasons for requesting the commitment. In this case, Jonathan's mother signed the petition.

Jonathan became extremely upset when he heard this, and demanded to see the patient-advocate lawyer (all patients are given the phone number of this professional who is not hired by the hospital and whose business is to assist and protect the patient).

The lawyer, after talking to Jonathan, agreed to take the case to court. The hospital had a room that was a judge's chambers and Jonathan, his lawyer, the treating psychiatrists and his family participated in the hearing. Because his family was afraid to have him back in the condition he was still in, the judge asked where he would go if he were released. Jonathan really had nowhere else to go, and finally agreed to stay in the hospital for the remaining period of the long-term commitment.

Naturally every case is different. Jonathan's family was lucky in that he had been seeing a psychiatrist who was willing to make a house call and there was a documented history to support the claim that he needed help. If a family member is faced with a first episode and hasn't the name of a psychiatrist, he or she can call the family doctor and ask for help or for a referral to a psychiatrist who might make a home visit. Also, by calling the admissions office of the nearest psychiatric hospital (or emergency room) a person can obtain some information as to the procedures for commitment in that state. The police can fill you in, too. One more suggestion: check the telephone book to see if your state has a Mental Health Information Service, and if so, give the office a call. The people there will no doubt be in a position to give valuable advice.

WHICH HOSPITAL IS BEST?

Years ago, the person in need of psychiatric treatment in a hospital went one of two places: a state facility, or a private—and very expensive—sanitorium. But today there are more options. Community hospitals (public and private) are carving out psychiatric inpatient services for short-term care, and they generally deliver a satisfactory level of service. University-affiliated teaching centers have excellent reputations that are largely dependent on their clinician/researcher teaching staff; on the other hand, it is the residents and interns—the least experienced members of the department—who tend to the patients (see pages 203–5 for a discussion of this type of hospital). Private psychiatric hospitals range in quality from those that offer excellent treatment to those whose unsoothing under-the-breath mantra is "money first, patient next." If the patient is a veteran, an admission to a Veterans Administration hospital is a possibility, but criteria for admission are becoming more stringent. In some cases patients are accepted for treatment only if the condition is considered service-related. Another possibility is that the patient may live in a catchment area that is serviced by a Community Mental Health Center with an inpatient service. Finally, there are the state hospitals. Most people cringe at the mention and see the state hospital as a last and desperate resort, but there are some state hospitals that offer excellent care, as well as those that too closely resemble the Bedlam of old.

But don't let private rooms and fancy facilities be the assurance of quality. The diagnostic abilities and the treatment philosophy of the psychiatrist running the unit are far more important. Admittedly, these are difficult matters to assess, but the doctor and/or staff members should be willing to explain the evaluation procedure and the goals and objectives of the hospitalization.

In Chapter 2 we outlined the diagnostic criteria for mood disorders and discussed the dilemmas that face the psychiatrist in establishing a diagnosis—particularly in the acute state (see pages 34–37 on misdiagnosis). Although DSM–IIIR is not infallible, if it is not being used in the diagnostic process, chances are the patient is not receiving up-to-date medical care. The following checklist of questions should aid a family in assessing the quality of care their relative is receiving:

- Has the family been invited to the hospital to expand on or explain the history of the patient's disorder?
- Has the family history been explored? (If not, this may be an indication that rigorous diagnostic procedures are not being observed.)

- Is there an adequate number of nurses and aides to oversee the depressed patient who may be suicidal? What is the procedure for this? (See pages 205–6 on constant observation.)
- How will the manic patient be dealt with? What is the policy and procedure for seclusion and restraint? (See discussion later in this chapter.)
- How frequently is the patient seen by a staff psychiatrist?
- What are the arrangements for medical consultation? Is there an internist assigned to the service?
- Is there an attempt to educate and inform the patient and family members as to the nature of the disorder and the benefits and risks of acute and long-term treatment?

One very important assurance of hospital quality is accreditation by the Joint Commission on Accreditation of Hospitals. JCAH, as it's called, is an outgrowth of the Hospital Standardization Program established by the American College of Surgeons in 1918. A hospital invites a survey team from the Commission to visit and evaluate the hospital's performance and safety features. The team also examines the therapeutic environment, the number and quality and credentials of the staff, the record keeping and the administration. Hospitals that pass the inspection receive a three-year accreditation.

Any hospital that does not have a JCAH certificate should be given a wide berth. Medicare and Medicaid actually specify that the hospitals participating in their programs must be certified by either JCAH or the Health Care Financing Administration, and most insurance companies do not reimburse bills from a hospital that does not have a JCAH accreditation. Look in the lobby or entranceway for the certificate, or ask someone in the hospital's administration office to tell you where it is. Also, you could call the Joint Commission on Accreditation of Hospitals in Chicago at (800) 621-8007 (Illinois residents call (800) 572-8089); or write their Department of Corporate Relations, 875 North Michigan Avenue, Chicago, IL 60611.

An excellent way to check out the quality of care in the hospitals in an area is to call the local chapter of a manic-depressive support group or family organization (see appendices). They can give you the names and numbers of family members who've had experience with the area's mental health hospitals and who are in a position to warn and advise. Also, you will no doubt gain support and a sympathetic ear.

ADMISSIONS PROCEDURES

We've discussed voluntary and involuntary hospitalizations, and we've outlined the different choices on the hospital horizon, but the specific, concrete steps that lead from an episode of illness to a person's actually walking into a psychiatric unit for treatment may seem a bit blurry and confusing. The two situations that follow should help clarify the hospital admissions procedures.

Adam McDonough is a thirty-five-year-old advertising executive who became increasingly withdrawn and irritable. He found himself unmotivated at work and began to spend hours sitting at his desk accomplishing little. His wife noticed that he wasn't sleeping at night, and that at times he became very teary. She called their family physician, who, after examining Adam, referred him to a psychiatrist. Adam was very resistant about going to see a "lunatic's doctor," but his wife was able to press the point and he did keep the appointment.

Adam described his symptoms to the psychiatrist and began to discuss his feelings of worthlessness. He admitted haltingly that he'd had thoughts of taking his own life so that his wife could be free of him. He hadn't the energy to fight through his feelings.

The doctor realized that Adam was experiencing a major depression and felt that as there was a possibility of suicide, he should be treated on an inpatient service. The psychiatrist called the director of a private teaching ward and asked if there was a bed available. He presented the case and the director agreed to admit Adam. He asked that Adam's wife call the administrator of the hospital so that the insurance policy could be checked.

After the phone call, Mrs. McDonough was asked to bring Adam to the admissions office of the hospital. There, he was met by the resident assigned to him. The resident spoke to Adam and asked him to fill out several forms: one was a voluntary commitment form, and others authorized general treatment at the hospital. He was then escorted to his room.

Diane Polisi is a twenty-two-year-old receptionist at a design firm. She is high-spirited and fun-loving, so when she began coming into work in the morning enthusiastically describing her "all-nighters" at the discos, her coworkers commented on the energies of youth and didn't notice that anything was wrong. By the end of the week, though, she began to talk faster and faster and she began embarking on several self-appointed projects such as straightening all the files in the storeroom and rearranging all the furniture in the conference room. She then began to call client after client, as she felt she should "drum up some business." The manager of the firm walked in and overheard her exhorting a client into a fanciful promotion and realized something was very wrong. She spoke calmly to the now-agitated Diane and told her she was calling her sister who worked nearby. Her sister drove her to the emergency room of the public hospital.

At the hospital, the resident on duty interviewed Diane and her sister and made note of some of the manic symptoms. He felt that Diane should be hospitalized for further evaluation and treatment. Since Diane's firm had a Blue Cross/Blue Shield policy, and as the beds for a public hospital were really intended for people not covered by private insurance, the resident asked the social worker in the emergency room to call the local private hospitals and arrange for a bed for Diane. In the meantime, he gave Diane a physical exam and an injection of haloperidol to diminish the level of agitation she was experiencing and to reduce her racing thoughts. Six hours later she was transferred by ambulance to the private hospital.

Adam's wife and Diane's sister had little experience with mental illness and were totally unfamiliar with the subjects of public versus private hospitals, but these experiences taught them that there are professionals who deal with this all the time and who will help people steer through the system and obtain appropriate medical attention.

WHAT TO BRING TO THE ADMISSIONS OFFICE

A telephone call to the admissions office of the hospital will fill you in on what's required for the admitting procedure. In all probability you need to bring and to know the following:

- The patient's insurance card (or cards if he or she has several policies); a Medicare and/or Medicaid card if the patient has one
- The Social Security card or number of the person who will bear the responsibility for the bill
- The name, address and telephone number of the patient's employer and of his or her spouse, if any
- The name, address and telephone number of the person to be notified in case of an emergency
- Information about the patient's military service (only if he or she is seeking admission to a Veteran's Administration hospital)
- A checkbook (some hospitals require a deposit) or credit card

INSURANCE AND COSTS

There's an unpleasant reality here: a hospital is a business—the administration seeks reimbursement for the services provided. Therefore, the extent of the patient's insurance coverage is very important. How many days in a psychiatric hospital are covered? Are psychiatric hospitals covered at all or is the policy intended for a psychiatric unit in a general hospital? Will the insurance company reimburse if the hospital has no JCAH accreditation? Is there a ceiling to the dollar amount reimbursed? How much of the doctor's fee is covered? What is the deductible? Granted, the small print on policies is difficult to understand (see Chapter 11 for a more complete picture of insurance policies), so you should ask the insurance agent or the person responsible for employee benefits to translate and clarify the coverage. If you have several policies, you'll need to know when and if one picks up for the other. If your coverage is inadequate, the business office may be able to initiate a Medicaid application, help arrange a bank loan or negotiate another payment mechanism. Families should be aware that there is a form of hospital "catastrophic medicaid" that covers patients who are not currently Medicaid recipients and whose expensive inpatient hospital care exceeds 25 percent of their income. This coverage is valid for only six months from the date of application and only inpatient care is covered. The more information you have going in, the more secure you will feel when the issues of money and insurance are raised.

What would three weeks of psychiatric hospitalization cost? The charges of a city, county or state public hospital vary according to the patient's income, but a patient admitted to a private, nonprofit (university-affiliated) hospital in the New York City area in 1986 would incur bills for this period of about $10,752. Additionally, the patient might be billed for selected services that are separate from the hospital bed rate. Charges for specific treatments would approximate these:

Physical examination	$75.00
Laboratory tests	143.75
Electrocardiogram (EKG)	80.00
CAT scan	316.00
ECT (10 treatments)	3,500.00
Therapy fees (individual medical psychotherapy)	675.00
Consultation fees	120.00

Thus, fees approximating $15,661.75 should provide powerful motivation for anyone to look into his insurance situation. If a person does not have coverage and lacks financial resources, a public hospital will take care of the treatment and initiate a Medicaid application.

AFTER ADMISSION

After the patient signs authorization-for-treatment papers, he or she is escorted to the unit. The family or an accompanying friend may go along and help the patient settle in. In most situations, the nursing staff handles the orientation and intake procedure. During this discussion the patient is informed about the daily schedule, the hospital rules, the therapy programs, meal schedules and visiting hours (to the extent his or her clinical status permits them). Most hospitals provide a brochure that explains these matters. Items that are sharp, heavy and potentially dangerous to the patient or anyone else on the unit are usually returned to the family or held for the patient.

Next the nurse takes a medical and psychiatric history and begins to explore the relationships the patient has with his or her family members. The care plan that the nurse writes outlines how much watching the patient needs and reports medical problems that need attention. The nurse's intake not only helps orient the patient to his or her new surroundings, it also gives the people who are working most closely with the patient a chance to get to know him or her. In many ways it is not only an assessment, but a valuable personal introduction.

Once the intake is complete, the psychiatrist responsible for the patient begins a medical and psychiatric work-up. In some hospitals the private psychiatrist who admitted the patient to the unit will be his private attending physician, and will thus be very familiar with the patient's history; but in the case of a unit that assigns its own staff to each new patient, the work-up requires the assembling again of many facts. If the patient is unable to assist the doctor with this admittedly extensive amount of information, the accompanying family member should be prepared to give details about the following:

- What was the patient like before the problem arose?
- What was the development of the problem? What changes did anyone notice in the patient's behavior?
- What kind of medications or treatments did the patient have prior to this hospitalization? What side effects did he or she experience? Were there any prior hospitalizations? When?
- Are there any existing medical problems? Does the patient have any allergies?
- Is there a history of learning disabilities, social adjustment problems, drug or alcohol abuse?
- Is there a history of mental illness in the family? Is there a history of alcoholism in the family? (These two questions could possibly help pinpoint the diagnosis of an affective disorder— as painful as it is, try to give the doctor very detailed information about any other family members with psychiatric or alcohol problems.) If anyone in the family has been treated for a similar condition, what medications did they respond to? (Response to medication is often genetic, so this information is extremely important.)

The psychiatrist explores the "mental status" of the patient by asking questions and then assessing his or her mood, emotional state and thought processes. The doctor determines whether the patient knows the day, the month, the year, whether he knows who he is and to whom he is talking and whether he knows the name of the place he's in. The patient's memory, concentration and ability to think abstractly are also tested.

The patient's history of illness, the current symptoms, the previous episodes of illness and the mental status exam lead the psychiatrist to a list of possible diagnoses. Further information and history, possible psychological testing and the results of the physical examination and laboratory tests lead to a more conclusive diagnosis.

THE PHYSICAL EXAMINATION

All patients who enter a hospital are given a physical exam and certain routine screening tests such as blood tests, urinalysis and a chest X-ray. The findings of these tests may point to a physical origin of the psychiatric problem, or may unearth a coexisting medical problem, but will definitely guide the physician in the choice of psychotropic medications. For instance, a patient with kidney disfunction may be unable to take lithium and the psychiatrist may instead prescribe carbamazepine (Tegretol); a patient with a history of grand mal seizures is prescribed a neuroleptic that would have less of a potential for lowering the seizure threshold (all neuroleptics lower it to a certain degree). Depending on the clinical picture, the psychiatrist may call for a medical consultation with a neurologist, an endocrinologist or a cardiologist.

Once the diagnosis is established, the treatment begins. Under the psychiatrist's direction, a team of other professionals—psychologists, social workers, nursing staff and occupational and activities therapists—continuously review, discuss and treat the patient.

THE HOSPITAL TEAM

Who are the different professionals and other staff members who treat the patients in a psychiatric hospital? What kind of training do they have? How can they help? The following brief descriptions should answer these questions.

The *psychiatrist* is a medical doctor who specializes in the diagnosis and comprehensive treatment of mental and emotional illnesses. After completing four years of medical school, he or she completes a four-year residency training program in psychiatry (at least six months of the first year is spent in general medicine). The residency is situated in a hospital approved by the American Board of Psychiatry and Neurology and the resident is supervised by experienced psychiatrists while learning differential diagnosis and specific approaches to the treatment of major psychiatric disorders. The education encompasses medical treatment approaches as well as psychotherapeutic approaches—individual, family and group. A psychiatrist, as a physician, is the only mental health professional who can prescribe medications and perform electroconvulsive therapy.

The *clinical psychologist* is also called "Doctor," but here the title refers to a Ph.D. degree in clinical psychology. The psychologist not only completes three years of course work, but also an internship in a psychiatric hospital or mental health clinic. In addition, most programs require a dissertation on a research topic. While a psychologist cannot prescribe medications, he or she is trained to do psychological testing, psychotherapy and research.

The *psychiatric nurse* is a registered nurse who has been specifically trained to work with people who have psychiatric disorders. He or she is the professional who spends the most time with the patient. Not only does the nurse dispense the medications ordered by the psychiatrist, but he or she closely monitors side effects. The nurse's daily report gives the rest of the treatment team valuable information about the patient's medical and mental status. Some nurses have Master's degrees, and some are nurse practitioners trained to do psychotherapy.

The *psychiatric social worker* can be invaluable to the family as well as the patient. After four years of college, the psychiatric social worker completes a two-year course with an internship in a psychiatric setting and is awarded the degree Master of Social Work (M.S.W.). Not only can this professional conduct psychotherapy sessions, but he or she assesses and coordinates the needs of the patient and the family during and after hospitalization. The social worker may arrange a place in a group home or halfway house if the patient requires it; or the social worker may initiate disability, SSI, Medicaid/Medicare applications where they are appropriate. If the initials A.C.S.W. appear after a social worker's name, it means that he or she has met the requirements of and is certified by the Academy of Certified Social Workers.

The *occupational therapist* (O.T.) has specialized training in evaluating an individual's employment and social skills and his or her ability to conduct the commonplace activities of daily living. The O.T. organizes structured activities and group tasks that aid concentration, socialization and living skills. Some of these group and individual activities focus on job interviews, writing skills, cooking skills and the running of a household. An occupational therapist completes either a four-year undergraduate program leading to a Bachelor of Science with a major in occupational therapy, or a Master's degree program in occupational therapy with six months of supervised clinical experience. An O.T. with either of these degrees may become registered by passing an examination administered by the American Occupational Therapy Association.

Many psychiatric units also have *activities therapists* who may specialize in art therapy, dance or music therapy or recreational therapy. They are graduates of accredited bachelor's or master's programs that emphasize the therapeutic application of the art or physical education. The activities programs are devised to encourage self-awareness and the exploration of feelings as well as to provide the patient with an opportunity to engage in a structured, shared leisure activity that promotes socialization and the improvement of interpersonal skills. The activities therapist understands the treatment goals for each patient and attempts to reinforce them through the projects undertaken.

In addition to the professionals just mentioned, the patient comes into close contact with other hospital personnel: the physician's assistant who may do physical exams, mental health aides and nursing aides. In a good hospital, these people not only do their jobs but also offer patients encouragement and reassurance.

THE STAFF-IN-TRAINING ON A TEACHING WARD

In a nonacademic hospital setting the staff psychiatrist usually directs the evaluation and treatment of the patient, but on university-affiliated training units, there are fellows, chief residents, residents and medical students who may have a more direct day-to-day involvement with the patient and the family. There are advantages and disadvantages to this system. John McPhee, in an article for *The New Yorker,* cites the advantages:

> The hospital's quality as a congregation of working doctors has been elevated by the presence of the residency in part because, as a teaching hospital, it is a place where more questions are going to be asked than would be asked if the residency were not there. In teaching rounds, scheduled conferences, and other forms of interaction, the residents engender a running dialogue that tends to draw specialists together.

McPhee goes on to quote a residents' teacher, Dr. Alan Hume: "If someone asks me a question and I don't know the answer, I come back tomorrow with an answer. This makes me a better doctor, and the patient gets better care. The resident is a built-in audit. . . ."

The disadvantage is that the least experienced staff member has the most contact with the patient.

A psychiatric fellow is someone who has completed a psychiatric residency and has elected to specialize in an area of clinical activity or research under the tutelage of a senior psychiatrist. He or she often provides valuable expertise in diagnosis and treatment.

The chief resident on a unit is in the final year of residency and is chosen from among his or her peers to assist in the administration of the unit and in the teaching of less senior residents.

A resident on an inpatient service may be in his or her second, third or fourth year of training. On a university-affiliated training ward, the resident is the primary therapist and is chiefly responsible for the management and care of the patient. The director of the unit, the staff psychiatrists and the chief resident supervise the resident's work.

A medical student does a clerkship on a psychiatric unit during the third year of medical school. He or she usually becomes very involved with one or two patients. Although the least experienced member of the medical team, the student can be a valuable ally who has the time to gather a detailed and possibly revealing history of the patient and the illness. This can help the staff to develop a better therapy formulation and treatment plan. A good medical student can listen well and offer support and the human touch.

THE DAILY AND WEEKLY SCHEDULE

Treatment for depression or mania should begin with an integrated plan to ameliorate the symptoms of the illness, help the patient re-establish a sense of self-esteem, educate the patient and the family as to the nature of the illness and develop a practical outpatient treatment that will serve to prevent rehospitalization. The many meetings, medical rounds and social and therapeutic interactions during the hospital day are aimed at accomplishing this agenda.

Typically each morning the staff assembles for "rounds." This is the medical vernacular for the nurses' report on the medical and behavioral status of the patients on the unit. If there are any questions about changes in the treatment plans, or concerns about a response to medication or a family visit, they are brought up at this time. The residents may report on their patients as well.

Many inpatient services divide the patient responsibilities into two teams. Detailed discussions of each patient are conducted in team meetings several times a week. Should a problem arise concerning a diagnosis or psychiatric medication, a psychiatrist with an expertise in these areas is called in for a consultation. In addition, supplemental medical rounds are conducted for patients experiencing neurological or medical problems.

Individual, group and family meetings are scheduled throughout the week, and the occupational and activities therapists offer recreational, skills and various art groups. Naturally, there are hours set aside for grooming periods, meals and visiting hours. (An example of a weekly schedule appears on the next page.)

WHEN CONSTANT OBSERVATION IS NEEDED

Some patients are watched more closely by or have more contact with the nursing staff. This is because the medical staff has determined that the patient is suicidal or aggressive toward other patients, or is so confused and disorganized that the patient cannot take care of his

	Monday	Tuesday	Wednesday	Thursday	Friday
8:00	Breakfast	Breakfast	Breakfast	Breakfast	Breakfast
9:00	Community meeting	—	—	—	Community meeting
10:00	Patients meet with their primary therapists	Group therapy	Patients meet with their primary therapists	Group therapy	Patients meet with their primary therapists
12:00	Community lunch	Community lunch	Community lunch	Community lunch	Community lunch
1:00	Expressive writing workshop	Art therapy	Social skills group	Recreational therapy	Social skills group
2:00 to 5:00	Visiting hours	Visiting hours	Visiting hours	Visiting hours	Visiting hours
4:00 to 5:00	Family meetings	—	Family meetings	—	Family meetings
6:00	Dinner	Dinner	Dinner	Dinner	Dinner
6:00 to 8:00	Visiting hours	Visiting hours	Multiple family group visiting hours	Visting hours	Visiting hours

or her own needs without close contact. Part of the treatment plan, then, is a period of time under close or even constant observation. Constant observation usually means that a nurse or assistant is assigned to stay within an arm's length of the patient at all times and make frequent eye or verbal contact with that patient.

THE SECLUSION ROOM AND PHYSICAL RESTRAINT

The fast ideas become too fast and there are far too many . . . overwhelming confusion replaces clarity . . . you stop keeping up with it—memory goes. Infectious humor ceases to amuse—

your friends become frightened . . . everything is now against the grain . . . you are irritable, angry, frightened, uncontrollable and trapped in the blackest caves of the mind—caves you never knew were there. It will never end. Madness carves its own reality.

This patient's description of a manic episode should help people understand that a person experiencing psychosis can be overwhelmed by noises, environmental stimuli and people. A normal conversation may sound like artillery fire, and anything can be interpreted as a direct threat. The patient may feel the need to hide or retaliate as protection. The patient may hear voices telling him to kill himself, and he may become so frightened that only a quiet and protected room will help remove the painful stimuli, help the patient feel safe and protect him from hurting himself or others. That is why most psychiatric units have a room where a patient can be isolated until he or she is calm and able to be with people. It's called a seclusion room.

Physically it is a room stripped of any sharp or heavy objects that could be used by the patient to hurt himself or the staff who come to check on him. The walls may be covered with padding, and there is a mattress on the floor for the patient to rest and sleep on (a bedframe has too many sharp angles). The door locks, but a window in it allows staff members to observe the patient. The seclusion room often does more to lock the world out than to lock the patient in, and its use is governed by many regulations.

The seclusion room can be used only to prevent a patient from hurting himself or others, and only when other therapeutic treatments are ineffective. A doctor must write the orders for seclusion, the patient's behavior must be observed and documented frequently, vital signs (blood pressure, pulse, respiration rate and temperature) must be taken periodically, and if the patient is not sleeping, he or she must be released, walked around and taken to the bathroom every two hours.

The nursing staff is instructed to greet the patient, tell him or her why the seclusion time is necessary and listen to the patient's response. The intention is to explain what is happening and allay the patient's anxiety.

If a patient is very manic and out of control, it is not easy for the staff to monitor his or her physical state or administer medications. If the patient was given an antipsychotic medication, the blood pressure and pulse must be taken in order to ensure that the blood pressure does not fall too low. In this case, aides and security guards are summoned to restrain the patient. One member of the staff talks to the patient and explains what they intend to do, and assures the patient that he or she will not be harmed, nor will the patient be allowed to harm anyone else.

In the event that a patient refuses medication, the clinical director of the unit and the patient advocate must be informed, and a decision must be made concerning involuntary medication of the patient. Most states allow involuntary medication if the situation is judged an emergency.

WHEN YOU VISIT

Few people like to visit patients in hospitals—people are in pain, the surroundings are rarely attractive, and it doesn't take long before you think: that could be me. So we realize that a visit with someone on a psychiatric unit is not just unpleasant—it's downright frightening. Even mental health professionals report an insecure feeling the first time they visit a locked unit and hear the door close behind them. Don't worry; it passes. But we do think a discussion about what you'll see and how to act and interact with family members and the other patients on the unit will do much to alleviate the anxiety.

We've all passed people on the street who seem strange or out of touch with reality, but a psychiatric unit certainly has a concentrated population of such people and you won't be able to avoid coming face to face with someone as you make your way through the unit. The big questions that come to mind are: How do I act? Should I smile and say hello? What do I do if someone approaches me?

Most of the apprehension people feel when confronted by a person acting strangely comes from the fear that the individual will harm them. In fact, you are probably safer on a psychiatric floor than on a city street. For the most part, people who are patients are fearful themselves—of external stimuli, of sounds, of you. So treat people naturally and gently and respond to them directly. If a patient in a confused state asks, "Are you my grandmother?" you could help establish reality by answering the truth, "No, I'm here to visit my sister." If someone does bother you, simply tell the nurse on duty and politely disengage yourself from the situation.

A lot of emotions are dredged up when you visit your relative in a hospital, but if you understand how the illness is affecting the patient's ability to communicate, the visit can be more constructive and helpful—it will also be less painful for all concerned.

It is often the case that a person in a depression responds to questions or conversation remarkably slowly. It may take quite a while for the patient to respond to the question, "How are you feeling today?" Most relatives view the long pauses as a sign that the patient does not wish to be with or communicate with them. Anyone who must wait a prolonged period for a simple response feels embarrassed, frustrated, devalued and angry. But this thought latency is a classic sign of depression, a slowing down of biological processes. It might be helpful to acknowledge to the patient that you understand that it is taking him or her time to respond. This may lessen the patient's burden when trying to communicate with you.

Another common feature of severe depression is a loss of appetite; your relative may stop eating. Rest assured that your relative is being watched closely for weight loss (he or she will be weighed several times a week), and if it becomes too pronounced, a naso-gastric tube will be inserted to maintain the vital functions until the medications have a chance to restore normal appetite.

One more thought: a gentle sense of humor is a blessing at a time like this, but don't attempt to turn into a comedian in front of the patient. You probably won't be able to raise your relative's spirits with jokes and chipper phrases, and he or she may read other things into your attempt at humor or feel you are making him or her the butt of the joke. Just be constant, positive, warm (but not intense) and firm in the knowledge that the depression will pass in time.

If your relative is in a manic phase and was recently hospitalized, it might be advisable to call the unit staff and find out when you should visit. There may be a dramatic improvement in several days, but people respond variably to medications and the primary symptoms of mania may linger for several weeks. If this is the case, natural conversation is difficult because the patient is flooded with ideas and may want to involve you in a lot of unrealistic plans. The patient may also insist that he or she doesn't belong in the hospital. You may feel overwhelmed or angry.

Most family members react to the patient's energy level and tell him or her to calm down. Rarely does this have any effect. One possible intervention, though, is to express your feelings to the patient. Tell him you are overwhelmed by the rapid speech, you are confused, and you are having trouble following what he is saying. If you cannot communicate with the patient, tell him or her that you'll return soon and that you hope you can talk more then. Reassure him that you will visit regularly.

The patient may be very angry with you for helping to hospitalize him, and this is very hard to deal with. You might say something like, "I brought you here because you were unable to control your impulses and I thought it was best for you and me. I also understand that you feel on top of the world, but I feel you need treatment now." Don't expect to win back friendship immediately—no matter what you say. Give it some time and keep in mind that you took a stand because you realized that your relative was in a very precarious position. The picture will change as soon as the manic phase is under control.

WHO CAN YOU CALL TO CHECK ON YOUR RELATIVE?

Naturally you'll want to check in and ask the staff how your relative is feeling; you'll also want to "test the waters" and determine if a visit is advisable that day. The nursing staff has close contact with your relative and is in the best position to answer your questions. Find out which nurse on which shift is assigned to the care of your relative and ask him or her when would be the best time to call. Elect one family member to make the call so as not to overburden the nurse.

THE COLD SHOULDER TREATMENT?

If you feel you are getting the cold shoulder from any of the staff members, or are not satisfied with the treatment you see administered to the patient, speak up. Perhaps there's been a misunderstanding or a lack of communication. If you receive no satisfaction, make an appointment to speak to the director of clinical services. He or she should be able to resolve the situation, but if not, consult the admissions brochure you were given at the beginning of the hospital stay and look for the name of the patient representative. This person is a direct link to the hospital's administration and should be able to help find a solution to the problem.

COMING HOME: DISCHARGE AND AFTERCARE

Once the acute symptoms of the affective episode resolve, the staff meets to determine a discharge plan and date. The social worker evaluates the situation in the community to which the patient will return. Most often the patient has a family or apartment; in the event that the patient has neither, the social worker will attempt to find a group home or halfway house and make the necessary application after discussing it with the patient.

Most people leave the hospital on a medication that requires regular visits with a physician. If the patient did not have a private psychiatrist before entering the hospital, or cannot afford a referral to a private psychiatrist, he or she will be referred to a community mental health center or a local clinic. Clinics normally charge a sliding-scale fee based on the patient's ability to pay. The social worker at the hospital makes the first appointment, and the patient is asked to sign a release form so that the record of hospitalization can be transferred to the clinic.

This transition from the closely supervised hospital setting to a normally overcrowded clinic can be an uncomfortable one for the patient. Unfortunately, the quality and organization of aftercare services is not always what it should be. Ideally the patient should be evaluated and treated by the same doctor, one who has an expertise in the treatment of affective disorders. The treating team, whether it includes psychiatrists, psychologists, social workers or other mental health professionals, offers a coordinated treatment plan.

This is all too rare. A more common scenario is that the patient sees a doctor who comes in from time to time to renew the medications prescription (but who may not be following the patient closely). Meanwhile, the patient is seen more frequently by a mental health professional who may have no training in the neurosciences and little understanding of the course of the disorder and its medical treatments.

In the event that a patient is unhappy with the referral he or she received, a call to the referring doctor who treated the patient in the hospital may encourage the doctor to call that clinic and intervene, or arrange for a referral to another kind of clinic.

It should be obvious from all of the above that there is little if any follow-up of the patient's care once he or she leaves the hospital, prescription and appointment in hand. The reality is that no one at the hospital will know what happens to the patient unless he or she stops taking the medication and eventually returns to the hospital. It is vital, then, that the patient have the support of family members who can ensure that medications are taken and appointments are kept. They can also help the patient critically assess the quality of the aftercare. When no family is around to be involved, a patient's participation in a support group may make all the difference.

A man who had been hospitalized with a bipolar disorder wrote and urged us to stress several points that would help people with the illness avoid hospitalization. He outlined three, and we quote his words:

1. Patients must come to accept the fact that no one in the world can do them any good if they fail to help themselves.
2. The family and the patient must work together with the doctor. Most patients—more than they want to admit—need family or a close friend, to help monitor their taking the medication and their going to see their therapist.
3. This is important: try to admonish patients that because of the precarious and tricky nature of manic-depressive illness, the patient must be ready to accept advice—if necessary MAKE A CONTRACT WITH A FAMILY MEMBER OR FRIEND—to be warned when "danger signals" are in evidence. For example, when the patient is saying or doing inappropriate things; when the patient is taking unreasonable risks, or manifesting abnormal behavior of any sort. At this point the medications can be altered and a full-blown episode (and thus the probability of another hospitalization) can be avoided.

Sound advice from one who's been there.

11

UNDERWRITING THE ILLNESS: THE WORLD OF INSURANCE

Between the interaction of the professional and the patient; between the admission to a hospital and the release . . . lies the bill. Yes, money hovers over and tracks silently behind the receipt of mental health care.

We don't know many people who could specify what their coverage would be in the event of hospitalization, or many people who realize that mental health coverage is far less than that for a physical illness (or that it's mostly earmarked for inpatient, not outpatient, care). Therefore, this chapter is really a minicourse on insurance and the economic realities of the mental health marketplace. We'll cover private insurance first and then move on to the safety nets of government coverage.

PRIVATE INSURANCE

The Blues and the Commercials

The health insurance movement in this country began just before the Great Depression when Justin Kimball of Baylor University offered prepaid hospital protection to the public school teachers of Dallas. For three dollars each semester the teachers were covered for up to twenty-one days of a hospitalization. It didn't take long for this novel concept to catch on, and other cities soon began to offer similar plans. An organization in Minnesota first began to use the now familiar Blue Cross name and symbol, and in 1939 the state of California initiated a plan that was to become the prototype of Blue Shield—

the insurance that covers doctors' bills. Today, in many states, these two organizations have merged and are referred to as Blue Cross/ Blue Shield.

An individual, an employer, a labor union or a group can buy private, prepaid medical insurance from the nonprofit and state-regulated Blue Cross/Blue Shield, or from commercial insurance companies such as Aetna, Mutual of Omaha, Prudential and others. The commercial companies also issue life, home and fire policies; the Blues stick to the field of health.

Since 1971 many states have mandated that insurance policies must offer a minimum benefit package for mental health care. Thus, the state of Maine ruled that a group policy must cover at least sixty days' inpatient care per year (in a licensed, accredited community mental health psychiatric inpatient unit, general hospital psychiatric unit, a psychiatric hospital or a public hospital) and forty visits per policy year to a psychiatrist, psychologist, psychiatric social worker or psychiatric nurse. The state of Colorado's law ensures at least forty-five days of full hospitalization per year in a licensed general or psychiatric hospital, and allows a minimum of $1,000 in outpatient services, but will reimburse only outpatient services given by a psychiatrist, a licensed psychologist or a mental health professional under the supervision of a psychiatrist or psychologist. These mandates were intended to establish the minimum, or floor, for psychiatric benefits. Unfortunately, they have for the most part been written into policies as the ceilings. But it's easy to see how important it is to know a policy. If a patient enters a hospital that has lost accreditation, or overstays the time specified as covered or seeks therapy from a professional not licensed according to the policy standard, he and his wallet are in trouble.

Most people are covered by group plans through their place of employment, professional association or union, and these group policies are generally more generous (and cheaper) than individual ones, but not always when it comes to psychiatric coverage. An employer usually has a choice as to how comprehensive the psychiatric benefits will be, but unless an employee works for the federal government or a large corporation that offers very good benefits, or lives in a state that mandates more, he or she can expect that about twenty to sixty days per year of a psychiatric hospitalization will be covered, along with about $1,000 for outpatient consultation or counseling. Most of the payments for outpatient therapy visits and medication come from the employee's own pocket.

If a person is unemployed or self-employed and cannot purchase group insurance through a professional association, he or she should purchase an individual policy—either from the Blues or from a large, established commercial company—but keep in mind that individual policies cost more and are less generous with benefits. The psychiatric coverage will most likely be very limited (with no option of increasing the coverage) and there will no doubt be a form/questionnaire to fill out that examines closely the psychiatric history of the would-be policyowner and his or her family. One application we looked at asked, "Have you or any named dependent within the past five years had any mental or physical disorder . . . ?" Answering truthfully does not guarantee a turndown for coverage; it does make things a bit more complicated, and as with certain preexisting physical illnesses, benefits may be eliminated for a certain period of time. In one state, Blue Cross has an eleven-month waiting period for a preexisting illness. This means that a person can have a history of manic-depression and buy a basic policy, but hospitalization in the event of another episode would not be covered for an eleven-month period.

It gets worse. When asked in a 1979 study of major health insurance companies doing business in Wisconsin how they would deal with a person who had a diagnosis of manic-depression, 20 percent of the companies said they would decline all cases regardless of how long the person had been well or the number of episodes. One company would consider coverage two years after recovery for the person with a single episode; the others would require waiting periods of five to ten years. If there had been multiple episodes, 40 percent of the companies would deny all coverage, and the others would require waiting periods of five to fifteen years.

A person with a history of mood disorders who leaves a job and has not yet found another may be able to sidestep the preexisting illness clause that would disqualify him from immediate psychiatric coverage, but he must act in a timely fashion. Once the person leaves the job where he is covered under a group plan, coverage ends after a specified grace period, but he often has the option to convert the group policy to an individual or family policy *without a physical examination or any questions asked*. It is important to make that conversion and pay the premiums on the now-converted individual policy. If not, the person with a history of manic-depression may find it next to impossible to get access to mental health insurance until he or she is employed again and enrolled in another group plan.

As one explores the world of insurance more thoroughly, one hears the terms "first-dollar" coverage and "deductibles and coinsurance." These terms determine how much out-of-pocket expense a patient will have in the event of treatment. "First-dollar" coverage generally has a higher premium and may not cover the same amount of services as a policy that has a deductible and coinsurance, but once the premium is paid, the patient can stop worrying about paying other expenses. A "deductible" is the specific dollar amount the insured person must pay before the policy takes effect; "coinsurance" refers to the percentage of all costs that the insured individual must pay. A plan with a deductible has a lower premium, covers more services and tends to deter a person from running to the hospital for nonessential treatment. Naturally a person will want to make sure the deductible is only a slight deterrent so that it doesn't discourage the policyholder from obtaining needed care. Many of these plans pay 80 percent of the bills, while asking the insured party to cover the remaining 20 percent.

Health Maintenance Organizations (HMOs)

Another option in the private group insurance arena is the health maintenance organization—the HMO. While the Blues or commercial insurance underwrite some of the patient's health care, it's up to the patient to find the medical personnel to supply it. Then he or she has to file the claims and hope the treatment was within the boundaries of the policy. The idea behind the HMO is that the health insurance and the health services are provided by the same organization, and there is follow-through and integration of treatment. A member pays a fixed monthly or quarterly premium and receives health care from a team (or teams) of doctors, nurses, technicians and other health professionals—often under one roof—but there are no deductibles, few if any copayments and absolutely no forms to send in to the insurer. All medical records are kept in a central office, and the emergency room services are available twenty-four hours a day.

HMOs are federally regulated and must meet certain standards. The federal government supports the idea of this kind of health care, and HMOs are allowed to participate in the Medicare program. The government has also decreed that every employer with a health-care plan must offer HMO membership as an alternative if there is an HMO operating in the area.

The psychiatric benefits vary from region to region. The average coverage is for thirty days of psychiatric hospitalization, and about twenty sessions of outpatient, short-term therapy—*not* adequate for manic-depressive illness. A large HMO has psychiatric professionals on staff at the center. The smaller ones contract for the services of psychiatrists and other mental health professionals. The disadvantage to this system is that the quality of the doctors varies, and the patient cannot choose the treating physician. One of the advantages to the HMO system, however, is that an individual with a mood disorder who leaves or loses his job can usually convert to an individual policy that still provides the psychiatric hospitalization coverage as well as twenty outpatient sessions. In other words, the outpatient coverage is not cut.

A variation on the HMO theme is the IPA—Individual Practice Association. This type of plan contracts with private physicians at their private practice offices. The patient sees the doctor there and might have a wider choice of doctors closer to home. The drawback is that it is doubtful that individual practice HMOs will offer the comprehensive range of services associated with a group-practice HMO center.

Several hundred group programs are operating around the country, and approximately fifteen million people currently subscribe to this kind of health insurance plan. If you would like to find out if an HMO exists in your area, write or call: The Office of Health Maintenance Organizations, Room 9–03, 5600 Fishers Lane, Rockville, MD 20857, (301) 443-1993.

How Does Your Policy Read?

From all of the above, it's clear that there are many different policies covering (or not covering) different aspects of psychiatric care. It's vitally important that an individual with an affective disorder and his or her family understand their coverage. Christine Ammer, in a book called *The Common Sense Guide to Mental Health Care* (Lewis Publishing Company, Brattleboro, VT, 1982; now available from Viking-Penguin, New York) advises people to check a policy for the answers to the following questions:

- Is diagnostic consultation (evaluation or assessment) covered? If so, in the practitioner's office or only in the hospital? By a psychiatrist only or a psychologist or other mental health professional? Does it include psychological testing?
- Is treatment for any nervous or mental disorder, regardless of previous illnesses, covered?
- Are office visits to a psychiatrist covered? What about to a psychologist or social worker or other counselor?
- Is electroconvulsive treatment covered in the hospital? In an outpatient setting? What about the anesthesiologist assisting the doctor with ECT?
- Is hospitalization in a general hospital covered? In a psychiatric hospital? (We know of one family whose policy specified that there had to be an operating room in the hospital to qualify. Their son was admitted to a psychiatric hospital, and the insurance company refused to reimburse.)
- How long can the hospitalization last and be covered?
- Is the cost of prescription drugs covered?
- Is partial hospitalization covered? Day care, night care, halfway house?
- Would an ambulance to the hospital or in a transfer situation be covered?
- Is rehabilitation therapy (vocational or otherwise) covered?
- Is genetic counseling covered?

The High Cost of Inadequate Coverage

Be prepared, for all the reasons we've already mentioned, not to feel at peace when you examine the psychiatric benefits in your policy. With few exceptions, the insurance coverage available for mental illness is woefully inadequate and discriminatory. The insurance companies are afraid of an overutilization of psychiatric services, and so they arbitrarily limit the coverage. But they are failing to look at the facts.

First, people don't run to psychiatrists for the fun of it. As a matter of fact, the *New York Times* reported that about 15 percent of people who have coverage pay their psychiatric care bills out of their own pocket rather than process them through the workplace. Stigma provides a powerful brake on overutilization.

Most interesting is that insurers are closing their eyes to what they of all people know: early intervention and referral to outpatient treatment averts the huge expense of inpatient care. In fact, insurance companies would save money if they increased the coverage for outpatient care. Why? Because it is estimated that 60 percent or more of the visits to general medical doctors are made by patients who have an emotional rather than an organic basis for their physical symptoms. When the patient is not diverted to the correct psychiatric specialist, the general medical doctor may order expensive lab tests and X-rays. These costs are covered by insurance, but the tests usually do nothing to help pinpoint the correct psychiatric diagnosis. The results of eleven studies pinpointed an overall 25 percent decrease in later use of medical services when outpatient psychotherapy was provided.

Mental illness costs American industry more than ten billion dollars annually—dollars lost through reduced productivity of the millions in the workplace suffering from some form of psychiatric problem. The Equitable Life Assurance Society developed an "Emotional Health Program" that encouraged employees to see mental health professionals. They found that for every dollar of treatment cost incurred, there was a three-dollar return in increased productivity.

Insurance agents are quick to point out that the "worried well" spend years in psychoanalysis or psychotherapy and the system cannot support their "self-education." They're confusing the issues. Thirty days a year of hospitalization and five to twenty outpatient therapy sessions is *not* adequate for many people with relapsing or chronic psychiatric disorders. Studies show that outpatient psychotherapy, including family psychoeducational treatment, can significantly reduce the rate of relapse and rehospitalization, and yet insurance companies do not cover these forms of treatment. Unfortunately, health insurance is about acute illnesses, not chronic ones, and in this cost-containment era, the trend is to cut back on benefits and limit the services covered.

What can patients and families do? Educate themselves about the insurance issues and band together. We know several psychiatrists who, with family groups, are speaking with insurance companies. They are pointing out that increased outpatient care and community services usually mean decreased inpatient care. And it's the inpatient care that is so costly.

The National Alliance for the Mentally Ill has appointed a committee to examine the issues of insurance for people with a chronic psychiatric illness, and they are accumulating information in order to make recommendations to their local affiliates. State laws on psychiatric insurance can be changed, and there are politicians and media people who are sympathetic to this issue. Find out who they are and work together. A booklet called *For Ayes Only* outlines the process of legislating a bill through the state mandating minimum mental health coverage. It also contains some invaluable information to add fuel to the argument. It's available for a small fee from the National Mental Health Association, 1021 Prince Street, Alexandria, VA 22314-297, (703) 684-7722.

PUBLIC INSURANCE

The federal government (through state programs) provides two main forms of public health insurance: Medicare and Medicaid; and two forms of disability insurance: Social Security and Supplemental Security Income. Members of the armed services and their dependents are covered by a third form of public insurance.

Medicare

Medicare is the program administered by the Social Security Administration for people over sixty-five, for some younger people who are disabled and for people of any age with permanent kidney failure.

To be eligible for Medicare you must be one of the following:

1. 65 or older and eligible for Social Security or the qualified railroad retirement system.
2. Not eligible for Social Security or railroad retirement benefits, but of age 65 before 1968. Or of age 65 after 1967, with a certain minimum number of quarters of Social Security coverage.

3. 65 or older and not eligible under the above stipulations but willing to enroll and pay the required premiums.
4. Under 65 and have received disability payments for at least twenty-four months.
5. In Federal employment for a minimum length of time and meet the requirements of the Social Security disability program.

There are two parts to the Medicare package: Part A, also referred to as HI (Hospital Insurance); and Part B, medical insurance called SMI (Supplementary Medical Insurance). SMI helps pay for outpatient care.

Part A is financed by Social Security contributions from employers, employees and the self-employed. (If an employee has received a weekly paycheck, he or she is familiar with the Federal Insurance Contribution Act [FICA] deduction.) This hospital coverage is then free to anyone eligible. Part B is financed by the monthly premium paid by those who wish to buy it. If a person is over 65 but has not worked long enough to be entitled to the hospital insurance provided by Medicare, he can buy into Medicare, so to speak, but he will have to buy Parts A and B. There is no option of not paying for Part B.

Medicare is a safety net, but as with any net, there are as many holes as solid structure. There are deductibles, coinsurance, items and services that are not covered and certain limits on how much Medicare will reimburse. In addition, no benefits are covered unless Medicare says they are "medically necessary" and they are furnished by providers certified or approved by Medicare. Medicare pays 80 percent of "responsible charges" for lab tests, but does not pay for prescription drugs. Thus, lithium levels or thyroid function studies will need 20 percent financing by the patient. However, Medigap policies (see below) may help with the prescription drugs.

Medicare coverage of mental illness is, much to a lot of people's anger and regret, negligible. In fact, Part B benefits don't even rate the word negligible: they allow $250 for office visits a year! The hospital insurance of Part A limits its coverage to 190 days of inpatient psychiatric hospital care *during the entire lifetime of a beneficiary*. The message needs no translating, and it's a cold one indeed.

No one can afford to rely on Medicare to cover the costs of treatment today, and most people do buy some sort of private Medigap policy to fill in where Medicare leaves off. A policy such as this may pay some or all of the deductibles and coinsurance, or extend the hospital days and pay for some prescription drugs. Many insurance policies that cover people before they are 65 can be converted to a Medigap policy, and this should be investigated.

You apply for Medicare at your local Social Security office, and you can keep current on the law by reading the most recent Social Security Handbook. Write to the U. S. Government Printing Office, Washington, DC 20402. A very sympathetic and well-written guide to the labyrinth of Medicare is *The Medicare Answer Book* by Geri Harrington. It was published by Harper and Row, New York, in 1982.

Medicaid

Medicaid is a form of public assistance for low-income persons— the medically indigent. The program is financed by federal, state and local taxes, and administered by local public assistance offices.

The Medicaid patient is not responsible for deductibles and coinsurance, and all inpatient or outpatient hospital care, doctors' fees, lab tests, X-rays and skilled nursing home care are covered. Sometimes adult daycare and prescription drugs are covered also (the benefits vary from state to state). But while Medicaid covers all charges from qualified providers, it reimburses the professionals and the facilities with sums well below their normal fees. Consequently, many doctors and hospitals do not accept Medicaid patients.

Some people qualify for both Medicaid and Medicare, and anyone receiving the Supplemental Security Income that we'll discuss below is automatically covered by Medicaid. To find out if you're eligible, contact your local public assistance office. Look in the telephone book under City Government Departments and scan down the sub-listings until you find Social Services.

Disability

The Social Security Administration disability program provides monthly cash benefits for those disabled workers (and their dependents) who have contributed to the Social Security trust fund through the FICA tax on their earnings. These people have an "earned right" to disability insurance benefits. You may qualify if a physical or mental condition prevents you from working for at least twelve months.

The years of work credit needed for disability checks depend on your age when you become disabled:

- *Before 24*—You need credit for 1½ years of work in the 3-year period ending when your disability starts.
- *24 through 31*—You need credit for having worked half the time between 21 and the time you become disabled.
- *31 or older*—You need the amount of credit shown in the following chart.

Born after 1929, become disabled at age	Born before 1930, become disabled before 62	Years of work credit you need
31–42		5
44		5½
46		6
48		6½
50		7
52	1981	7½
53	1982	7¾
54	1983	8
55	1984	8¼
56	1985	8½
57	1986	8¾
58	1987	9
60	1989	9½
62 or older	1991 or later	10

If you are a disabled worker 31 or older, generally you must have earned at least five years of work credit in the ten years immediately before you become disabled. *Exception:* If you are disabled by blindness, the required credit may have been earned at any time after 1936; you need no recent credit.

If you are disabled, certain members of your family may receive benefits from Social Security also: unmarried children under eighteen, disabled children eighteen or over if they were disabled before the age of twenty-two and a spouse if he or she is sixty-two or older or has an eligible child in his or her care. A divorced individual is entitled to a former spouse's benefits if he or she was married to the worker for ten years prior to the date the divorce became final.

A determination as to whether an applicant's claim to disability is valid according to the law is made by a special disability determination unit. A physician participates in the decision-making process and reviews reports from treating physicians, hospitals and other medical sources. Therefore, when you apply for disability and survivors' Social Security at your local Social Security office (check the telephone book under Social Security), you'll need to bring a letter from your physician, your physician's name, address and telephone number and a list of dates when you were examined by that physician and other treatment providers such as hospitals.

In 1984 there were 3.8 million people receiving disability, about 11 percent of whom had mental disorders. The stringency in determining whether a person should receive disability has fluctuated from year to year. In 1980 Congress got a little jittery about the rapid growth of the disability program and passed a law requiring the Social Security Administration to review each beneficiary's eligibility every three years. If a person appeared well on the day of the interview, he or she was eliminated from the rolls—very often unfairly, too often causing excessive anxiety and human suffering. In September 1984, both houses of Congress unanimously approved legislation to overhaul the program and voted that the amount of stress the person can withstand must enter into the decision-making process. This more empathetic understanding of the problems the mentally ill face is a definite step in the right direction.

SSI

Supplemental Security Income (SSI) is a federal program designed to provide a floor of income for the aged, blind or disabled who have little or no income and resources. It is administered by the Social Security Administration and is financed by general tax revenues. There are no periods of work required—a person qualifies solely because of need. Medicaid medical insurance is provided also. As with disability, a determination and review of the claim is made by a special committee.

In order to apply for SSI a person must not have countable resources in excess of $1,800 (individual), or $2,700 (as a couple). Certain resources, however, are excluded when determining whether one is eligible for SSI: a home used as a principal domicile, a car if it is used to provide necessary compensation, gifts, prizes and awards, et cetera (see #2155 of the 1986 Social Security Handbook for the complete listing). A listing a few pages further on in the Handbook states that "One wedding ring and one engagement ring are excluded regardless of value"; we rather appreciated the bureaucratic sentiment. A person applies for SSI at the local Social Security office by filling out some forms. The personnel at the office will need to see proofs and documents that would show the applicant's assets, such as bank books, insurance policies, paycheck receipts, other proof of income and car registration.

People on SSI are paid at different monthly rates. The levels are determined by whether an individual lives alone, lives with others but pays his or her own expenses or lives in the household of others and receives support and maintenance. These payments are not huge. In 1986 a recipient who lived alone in the state of New York received a monthly SSI check for $408; one who lived at home supported by his or her family received a check for $241. Other states may pay even less. If the person gets a job the payments are reduced or cut. Being eligible for SSI means that the person is also eligible for Medicaid and may be eligible for housing programs, vocational rehabilitation and food stamps.

If a person is truly disabled and believes he is entitled to the benefits of SSI, he's going to need a lot of persistence. Sometimes a claim is not hard to document and is very apparent. Other claims may be denied for many reasons. The law defines a disability as "the inability to engage in any substantial gainful activity by reason of any medically determinable physical or mental impairment which can be expected to result in death or has lasted or can be expected to last for a continuous period of not less than twelve months." The problem phrase here for psychiatric disabilities is the one that stresses "medically determinable physical or mental impairment." Because it is extremely difficult to count the days or assess the outcome of a mental disorder, an applicant for SSI or the representative making the claim for him or her should know about the appeals process.

Should an applicant receive a denial, he or she has sixty days to submit a request for reconsideration to the district office. A Legal Aid service lawyer can help prepare this (the law provides for payment of legal fees in an amount up to 25 percent of the award approved for Social Security claims). If the claim is then denied at the reconsideration level, a request should immediately be made for an administrative law judge hearing. In 1980, 58 percent of the claims heard by a judge were allowed despite their having been denied twice before the hearing. Keep all this in mind to bolster your defense as you press against and through the system.

Christine Ammer, in *The Common Sense Guide to Mental Health Care,* again provides some good tips for dealing with the Social Security office. She suggests that you try to call early in the morning or early in the afternoon and late in the month if you don't want to receive a busy signal, and that you bring a snack and something to read when you go to the office. Bring all correspondence you've had with the Social Security Administration, information about your doctor (name, address, telephone number and dates when you saw the doctor) and other treatment sources and a letter from the doctor confirming your disability. Then, write down the names of any people you speak with on the telephone or in the office, and never, never ignore any correspondence from Social Security. Should you fail to respond to a letter, your claim may be denied on grounds of "lack of cooperation."

CHAMPUS

CHAMPUS stands for Civilian Health and Medical Program of the Uniformed Services, and it is the insurance plan that covers members of the armed forces and their families. During their service, military personnel and their dependents are treated free for any physical or mental illness, and afterward for service-connected conditions. At one time CHAMPUS provided the most comprehensive psychiatric coverage in the country: unlimited hospitalization and outpatient care. In 1974, however, the Department of Defense set a 120-day yearly limit on hospitalization and covered forty outpatient visits per year. Months later, they about-faced and raised the outpatient limit to sixty visits per year. In 1984, in order to control costs, a cap of sixty days of inpatient care per year (except "under extraordinary circumstances") was mandated. The benefits end upon discharge or retirement.

A retired member of the armed forces entitled to retirement pay may apply through his or her individual service branch for the Survivor Benefit Plan. This helps plan for the care of a disabled spouse, child or other family member after the veteran's death.

We just want to state that on a good day we're often confused by the ifs, ands and buts of the policies and plans, the bureaucracy and the rapid change in laws. How then, we wondered, could someone in a disabled state sort all this out? Well, with a lot of help. Your best bet is to talk to a social worker, either at the hospital before discharge, or at a clinic or community mental health center. These professionals are aware of the laws and programs and know how to initiate petitions for Medicaid/Medicare, disability and SSI. If you're fortunate enough to have a family member, friend or advocate who will help you negotiate the system, with patience and time you'll get what you need to have and get where you need to go.

FOUR

COMING FULL CIRCLE

12

RECOVERY AND
THE WORLD OUTSIDE

When a person with an affective disorder obtains information and treatment, and comes to accept what has happened to him because of the illness, he has added very necessary ballast to his life. Much of the initial phase of stabilization and education involves a member of the mental health profession. But the next phase finds the patient turning outward and interacting with his or her family members, office colleagues and social networks. The details of the disorder, and perhaps also an absence from the home and workplace, must be explained. How will my spouse and I explain it to our children? Should I tell my boss? How do I repair and rebuild? Where do I go from here? These are just a few of the questions to which answers must be found.

Now we come full circle—the patient who was very much in need of information is now the person who must decide who to inform and in what way. Here are some ideas that may ease the tensions surrounding these issues.

HOW TO TELL A CHILD

It is difficult enough for a husband or wife to deal with an ill spouse, but when there are children in the home the strain and the complexity of the situation multiply. Most parents have a tendency to want to shield children from the unpleasant realities of life—"There's time enough for that when they're older" is the rationale. But most people underestimate children's extreme sensitivity to a parent's mood and their capacity to imagine things more terrible than reality. When a depressed parent becomes silent and inactive, no longer able to care for the children or look after the household, the children are bound to become confused and anxious; if the parent suddenly begins to act in a wild and erratic way, with explosive emotional outbursts, the children will become skittish, filled with fear and resentment. Unfortunately, children also have a huge capacity for guilt and self-blame. They may assume they caused the parent's problem. They can't understand what has happened to the parent they knew and counted on, and they no longer feel secure, protected and loved.

A simple explanation from the well parent would do much to help the child deal with the fears and replace untoward imaginative fantasies with firm and guilt-free facts. A mother in St. Louis told us that she explained everything to her children at the beginning of what was to become a series of hospitalizations for their father, who was manic-depressive. She wrote to us recently and summarized the responses of her fourteen-year-old son, Tim, to his father's illness:

> Tim is extremely bright and knowledgeable about manic-depressive illness. He said that in his earlier years he was very afraid of his father when he was in a manic mood and he felt great relief when his Dad was depressed as he slept most of the time and didn't bother the children very much. As he got older and was better able to understand the information about the illness that I had been constantly feeding him, his response became less that of dread and more of loving concern for his father's welfare. Remember, though, that as Tim was getting older, his father was becoming more stabilized and Tim's understanding combined with his Dad's stability helped immensely in establishing a very good rapport between both of them. Some of Tim's comments are that he doesn't fear his Dad anymore. Because of his constant education about the disorder, he regards the illness as no more complicated than any other medical problem he may encounter. Being fully aware of the genetic factors involved, Tim is firmly convinced that under no circumstances would he fight treatment if he experienced an onset of manic-depression. He has seen first-hand the devastation this illness creates and wants no part of it. He has also witnessed the massive change in his father's whole personality because of stabilization and he is extremely proud of his Dad's accomplishments under oftentimes great duress.

Children who share their parents' joys *and* sorrows often develop strength and a sense of self-worth.

Author Helene Arnstein, in *What to Tell Your Child About Birth, Death, Illness, Divorce and Other Family Crises,* offers some fine phrases for telling even a very young child what is going on. She relates how a father helped his five-and-a-half-year-old whose mother was hospitalized for depression by saying:

> Tommy, Mommy cried a lot before she went to the hospital, and she didn't seem to pay as much attention to you as she used to. She just felt tired and sick. Feelings sometimes get sick just the way bodies do. Do you remember the time when you had the measles? You didn't *seem* to love anybody because you felt so bad. Well, Mommy loves you but she cannot show it because *she* feels so sick. When she feels better again and comes home, Mommy will be able to play with you and hug you, and you'll know she has never really stopped loving you and me.

After explaining the situation, a parent should wait patiently for the child to ask questions, and answer them honestly. It should not be assumed that a lack of questions or curiosity implies that the child is too young to understand, or that there is not turmoil churning within. In fact, the silence may be the clue as to how upset the child really is.

A child who witnesses a parent's being forcibly removed from the home and taken to a hospital will be terrified (this scene is a searing one for an adult witness also). Ms. Arnstein advises a conversation something like this:

> Daddy (or Mommy) didn't know just then what was best for him. He didn't know that the hospital is the safest and most comfortable place to be in while he is getting well. You know, there were times when you too had to do things you didn't want to, but which we knew were good for you. It was that way with Daddy, too. Other people needed to decide what was best for him.

Teenagers have other concerns. They may fear bad blood in the family and ostracism from classmates and dates; their shame and embarrassment may keep them away from friends. Because teenagers find it particularly embarrassing to discuss emotional problems with parents, it might be best if they spoke to an informed doctor, social worker or other adult who understands the illness and can listen and respond well to an adolescent boy or girl.

If a child with a hospitalized parent can imagine what the hospital looks like, can envision some of the personalities of the staff working with the mother or father and can understand what the parent does during the day, he or she will feel reassured that the parent is being cared for, will get well and will return home again. This is not to suggest that the child visit the hospital, but when the well parent actively describes the hospital setting, the child is usually more comfortable with the temporary changes in the home life. When the parent does return, however, the child is going to have a lot of mixed feelings: relief, anger, anxiety and embarrassment. The well parent should not insist it be a joyous reunion unless the child attempts to make it one, and the child should be warned that the recovering parent needs a lot of rest and time to adjust to the homecoming. Everyone needs some time to get used to each other again and to let the harshness of the preceding crisis fade a bit.

TO TELL OR NOT TO TELL AN EMPLOYER

People who have mood disorders react differently. Some people, once treated, are able to function well; others experience recurrences that cause problems when they return to work. Much depends, of course, on the employer's attitudes concerning illness. Does the employer generally react with suspicion or understanding when an employee becomes ill?

For the most part, an employer is concerned with productivity. He or she prefers employees who come into work every day, work hard and take a minimum of sick days (employees who utilize insurance benefits raise the company's premiums). But there are employers who may understand a worker's problems, especially if the worker has been valuable to the company. Recently more companies are becoming enlightened, and some are sponsoring programs to deal with alcoholism, drug abuse and emotional problems.

A person with a recurrent disorder must weigh all the factors and decide either to make a full disclosure or no disclosure at all. There is little value in minimal disclosure as it leaves open the possibility of the employer's assuming that the situation is worse than it is. The employer may also link unrelated aspects of work performance to problems with the disorder. It's unfortunate, but there are risks to disclosing information about psychiatric disorders—stigma is not a thing of the past. No one can offer blanket advice about the best course of action, and we caution you to proceed thoughtfully.

If a person wishes to inform an employer, he or she should make an appointment at a time that will ensure privacy and attention. The employee can say that he or she has an affective disorder that is a medical illness that affects sleep, activity level and concentration—that it is treated with medication. The employee might add that he or she is in treatment with a physician who is administering the medication, and while no one can guarantee that there won't be brief periods where these functions aren't disturbed, for the most part the doctor and the employee are closely monitoring the problem. No doubt the employer will have questions, and the employee should do his best to answer them in a straightforward manner.

Naturally, if there is a sudden hospitalization, a family member or friend will notify those in charge at the workplace. Early in the episode many details (such as what will happen and how long it will be before the patient can return to work) are unknown. Perhaps it is wisest not to say too much before some facts and progress are known. The friend or family member should simply say that Mr. D. has not been well lately, has been hospitalized and is being evaluated and that the employer will be kept informed. As soon as the picture is clearer, the employer should if possible be told when to expect the employee back at work.

Many people who have dealt with the problem of whether or how to tell an employer wrote to us. They received varying responses to their disclosures:

"I had to explain where I had been for a month, so I told them. They took it well. It seems someone told them already."

"I told them and apologized for my illness. They responded with understanding but I resigned, and my resignation was accepted."

"I did tell them and their response was very positive. They bent over backwards to help. Everything possible was done to make my job easier."

"I didn't tell my employers but they seemed to know. Insurance payments through the firms are not 'secret.' There have been three lay-offs in the past five years in which I have been included."

"After I was diagnosed I was terminated. I was told they couldn't take a chance with me (I might commit suicide). I am very careful not to reveal anything on future applications."

"I said, 'I need to clue you in on something. I have an illness called manic-depression and it sometimes interferes with my concentration. I take medication—lithium—and I do not consider it a handicap. I just want you to know.'" (The employer's reaction was to caution the employee to write things down so she wouldn't forget them.)

"I told my employer largely in medical terms and I stressed the analogy to high blood pressure or diabetes. My employer was sympathetic and reestablished my job. I later received a promotion."

"I told them I had manic-depression, that I took medications for it, and that I should be able to work without difficulty. With two exceptions, the response has always been negative. When job hunting, the mention of this topic seems to provide a sure guarantee for not getting a job."

"I never mentioned it before I was hired. After that, I gradually made remarks about my past and let them know I had been hospitalized. Employers have never hesitated to hire me back after a bout in the hospital or after I had my children. I must be a productive worker in spite of the disorder."

SUPPORT GROUPS

One of the greatest boons to people suffering with manic-depression and depression is the recent proliferation of support groups. They offer individuals with a chronic psychiatric illness *and* their family and friends information, assistance, acceptance and a chance to join forces with others to lobby for better research and legislation. Many groups are developing antistigma campaigns in order to improve public understanding of the serious psychiatric disorders. The National Depressive and Manic Depressive Association, the National Alliance for the Mentally Ill and Recovery, Inc. are the three major support organizations, with affiliates throughout the country.

Although they all offer education and support, there are differences among the organizations. The National Depressive and Manic Depressive Association, with almost eighty affiliates across the United States, is an organization of individuals who have been diagnosed as having mania, depression or both, and their family members. Monthly meetings feature lectures by experts in the fields of depression and mania, as well as "rap" sessions where people can talk about their problems and share information about the solutions they've found.

The National Alliance for the Mentally Ill (NAMI) was founded in 1979 and now has over 700 affiliates. This organization has become a powerful force with state governments and in Washington, and members testify before congressional hearings quite often. Their affiliates, or Alliances for the Mentally Ill (AMIs), consist mostly of family members of schizophrenic patients, but their programs do include patients and families with affective disorders.

Recovery, Inc., founded in 1939, is the oldest of these organizations. It was begun by a Chicago-based psychiatrist, Dr. Abraham Low, for formerly hospitalized psychiatric patients. Today more than one thousand chapters worldwide serve anyone with emotional problems. The weekly meetings, led by former patients, are based on a method of temper control, behavior modification and cognitive reconstruction. Recovery, Inc. is the only support group where diagnosis, medication and treatment are not discussed at meetings. However, cooperation with the treating psychiatrist is encouraged.

A newcomer to the list of support groups is Depressives Anonymous: Recovery from Depression. This organization uses a self-help method originated by Dr. Helen De Rosis, which involves specifying particular problem areas in a person's life that can be broken down into manageable units and overcome by applying a four-step approach. Depressives Anonymous offers a course for health professionals and lay people who wish to start a group of their own.*

People who have joined support groups speak enthusiastically about the benefits. One member said: "There is a great deal of comfort in finding other people like you with the same experiences and problems. We learn from one another and are a great comfort to each other during crisis situations." Many people find it therapeutic to share what they've learned and to offer encouragement and support to others. It raises a person's self-esteem. Another member put it this way: "Helping someone with the same disorder helps me lessen my dislike of my own disorder. It's better to be active than passive."

Most of the groups publish regular newsletters that keep members informed of monthly schedules and meetings, report on areas of research and legislation pertinent to the membership and review books that are thought to be helpful.

These are all ample reasons for seeking out a support group, but even greater possibilities exist when people join together in advocacy of research, destigmatization and better services and support. There is power in numbers, and until recently people with psychiatric disorders were among the least powerful. Because they had no voice, they were at the mercy of by-the-whim decisions about funding and legislation. The cost of mental illness to the American economy exceeds $36 billion in direct costs *per year,* and yet between 1967 and 1977 the federal funding for research on mental illness fell by half. This country spends $203.00 in research for each cancer patient yearly, $88.00 for each heart patient and a mere $5.27 for each person with a major affective disorder. The money is allocated by Congress and administered through the National Institute for Mental Health.

---

* Addresses of all state affiliates of the National Depressive and Manic Depressive Association and the National Alliance for the Mentally Ill are to be found in the appendix. The national headquarters of Recovery, Inc. is located at 802 North Dearborn Street, Chicago, IL 60610, (312) 337-5661. Depressives Anonymous: Recovery from Depression may be contacted at 329 East 62nd Street, New York, NY 10021, (212) 689-2600.

CHANGING THE PUBLIC'S ATTITUDES

Unfortunately, public spending is quixotic and has always mirrored the support and spending trends of the private sector. Of the more than 22,000 private foundations in America, only a handful—namely the McArthur Foundation, the Ittleson Foundation, the Scottish Rite, the Van Ameringen Foundation and the Brain Research Foundation— donate significant funds for psychiatric research.

The patient and family advocacy groups mentioned above are beginning to address this pitiful state of private and public funding. In July 1985 the National Alliance for the Mentally Ill announced the newly founded National Alliance for Research on Schizophrenia and Depression (NARSAD).* NARSAD intends to launch a public fund drive that will become the private funding arm for research in the field of mental illness. The private sector will have a chance to contribute. Meanwhile, NAMI advocates lobby in Washington and talk with legislators, testify before subcommittees, offer seminars and make the case for increased government spending for research.

NAMI has also targeted the areas of stigma and public education. This organization has enlisted the help of actors such as Kirk Douglas to film Public Service Announcements whose aim is to reduce stigma and encourage people to seek help. In a country where fewer than one in three people with a clinical depression seek treatment of any kind, and fewer than one in ten visit mental health specialists for help with depression, this kind of attention to the problem is urgent. The commercial shows Mr. Douglas straight-on, sitting in a chair. He says:

> It's been troubling me. Now, why is it that most of us can talk openly about the illnesses of our bodies, but when it comes to our brain and illnesses of the mind we clam up and because we clam up, people with emotional disorders feel ashamed, stigmatized and don't seek the help that can make the difference. Now let's start now, talk openly about mental illness, help us change those attitudes.

---

* The address of NARSAD is: NARSAD, c/o NAMI, 1901 North Fort Meyer Drive, Arlington, VA 22209.

This commercial, and the ones like it made by Louis Jourdan, Madge Sinclair and Susan Blakely, are simple and effective. They urge people not to let stigma keep them from getting the help they need.

The National Alliance for the Mentally Ill has launched a "media watch" campaign whose aim is to reduce stigma. When television commercials, talk show hosts or movies make jokes about mental illness or portray mental illness incorrectly, broadcasters and film-makers hear about it from AMI members. Usually one rational and polite letter does much to educate and alert media personnel to the disservice they are performing, but sometimes the one letter fails to enlighten. A giftware company in Southern California was manufac-turing a coffee mug that said: "Kiss me twice . . . I'm schizo-phrenic!" Chuck Harman, the Public Relations Director of NAMI, wrote the company that

> schizophrenia and other brain diseases are not laughing matters to the over 30,000 families who have joined our organization to receive support and to advocate for their mentally ill relatives. Would your company print similar words about other diseases, such as cancer or diabetes? I think not.
>
> I request that you immediately suspend production of the mug and remove those already distributed. The turmoil that pa-tients and relatives of the mentally ill experience is bad enough. Stigma compounds the problem.

The giftware company, after conferring with its lawyers, re-sponded that they were protected by the First Amendment and said: "Our plans are to continue the 'Kiss me twice—I'm schizophrenic' mug throughout 1986." They added that the "good taste of our products has never been questioned in the past."

Mr. Harman wrote back and acknowledged that they had every right to use the First Amendment argument, but so did the sixty thousand members of his organization. One of the members of an AMI, a father with two ill sons, called the president of the company and told him what it was like to live with mental illness and the harm that products like this cause. After that phone conversation, the company decided to suspend manufacturing of the mug.

Certainly the winds of change are stirring. Last year the National Institute of Mental Health launched a major educational campaign to publicize psychiatry's increasing ability to treat depression of all kinds. Coming after two decades of productive research on the psychobiology, epidemiology and treatment of affective disorders, Project D/ART—for Depression/Awareness, Recognition and Treatment—came into existence when the NIMH realized that too many people who suffer from depression do so needlessly. As many as 80 to 90 percent of persons with depression can be treated successfully; however, current evidence suggests that depression is poorly recognized, undertreated and/or inappropriately treated by the health care system.

Project D/ART aims to improve the identification, assessment, treatment and clinical management of depressive disorders through a national educational campaign focused on three major target audiences: the general public, primary care providers and mental health specialists. The program will reach the public through the media, and special materials will be developed for physicians and mental health specialists. It is an ambitious and exciting project in that it seeks to link the scientific leadership and expertise of the NIMH with the resources and knowledge of health education groups, professional organizations, private foundations, unions, insurance companies and the media for the common purpose of improving the early identification and treatment of depression.

Another organization was formed recently and is rapidly growing and making a difference. The National Mental Health Consumers' Association (NMHCA) is concerning itself with legislative, judicial and social issues affecting present and former mental patients. It is a broad-based self-help and advocacy organization that intends to improve the quality of life of people with psychiatric histories and empower these people to speak for themselves. The NMHCA operates a national clearing house that provides information and referral services to individuals and groups around the country.*

On May 12, 1986, a press conference and congressional recep-

* To contact the NMHCA, write or call: 311 S. Juniper Street, Room 902, Philadelphia, PA 19107, (215) 735-2465.

tion on Capitol Hill announced the establishment of the National Depressive and Manic Depressive Association (NDMDA). This was an important milestone in the history of mental health advocacy. For the first time, a group of patients have banded together to form a national organization. Their message? "We suffer from a treatable medical illness, not a character flaw." The national organization intends to:

- Improve the way society perceives this disorder and treats those suffering from it, especially in terms of medical insurance coverage and employer attitudes
- Stimulate further research on affective disorders
- Promote public and professional education about depression
- Provide support for people with depressive illness and their families

Local affiliates can do much to improve the situation and services allocated in their part of the world to people with manic-depression and depression. Some ideas might include:

- Survey clinics and hospitals to find out if an integrated up-to-date treatment approach is being utilized (compile a list of such places for members).
- Compile lists of doctors in the area who use a modern, integrated treatment approach and pass the names on to people who need them.
- Organize a speakers' bureau and book dates with local organizations and clubs. Educate the community.
- Invite the press to meetings, write articles about depression and manic-depression and arrange interviews with researchers and psychiatrists about new findings or studies.
- Develop antistigma campaigns and Public Service Announcements for radio and television.
- Pinpoint which state legislators might be sympathetic to the issues and arrange meetings with them. Inspire them to raise the issues in Congress and vote for better legislation, for research and insurance issues and commitment laws.

That evening in May at the congressional reception, Senator Paul Simon of Illinois opened his remarks by reminding the guests that he was from the same state as the most famous man who suffered from depression, Abraham Lincoln. He spoke of the fact that Lincoln had been so tormented by the illness that from the ages of thirty-two to thirty-four he had contemplated suicide. "What a loss that would have been for the nation," said Senator Simon. He paused and then asked quietly: "Would there have even *been* a nation?"

It's time now. We have the treatments, we have the talented researchers, we have a democratic nation that depends upon its constituency and listens to its concerns. The only thing that can stop the groundswell for change is indifference. Everyone—patients and family members—can play a part. First by seeking the proper treatment and by learning about the illness, then by giving support to others and joining together to foster research, fight stigma and promote public education.

This generation can do what none before had the knowledge or treatments to do. The suffering, neglect and stigma surrounding these disorders can be ended. The cycle *can* be broken.

APPENDICES

THE AFFECTIVE DISORDERS QUESTIONNAIRE

Copies of this questionnaire were sent to the leaders of manic-depressive support groups around the country, who then distributed them to their membership.

Age _____   Marital Status _____
Sex _____   Ages of Children _____
State of Residence _____
How were you diagnosed? (recurrent depression, manic-depression with hypomania, manic-depression with mania, etc.)

1. How long have you had an affective disorder?
2. At what age did you experience your first episode of depression, hypomania or mania?
3. Before you were diagnosed and learned about the disorder, how did you attempt to explain the early symptoms to yourself?
4. Do you remember experiencing unexplained mood swings or periods of hyperactive behavior when you were a child or adolescent? (Please specify age and describe.)
5. How often in a one-year period do you experience a depressive or manic episode?
6. What is the usual duration of each episode?
7. Does anyone else in your family have an affective disorder? What relationship are they to you?
8. With whom did you first consult—family practitioner, social worker, psychologist or psychiatrist?
9. Who made the diagnosis of an affective disorder?
10. Were you ever misdiagnosed? What diagnosis were you given?
11. How did you find the health professional who made the correct diagnosis?

12. What kind of treatment was prescribed—medications, individual therapy (supportive or insight-oriented), family therapy, a combination of medications and a form of therapy?

13. What medications do you take, and what are the daily dosages?

14. Was your response to the medications partial or complete?

15. What side effects did you or do you experience? (List medication first, then corresponding side effects.)

16. Did you ever go off the medications? Why?

17. What is your opinion about the medication you are taking?

18. Did your doctor explicitly describe the nature of the illness, the medications and their side effects?

19. What, in your opinion, constitutes a good doctor? What would you advise someone else to look for?

20. What has your experience been with individual psychotherapy, family therapy and group therapy?

21. What were the approximate monthly costs of treatment? Medications $ _____ Therapy $ _____

22. How did you pay for it?

23. How did you tell family and friends about the disorder?

24. Did it change their perception of you and your behavior, even during periods of well-being?

25. Did people ever urge you to try vitamins or nutritional therapy? Did they ever chide you for using medications? How did you respond?

26. Did you ever tell your employer about the disorder and how it affects you? How did you phrase the explanation?

27. What was the response?

28. How has the disorder affected your employment? In what field are you employed?

29. How has your social life been affected?

30. After the diagnosis and prescription of medication, did you ever consider pregnancy?

31. Understanding that medications are potentially harmful to a fetus, how did you and your doctor handle the management of medications during the period of conception and gestation?

32. During pregnancy, if no medications were used, did you experience mood swings?

33. What about the post-partum period?

34. Were you ever hospitalized?

35. In what kind of hospital? (private, city, state, VA hospital, community mental health center?) For how long?

36. What was the most helpful aspect of the hospitalization?

37. Was there any attempt to involve family members and educate them as to the nature of the disorder?

38. If not, would this have been helpful?

39. What kind of follow-up program was recommended after discharge?
40. Do you receive Supplemental Security Income (SSI)? Who helped initiate the application?
41. Can you give a descriptive account of how your thinking, mood and behavior change during the period of time in which you are depressed?
42. Can you give a descriptive account of how your thinking, mood and behavior change during the period of time in which you are hypomanic or manic?
43. What are the most enduring and problematic aspects of having this disorder?
44. Do you feel more creative without medications?
45. What books have you read about the disorder? What did you think of them? What journals or magazines do you read to keep current on the subject?
46. Do you find a support group helpful? Why/why not?
47. What do you think can be done about the stigma that people with psychiatric disorders face? Have you made any efforts in addressing the problem?
48. Is there anything you would like to say to us, or any issue you hope will be covered in this book?
49. About manic-depression and depression: What do you know now that you wish you had known when the illness first manifested itself?

If you have a written account of your personal experience with manic-depression or depression, we hope you'll send it to us for possible inclusion in the book.

If we found a phrase or description on this questionnaire that we thought would help explain the disorder to others or help make a particular point, would it be acceptable to you if we quoted it from an anonymous source? _____ Yes _____ No

ORGANIZING AND PUBLICIZING A MANIC-DEPRESSIVE SUPPORT GROUP

Should you decide that a manic-depressive support group would be helpful to you and the people in your community, contact the National Depressive and Manic Depressive Association, Merchandise Mart, P.O. Box 3395, Chicago, IL 60654, (312) 446-9009, for start-up materials and suggestions.

We recommend four handbooks that will aid the evolution of the group:

The Nonprofit Organization: An Operating Manual by Thomas Wolf. Englewood Cliffs: Prentice-Hall, Inc., 1984.

A clear and concise blueprint for structuring a nonprofit organization. The text explains how to build a better board, financial management, personnel management, long-term planning and effective fund raising.

Awakenings: Organizing a Support/Advocacy Group. Arlington: National Alliance for the Mentally Ill, 1982.

A guide to structuring an organization, including sample bylaws, articles of incorporation and recruitment letters and ideas.

Anti-Stigma: Improving Public Understanding of Mental Illness: A Community Communications Handbook. Arlington: National Alliance for the Mentally Ill, 1982.

A useful "how to approach the media" guide with very specific formats.

Editing Your Newsletter: A Guide to Writing, Design, and Production by Mark Beach. Portland: Coast to Coast Books, 1982.

A detailed and extremely helpful guide to launching a newsletter.

Once the preliminary organizational logistics are worked out, you will need to inform the general public about the group. There are several ways to go about this: you can design a flyer and distribute it through mental health clinics, psychiatrists, psychologists and social workers; and you can write a press release and mail it to local newspaper editors and radio and television broadcasters. These editors and broadcasters may then list the date of the meeting in the daily community events column, write an article about the new organization or announce your upcoming meeting over the air.

An entire communications network that needs ideas and information exists in each community in this country. The editors—the people who receive the notices—*will* view you as a reporter in the field, but there are contact formats and skills that one must understand in order to gain coverage. If you send a correctly constructed, properly worded press release, you increase the chances of obtaining publicity for your organization and spreading the message to the public.

WRITING A PRESS RELEASE

The press release is the announcement of your new organization, its intentions and information concerning its first meeting. It should basically follow the format shown on page 253, but there is plenty of room for variation in the body of copy. Tell the editor what is happening—when, where and why. Then follow this information with some background or facts.

The person who is listed as the contact in the upper right-hand corner should be accessible, available and able to speak articulately about the group and the disorders if an editor should call for more information or for an interview.

If your new group has letterhead stationery, the release should be typed double-spaced on it; if not, a plain bond paper will do as well. It can be duplicated by photocopying or offset printing. The release is usually mailed six weeks before the scheduled meeting, but it's always a good idea to check the deadline requirements for each publication.

To compile a list of the editors and announcers you should contact with the release, call the switchboards of the newspapers and radio and television stations (check your local Yellow Pages under "Newspapers," "Radio" and "Television—Cable"). Explain that you wish to publicize the starting-up of a manic-depressive support group and that you need to know who handles articles on health-related topics and who handles calendar listings for community events. Send each of these people a copy of your press release. But don't let it rest there. Follow up with a telephone call to see if that person received the release and to find out if he or she needs any further information. You can be warmer and more immediate on the telephone, you can tune the editor in, and you might just stir up enough interest to persuade the editor to do an article about your group. This would be a great coup as many people in the community who might really benefit from your efforts can read about the group in the paper, call you and get involved. Interested physicians and mental health professionals will also know how to get in touch with you and might offer their services to help launch the group.

Contact: Jackie Hauger
(202) 555-4321
FOR IMMEDIATE RELEASE
March 25, 1988

MANIC-DEPRESSIVE SUPPORT GROUP TO HOLD
FIRST MEETING—MAY 7, 1988

A newly formed manic-depressive support group will hold its first meeting in the auditorium at St. Luke's Hospital, 230 Maple Avenue, at 8:00 P.M. on Tuesday, the 3rd of May, 1988. The public is welcome and encouraged to attend.

Manic-depressive illness (bipolar affective disorder) or recurrent depression (unipolar affective disorder) currently affects more than twenty million Americans. Although the disorders have afflicted mankind since its beginnings, today there are new treatments and medications that can do much to attenuate the mood swings and help a person salvage career and relationship networks.

The manic-depressive support group intends to provide information, referrals, emergency aid and support to patients, their families and friends. Monthly lectures will feature psychiatrists, researchers and health professionals who will provide the most current information about the disorders. In addition, there will be smaller "rap" sessions in which patients and families can tell their own stories, trade information and give and gain support. Eventually, the group will join with the National Depressive and Manic Depressive Association in order to promote research and antistigma campaigns in this country.

For further information about the group and the meeting, please call (202) 555-4321.

NATIONAL DEPRESSIVE AND MANIC DEPRESSIVE ASSOCIATION LOCAL CHAPTERS

Manic-depressive support groups are starting up all over the country. To find out if a group exists in your area, contact the national headquarters: NDMDA, Merchandise Mart, Box 3395, Chicago, IL 60654; (312) 993-0066 or -0069.

ARIZONA
John Simer
Mental Health Association
  of Maricopa City
1515 E. Osborn Rd.
Phoenix, AZ 85104
(602) 274-0527

Vernon White
2655 E. Boston
Mesa, AZ 85203
(602) 833-0341

ARKANSAS
MDDA of Little Rock
P.O. Box 1770
N. Little Rock, AR 72114
(501) 771-1500

CALIFORNIA
Nancy Gothier
P.O. Box 223
Tustin, CA 92680
(714) 836-8080

Dorothy Palmer
1004 El Terino
Modesto, CA 95354
(San Fran. area)

Kent Layton
San Luis Rey Hospital
1015 Devonshire
Encinitas, CA 92024
(619) 753-1245
(San Diego area)

COLORADO
Carla Bergstrom
4035 Moorhead
Boulder, CO 80308
(303) 494-2506

**DISTRICT OF COLUMBIA
AREA**
DMDA
7614 Gralnick Place
Springfield, VA 22153
(703) 354-0495
(703) 569-4324

*The following four groups
are satellites of the preceding:*

Georgetown Group
St. John's Episcopal Church
32nd & Q Streets, N.W.
Washington, DC

Walter Reed Group
Walter Reed Army Medical Center
Georgia Ave., N.W.
Washington, DC

Wheaton Family Group
Wheaton Community Center
2424 Reedie Dr.
Wheaton, MD

Dominian-Barcroft Group
Dominian-Barcroft Hospital
2960 Sleepy Hollow Rd.
Falls Church, VA

FLORIDA
John Massollo
12901 N. 30th St.
Box 14
Tampa, FL 33612
(813) 974-3051

Dudley Cawthon, Jr.
351 N.E. 105th St.
North Miami Shores, FL 33138
(305) 891-0697
(305) 754-8941

Charter Springs MDDA
Joan Mathis
4921 N.E. 7th St.
Ocala, FL 32671

GEORGIA
Pam Lerner/
Gary De Bacher
P.O. Box 930553
Norcross, GA 30093
(404) 934-4798

HAWAII
Laurie Meech
400 Hobron Ln. No. 1702
Honolulu, HI 96815
(808) 947-4768

IDAHO
Carol Henze/
Ronda Johnson
P.O. Box 3649
Idaho Falls, ID 83403
(208) 523-9681

ILLINOIS
MDDA of Chicago
Marilyn Weiss
222 S. Riverside Plaza
Chicago, IL 60606
(312) 993-0066

Don Wells
328 Harris Lane
Bartonville, IL 61607

DMDA of Hinsdale
Marilyn Lohnstein
Box 535
Hinsdale, IL 60521

Family Support/Chicago
Milly Sokolec
222 S. Riverside Plaza
Chicago, IL 60606
(312) 993-0066

Alexian Bros./Chicago
Jean Kesseg
3753 N. Pontiac
Elk Grove Village, IL 60634
(312) 439-0999

Dave Linderborg
9 E. Cliff Dr.
Joliet, IL 60436
(815) 725-1000

Barbara Ryan/
Judy Poultrey
209 Concord Dr.
Normal, IL 61761
(309) 454-2740, 452-7665

Julie Harrison
3913 14th St.
Rock Island, IL 61201
(309) 793-2047

Barbara Danley
Education Services
South Clinic 2
602 W. University
Urbana, IL 61801
(217) 337-3399

Sue Patterson
Memorial Medical Center
800 N. Rutledge
Springfield, IL 62781
(217) 788-3508, 788-3505

INDIANA
Rob Bonner
4503 Washington Blvd.
Indianapolis, IN 46205
(317) 283-7362

Lois Dillon
1050 Camelot Manor
Portage, IN 46368
(219) 942-5772

KENTUCKY
Barbara Sanders
1119 Athenia Drive
Lexington, KY 40504
(606) 277-4909

Frank Marks
1100 Ambridge
Louisville, KY 40207
(502) 896-2185

LOUISIANA
Marie Kasten
5718 Chatam Drive
New Orleans, LA 70122
(504) 899-8282

Arlene and Mike Chenevert
1462 Wellington
Baton Rouge, LA 70815
(504) 275-6684

MAINE
June Labbe
399 Court St.
Auburn, ME 04210
(207) 783-2738

MARYLAND
Wendy Resnick, R.N., M.S.
Meyer 4-181
Johns Hopkins Hospital
600 N. Wolse St.
Baltimore, MD 21205
(301) 955-3246, 955-0067

Susan Simmons-Alling
9802 Montauk Ave.
Bethesda, MD 20817
(301) 530-7636

MASSACHUSETTS
Robert Berman, Ph.D.
180 Gardner St.
Arlington, MA 02174
(617) 643-5906

MICHIGAN
Judith Barta
113 Fairview
Ann Arbor, MI 48103
(313) 995-1463

Jim Erickson
1336 E. Pine River Rd.
Route 9
Midland, MI 48640
(517) 631-0635

Jo Ann Martin/
Bob Preuss
P.O. Box 132
Dearborn, MI 48121
(313) 934-3114

Linda Wronski
4520 Chippewa Dr.
Okemos, MI 48864
(517) 349-4579

MINNESOTA
Kevin Ferris/
Sue Nelson
P.O. Box 41424
Minneapolis, MN 55441
(612) 333-0219

MISSISSIPPI
Helen Walton
6271 Woodrun Dr.
Jackson, MS 39211
(601) 353-9691

MISSOURI
Dolores Segal
111-A N. Kirkwood Rd.
Kirkwood, MO 63122
(314) 965-7007

NEBRASKA
Barbara Hamilton
507 Woodbine Circle
Papillon, NE 68128
(402) 339-7779

NEW JERSEY
Pat McDonald
74 Magna Dr.
Gillette, NJ 07933
(201) 647-4460

Bergen County Chapter
Stuart Noss c/o MLPFS
50 Chestnut Ridge Road
Montvale, NJ 07615
(201) 573-4552

MDSG of Monmouth County
Ralph Strauss
25 Morris Ave., Bldg. 3, Apt. 23
Long Branch, NJ 07740
(201) 229-0310

South Jersey DMDA
Jerry Yellin
P.O. Box 367
Audubon, NJ 08106
(609) 547-7744

NEW MEXICO
Sara Brooks
1816 Indian School Rd.
N.W. #81
Albuquerque, NM 87104
(505) 247-9652

NEW YORK
Gary Goldsmith
MDSG—N.Y.
15 Charles St., 11H
New York, NY 10014
(212) 924-4979

Nassau Chapter
Larry Schultz
1212 Bay 27th St.
Far Rockaway, NY 11691
(718) 327-4569

Phil Garson
2 Bryant Crescent
White Plains, NY 10605
(914) 977-8255

Betty Schupner
212 Glenbrook Rd.
Nyack, NY 10960
(914) 353-0675

NORTH DAKOTA
Joanna L. Bope
63 6th Ave. N.
Fargo, ND 58102
(701) 772-1851

OHIO

Beth Klay
5 Techwood Place
Lima, OH 45805
(419) 222-8234

Linda Perkins
35105 Spruce
N. Ridgeville, OH 44039
(216) 327-1775

Jeanne Mohre
(Toledo Group)
5236 Alexander
Pemberville, OH 43450
(419) 287-4138

OKLAHOMA

Glenn Estes/Judy Short
6009 NW Expressway
Oklahoma City, OK 73190
(405) 682-2405 (J. Short)
(405) 722-9105 (G. Estes)

OREGON

Donna Kling
142 SW 8th St.
Corvalis, OR 97330
(503) 753-9385

PENNSYLVANIA

Kim Abbott
Philadelphia Medical Inst.
Jefferson Bldg.
1015 Chestnut St. No. 1303
Philadelphia, PA 19107
(215) 923-2583

TENNESSEE

Albert M. Carter
P.O. Box 8086
Chattanooga, TN 37411
(615) 892-7995

Tricia Williams
565 Leonora
Memphis, TN 38117

TEXAS

Artie Houston
P.O. Box 6362
Ft. Worth, TX 76115
(817) 654-7100

Pat Day
P.O. Box 224842
Dallas, TX 75222
(817) 654-7100

Mary Etta Clearman/
Patrick O'Sheehan
209 Westlake Dr.
Austin, TX 78746
(512) 327-0235

Dr. Cynthia Desmond
730 Inwood Dr.
Bryan, TX 77802
(409) 846-7627

Nadine R. Wood
554 Handover
Corpus Christi, TX 78412
(512) 993-0918

D. Lawrence
DMDA Houston
and Harris City
P.O. Box 270341
Houston, TX 77277
(713) 528-1546

Linda Comstock
Rt. 4, Box 280
Wichita Falls, TX 76301

Metta O'Kelley
4310 Tim Lane
Corpus Christi, TX 78412

VERMONT

Edwin I. Levin
Spruce Mountain Inn
Box 153
Plainfield, VT 05667
(802) 454-8353

VIRGINIA
Richard S. Shaughnessy
5002 Fran Pl. Apt. 303
Alexandria, VA 22312
(703) 354-0495

Elizabeth Youngblood
206 Norwood Dr.
Colonial Hts., VA 23834

WASHINGTON
Nancy Donigan
13437 Greenwood Ave. N.
No. 303
Seattle, WA 98133
(206) 363-7705

WISCONSIN
Bob Smith
P.O. Box 11511
Milwaukee, WI 53211
(414) 276-3122

Mary Ullmer
339 Bellevue St.
Green Bay, WI 54302
(414) 468-5955

CANADA

MANITOBA
Roy Finnen
248 Lanark St.
Winnipeg, Manitoba
(204) 489-6533

ONTARIO
Donna Noble
c/o Public Health Office
22 Prospect St.
New Market, Ont. LOH1G0
(416) 895-4511

Rachelle Grafstein
P.O. Box 503, Station R
2 Laird Dr.
Toronto, Ont. M4G4E1
(416) 486-8046

NATIONAL ALLIANCE FOR THE MENTALLY ILL AFFILIATES BY STATE

There are currently over 700 affiliates around the country, with an average of ten added each month. To find the organization nearest you, contact the state organization listed below or the national headquarters in Arlington, Virginia, at (703) 524-7600.

ALABAMA
Montgomery AMI
1743 Croom Dr.
Montgomery, AL 36106
(205) 272-2223

ALASKA
Alaska AMI
P.O. Box 2543
Fairbanks, AK 99707
(907) 457-3733

ARIZONA
Arizona AMI c/o Robert Richter
2515 E. Thomas S-16
Box 656
Phoenix, AZ 85016
(602) 273-0080

ARKANSAS
Arkansas AMI—Help and Hope Inc.
Hendrix Hall 125
4313 W. Markham
Little Rock, AR 72201
(501) 661-1548

CALIFORNIA
California AMI
2306 J St. 203
Sacramento, CA 95816
(916) 443-6417

COLORADO
Colorado AMI
1100 Fillmore St.
Denver, CO 80206
(303) 321-3104

CONNECTICUT
Connecticut AMI
284 Battis Road
Hamden, CT 06514
(203) 248-3351

DELAWARE
New Castle County AMI
3705 Concord Pike
Wilmington, DE 19810
(302) 478-4594

DISTRICT OF COLUMBIA
Threshold—DC
422 8th St. SE
Washington, DC 20003
(202) 546-0646

FLORIDA
Florida AMI
7096 Pine Bluff Dr.
Lake Worth, FL 33467
(305) 439-0539

GEORGIA
Georgia AMI
1362 W. Peachtree St. NW
Atlanta, GA 30309
(404) 874-7351

HAWAII
Hawaii Families and Friends of
    Schizophrenics, Inc.
P.O. Box 10532
Honolulu, HI 96816
(808) 487-5456

IDAHO
Idaho AMI
260 Skyline Dr.
Pocatello, ID 83204
(208) 232-5791

ILLINOIS
AMI Illinois State Coalition
P.O. Box 863
Glenview, IL 60025
(312) 297-9966

INDIANA
Indiana AMI
Box 8186
Fort Wayne, IN 46808
(219) 432-4085

IOWA
Iowa AMI
509 E. 30th St.
Davenport, IA 52802
(319) 322-5845

KANSAS
Kansas Families for Mental Health AMI
4811 W. 77th Pl.
Prairie Village, KS 66208
(913) 642-4389

KENTUCKY
Kentucky AMI
145 Constitution Ave.
Lexington, KY 40508
(606) 252-5518

LOUISIANA
Louisiana AMI
1633 Letitia St.
Baton Rouge, LA 70808
(504) 344-2208

MAINE
Maine State AMI
P.O. Box 307
Oakland, ME 04963
(207) 547-3639

MARYLAND
AMI of Maryland Inc.
2500 N. Charles St.
Baltimore, MD 21218
(301) 235-2511

MASSACHUSETTS
AMI of Massachusetts Inc.
34½ Beacon St.
Boston, MA 02108
(617) 367-8890

MICHIGAN
State AMI of Michigan
P.O. Box 51102
Livonia, MI 48151
(313) 425-1530

MINNESOTA
Mental Health Advocates Coalition of
    Minnesota Inc.
265 Fort Road
St. Paul, MN 55102
(612) 222-2741

MISSOURI
Missouri Coalition of AMI
10 Blackpool Lane
St. Louis, MO 63132
(314) 993-6937

MONTANA
Helena AMI
479 S. Park
Helena, MT 59601
(406) 443-6096

NEBRASKA
AMI of Nebraska
c/o John Woodall
122 Westridge Rd.
Bellevue, NE 68005
(402) 291-9483

NEVADA
Nevada AMI
P.O. Box 15445
Las Vegas, NV 89114
(702) 645-2859

NEW HAMPSHIRE
NAMI in New Hampshire
P.O. Box 544
Peterborough, NH 03458
(603) 924-3069

NEW JERSEY
New Jersey AMI
c/o Goldstein
Box 101 Hoes Lane
Piscataway, NJ 08854
(201) 463-4059

NEW MEXICO
AMI—New Mexico
P.O. Box 9049
Santa Fe, NM 87504-9049
(505) 983-2584

NEW YORK
AMI of New York
P.O. Box 746
New Paltz, NY 12561
(914) 255-5134

NORTH CAROLINA
North Carolina AMI
5105 Burr Oak Circle
Raleigh, NC 27612
(919) 781-5212

NORTH DAKOTA
Minot AMI (Reach)
505 19th St. SW
Minot, ND 58701
(701) 838-8905

OHIO
AMI of Ohio
360 S. Third Street #102
Columbus, OH 43215
(614) 464-2646

OKLAHOMA
Oklahoma AMI
c/o Hollis Terry
10404 Sunrise Blvd.
Oklahoma City, OK 73120
(405) 751-2885

OREGON
Oregon Alliance of Advocates for the
    Mentally Ill
5884 E. St.
Springfield, OR 97482
(503) 632-3251

PENNSYLVANIA
AMI of Pennsylvania
c/o Charles Pisano
1110 Cocklin St.
Mechanicsburg, PA 17055
(717) 766-8949

RHODE ISLAND
MHA Project Reach Out Mental Health
    Association of Rhode Island
89 Park St.
Providence, RI 02908
(401) 272-6730

SOUTH CAROLINA
South Carolina AMI
P.O. Box 2538
Columbia, SC 29202
(803) 736-1542

SOUTH DAKOTA
FRIEND AMI
Box 550
Aberdeen, SD 57401
(605) 226-1988

TENNESSEE
Tennessee AMI
1900 N. Winston Rd. #502
Knoxville, TN 37919

TEXAS
Texas AMI (Texami)
902 Terrace Mountain Dr.
Austin, TX 78746
(512) 327-4253

UTAH
Utah AMI
P.O. Box 26561
Salt Lake City, UT 84126
(801) 583-2500

VERMONT
AMI of Vermont
c/o Roch Thibodeaux
P.O. Box 1511
Burlington, VT 05402
(802) 862-6683

VIRGINIA
Virginia AMI
P.O. Box 1903
Richmond, VA 23215
(804) 344-4820

WASHINGTON
AMI of Washington State
P.O. Box 2174
Vancouver, WA 98684
(206) 892-6323

WEST VIRGINIA
AMI of West Virginia
c/o Judith Krall
25 Clinton Hills
Triadelphia, WV 26059
(304) 242-8850

WISCONSIN
AMI of Wisconsin
1245 E. Washington Ave.
Madison, WI 53703
(608) 257-5888

WYOMING
Wyoming AMI (WYAMI)
c/o Marjorie Haass
1123 Beaumont Dr.
Casper, WY 82601
(307) 234-4775

CANADA
AMI-Quebec Alliance pour les Malades
    Mentaux, Inc.
CP 145 Succ Cote-des-Neiges
Montreal, Quebec H35 255
(514) 731-8059

Regroupement des Parents et Amis du
    Malade Mental
432 BL St. Cyrille Quest
Quebec–P.Q. G15-153

PUERTO RICO
Asociacion Familiares y Voluntarios
    Pro-Participantes Centro
Psicosacirot de Bayamon
Antiquo Hosp Ruis Soler Carr #2
Bayamon, PR 00619
(809) 782-3970

Grupo de Apoyo Dinamico
    Comunitano
Box 4562
Carolina, PR 00628
(809) 702-2731

VIRGIN ISLANDS
St. Croix Concerned Citizens for
    Mental Health, Inc.
P.O. Box 937 Kings Hill
St. Croix, VI 00850

STATE INVOLUNTARY COMMITMENT STATUTES

This overview of state statutes was compiled by Edward B. Beis. It appeared in *Mental Health and the Law* (Rockville, MD: Aspen Systems Corp., 1983) and is reprinted with permission. Because state laws change, we advise your keeping up to date by calling a patient or family group or a mental health professional.

Alabama

Criteria
Mentally ill and as a consequence poses a real and present threat of substantial harm to himself or others as evidenced by a recent overt act.

Maximum Length of Disposition
None.

Alaska

Criteria
Mentally ill and likely to injure himself or others or in need of immediate care or treatment, and because of illness lacks sufficient insight or capacity to make responsible decisions concerning hospitalization.

Maximum Length of Disposition
Indeterminate.

Arizona

Criteria
Mental disorder and as a result poses a danger to himself or others or is gravely disabled.

Maximum Length of Disposition
Variable: 60 days to one year.

Arkansas

Criteria

Person has a mental illness, disease or disorder and as a result is homicidal, suicidal or gravely disabled.

Homicidal means the person poses a significant risk of physical harm to others as manifested by recent overt behavior evidencing homicidal or other assaultive tendencies toward others.

Suicidal means the person "poses a substantial risk of physical harm to himself as manifested by evidence of threats of, or attempt at, suicide or serious self-inflicted bodily harm, or by evidence of other behavior or thoughts that create a grave and imminent risk to his physical condition.

Gravely disabled "refers to a person who is likely to injure himself or others if allowed to remain at liberty or is unable to provide for his own food, clothes, or other shelter by reason of mental illness or disorder.

Maximum Length of Disposition

Initial 45 days. With additional 120 days.

California

Criteria

Mental disorder and as a result attempted, inflicted or made a substantial threat of physical harm upon the person of another, or himself or is gravely disabled ("a condition in which a person, as a result of mental disorder, is unable to provide for his basic personal needs for food, clothing or shelter").

Maximum Length of Disposition

194 days for persons dangerous to others; 28 days for suicidal persons; and no limit for gravely disabled except dissolution of conservatorship.

Colorado

Criteria

Mentally ill and as a result person is dangerous to others, himself or is gravely disabled.

"Mentally ill person" means a person who is of such mental condition that he is in need of medical supervision, treatment, care, or restraint.

"Gravely disabled" means a condition in which a person, as a result of mental illness, is unable to take care of his basic personal needs or is making irrational or grossly irresponsible decisions concerning his person and lacks the capacity to understand this is so.

Maximum Length of Disposition

12 months.

Connecticut

Criteria

Mentally ill and dangerous to himself or others or gravely disabled.

"Mentally ill person" means any person who has a mental or emotional condition which has substantial adverse effects on his or her ability to function and who requires care and treatment excluding drug dependence and alcoholism.

"Dangerous to self or others" means there is a substantial risk that physical harm will be inflicted by an individual upon his or her own person or upon another person.

"Gravely disabled" means that a person, as a result of mental or emotional impairment, is in danger of serious harm as a result of an inability or failure to provide for his or her own basic human needs such as essential food, clothing, shelter or safety and that hospital care is necessary and available and that such person is mentally incapable of determining whether or not to accept such treatment because his judgment is impaired by his mental illness.

Maximum Length of Disposition

Duration of mental illness.

Delaware

Criteria

Mental disease and poses a real and present threat to himself or others, or to property. Threat must be based upon manifest indication that person is likely to commit or suffer serious harm to himself or others or property if immediate care and treatment is not given.

"Mentally ill person" means a person suffering from a mental disease or condition which requires such person to be observed and treated at a mental hospital for his own welfare and which either (1) renders such person unable to make responsible decisions with respect to his hospitalization, or (2) poses a real and present threat, based upon manifest indications that such person is likely to commit or suffer serious harm to himself or others or to property if not given immediate hospital care and treatment.

Maximum Length of Disposition

6 months to indefinite.

District of Columbia

Criteria

Mental illness and likely to injure himself or others. "Mental illness" means a psychosis or other disease which substantially impairs the mental health of a person.

Maximum Length of Disposition

Indeterminate.

Florida

Criteria

Suffers from an apparent or manifest mental illness; has refused voluntary placement, is unable to determine for himself whether placement is necessary; is "manifestly incapable of surviving alone or with the help of willing and responsible family or friends, or alternative services, and without treatment is likely to suffer from neglect or refuse to care for himself and such neglect or refusal poses a real and present threat of substantial harm to his well being or it is more likely than not that in the near future he will inflict serious harm on another person, as evidenced by behavior causing, attempting, or threatening such harm, including at least one incident thereof within 20 days prior to initiation of proceedings."

"Mental illness" means an impairment of the emotional process, of the ability to exercise conscious control of one's actions, or of the ability to perceive reality or to understand, which impairment substantially interferes with a person's ability to meet the ordinary demands of living, regardless of etiology, excluding developmental disabilities, simple alcoholism or conditions manifested only by antisocial behavior or drug addiction.

Maximum Length of Disposition

Initial 6 month period with additional 6 month periods.

Georgia

Criteria

Mental illness and a substantial risk of imminent harm to self or others (as manifested by either recent overt acts or recent expressed threats of violence which present a probability of physical injury to himself or others) or is unable to care for his own physical health and safety as to create an imminently life threatening crisis.

Mental illness means having a disorder or thought mold which significantly impairs judgment, behavior, capacity to recognize reality or ability to cope with the ordinary demands of life.

Maximum Length of Disposition

Up to 20 months.

Hawaii

Criteria

Mental illness or substance abuse and dangerous to himself or others or to property and in need of care and treatment. Must also be least restrictive alternative.

"Mentally ill person" means a person having psychiatric disorder or other disease which substantially impairs his mental health and necessitates treatment or supervision.

"Dangerous to other" means likely to do substantial physical or emotional injury on another, as evidenced by a recent act, attempt or threat.

"Dangerous to self" means likely to do substantial physical injury to one's self, as evidenced by a recent act, attempt or threat to injure one's self physically or by neglect or refusal to take necessary care for one's own physical health and safety together with incompetence to determine whether treatment for mental illness or substance abuse is appropriate.

"Dangerous to property" means inflicting, attempting or threatening imminently to inflict damage to any property in a manner which constitutes a crime, as evidenced by a recent act, attempt or threat.

Maximum Length of Disposition
90 days.

Idaho

Criteria
Mentally ill and either likely to injure himself or others or is gravely disabled.

"Likely to injure self or others" means:

(1) A substantial risk that physical harm will be inflicted by the proposed patient upon his own person, as evidenced by threats or attempts to commit suicide or inflict physical harm upon himself; or

(2) A substantial risk that physical harm will be inflicted by the proposed patient upon another as evidenced by behavior which has caused such harm or which places another person or persons in reasonable fear of sustaining such harm.

"Mentally ill" shall mean a person who as a result of a substantial disorder of thought, mood, perception, orientation, or memory, which grossly impairs judgment, behavior, capacity to recognize and adapt to reality, requires care and treatment at a facility.

Gravely disabled shall mean a person who, as a result of mental illness, is in danger of serious physical harm due to the person's inability to provide for his essential needs.

Maximum Length of Disposition
3 years.

Illinois

Criteria
Mental illness and as a result the person is reasonably expected to inflict serious physical harm on himself or another in the near future, or is unable to provide for his basic physical needs.

Maximum Length of Disposition
180 days.

Indiana

Criteria

Mentally ill and gravely disabled or dangerous and in need of custody, care or treatment.

"Mental illness" means a psychiatric disorder which substantially disturbs a person's thinking, feeling, or behavior and impairs the person's ability to function. It includes mental retardation, epilepsy, alcoholism or addiction to narcotics or dangerous drugs.

"Gravely disabled" means a condition in which a person as a result of a mental illness is in danger of coming to harm because of his inability to provide for his food, clothing, shelter or other essential needs.

"Dangerousness" means a condition in which a person as a result of mental illness presents a substantial risk that he will harm himself or others.

Maximum Length of Disposition
Indeterminate.

Iowa

Criteria

Seriously mentally impaired and is likely to injure himself or herself or other persons if allowed to remain at liberty.

"Seriously mentally impaired" means a mental illness (every type of mental disease or disorder except mental retardation) and because of illness lacks sufficient judgment to make responsible decisions with respect to his or her hospitalization or treatment, and who:

(a) is likely to physically injure himself or herself or others if allowed to remain at liberty without treatment; or

(b) is likely to inflict serious emotional injury on members of his or her family or others who lack reasonable opportunity to avoid contact with the afflicted person if the afflicted person is allowed to remain at liberty.

Serious emotional injury is an injury which does not necessarily exhibit any physical characteristics but which can be recognized and diagnosed by a licensed physician or other qualified mental health professional and which can be causally connected with the act or omission of a person who is, or is alleged to be, mentally ill.

Maximum Length of Disposition
Indeterminate.

Kansas

Criteria

Mentally ill person who is dangerous to himself or others or who is unable to meet his or her own basic physical needs.

(1) "Mentally ill person" means any person who is mentally impaired to the extent that such person is in need of treatment and who is dangerous to himself or herself and others, and

(a) who lacks sufficient understanding or capacity to make responsible decisions with respect to his or her need for treatment, or

(b) who refuses to seek treatment. Proof of a person's failure to meet his or her basic physical needs, to the extent that such failure threatens such person's life, shall be deemed as proof that such person is dangerous to himself or herself, except that no person who is being treated by prayer in the practice of the religion of any church which teaches reliance on spiritual means alone through prayer for healing shall be determined to be a mentally ill person unless substantial evidence is produced upon which the district court finds that the proposed patient is dangerous to himself or herself or others.

Maximum Length of Disposition
90 days.

Kentucky

Criteria
Mentally ill person who presents a danger or threat of danger to self, family, or others and can reasonably benefit from treatment.

"Mentally ill person" means a person with substantially impaired capacity to use self-control, judgment or discretion in the conduct of his affairs and social relations, associated with maladaptive behavior or recognized emotional symptoms where impaired capacity, maladaptive behavior or emotional symptoms can be related to physiological, psychological or social factors.

"Danger" or "threat of danger to family or others" means substantial physical harm or threat of substantial physical harm upon self, family or others, including actions which deprive self, family or others of the basic means of survival including provision for reasonable shelter, food or clothing.

Maximum Length of Disposition
360 days.

Louisiana

Criteria
Mental illness or substance abuse which causes a person to be dangerous to self or others or gravely disabled.

"Mentally ill person" means any person with a psychiatric disorder which has substantial adverse effects on his ability to function and who requires care and treatment. It does not include persons suffering from mental retardation, epilepsy, alcoholism or drug abuse.

"Dangerous to others" means the condition of a person whose behavior or significant threats support a reasonable expectation that there is a substantial risk that he will inflict physical harm upon another person in the near future.

"Dangerous to self" means the condition of a person whose behavior, significant threats or inaction supports a reasonable expectation that there is a substantial risk that he will inflict physical or severe emotional harm upon his own person.

Maximum Length of Disposition
Indeterminate. Alcoholism 45 days (initial) and up to two 60-day periods thereafter.

Maine

Criteria
Mental illness and poses a likelihood of serious harm and inpatient hospitalization is best available means of treatment.

"Mentally ill individual" means an individual having a psychiatric or other disease which substantially impairs his mental health. Does not include mentally retarded or sociopathic individuals. Does include persons suffering from drugs, narcotics, hallucinogens or intoxicants, including alcohol.

"Likelihood of serious harm" means:

A substantial risk of physical harm to the person himself as manifested by evidence of recent threats of, or attempts at, suicide or serious bodily harm to himself, and, after consideration of less restrictive treatment settings and modalities, a determination that community resources for his care and treatment are unavailable; or

A substantial risk of physical harm to other persons as manifested by recent evidence of homicidal or other violent behavior or recent evidence that others are placed in reasonable fear of violent behavior and serious physical harm to them and, after consideration of less restrictive treatment settings and modalities, a determination that community resources for his care and treatment are unavailable; or

A reasonable certainty that severe physical or mental impairment or injury will result to the person alleged to be mentally ill as manifested by recent evidence of his actions or behavior which demonstrate his inability to avoid or protect himself from such impairment or injury, and, after consideration of less restrictive treatment settings and modalities, a determination that suitable community resources for his care are available.

Maximum Length of Disposition
1 year.

Maryland

Criteria

A person who has a mental disorder and needs inpatient care or treatment for the protection of self or others. Individual presents a danger to the life or safety of the individual or others.

Maximum Length of Disposition

Not available.

Massachusetts

Criteria

Person is mentally ill and discharge would create a likelihood of serious harm.

"Likelihood of serious harm" means:

(1) a substantial risk of physical harm to the person himself as manifested by evidence of threats of, or attempts at, suicide or serious bodily harm; (2) a substantial risk of physical harm to other persons, as manifested by evidence of homicidal or other violent behavior or evidence that others are placed in reasonable fear of violent behavior and serious physical harm to them; or (3) a very substantial risk of physical impairment or injury to the person himself as manifested by evidence that such person's judgment is so affected that he is unable to protect himself in the community and that reasonable provision for his protection is not available in the community.

Maximum Length of Disposition

1 year.

Michigan

Criteria

Mentally ill person who can reasonably be expected within the near future to intentionally or unintentionally seriously physically injure himself or another and who has engaged in an act or acts or made significant threats that are substantially supportive of the expectation or is unable to attend to basic physical needs, such as food, clothing, or shelter that must be attended to in order for him to avoid serious harm in the near future, and who has demonstrated that inability by failing to attend to those basic physical needs.

"Mental illness" means a substantial disorder of thought or mood which significantly impairs judgment, behavior, capacity to recognize reality, or ability to cope with the ordinary demands of life.

A mentally ill person is one whose judgment is so impaired that he is unable to understand his need for treatment and whose continued behavior is the result of mental illness that can reasonably be expected on the basis of competent medical opinion to result in significant physical harm to himself or others.

Maximum Length of Disposition
Indeterminate, following commitment periods of 60, then 90, days.

Minnesota

Criteria
Mentally ill, mentally retarded or chemically dependent person.

Mentally ill person means a substantial psychiatric disorder of mood, perception, orientation or memory which grossly impairs judgment, behavior, capacity to recognize reality, or to reason or understand, which:

(a) is manifested by instances of grossly disturbed behavior or faulty perceptions;

(b) poses a substantial likelihood of physical harm to self or others as demonstrated by:

i. a recent attempt or threat to physically harm himself or others; or

ii. a failure to provide necessary food, clothing, shelter or medical care for himself, as a result of the impairment.

This impairment excludes (a) epilepsy, (b) mental retardation, (c) brief periods of intoxication caused by alcohol or drugs, or (d) dependence upon or addiction to any alcohol or drugs.

"Chemically dependent person" means any person (a) determined as being incapable of managing himself or his affairs by reason of the habitual and excessive use of alcohol or drugs; and (b) whose recent conduct as a result of habitual and excessive use of alcohol or drugs poses a substantial likelihood of physical harm to himself or others as demonstrated by (i) a recent attempt or threat to physically harm himself or others, (ii) evidence of recent serious physical problems, or (iii) a failure to provide necessary food, clothing, shelter, or medical care for himself.

Maximum Length of Disposition
6 months.

Mississippi

Criteria
Person afflicted with mental illness if reasonably expected at the time determination is made or within reasonable time thereafter to intentionally or unintentionally physically injure himself or others or is unable to care for himself so as to guard himself from physical injury or to provide for his own physical needs. It does not include mental retardation.

Maximum Length of Disposition
Indeterminate.

Missouri

Criteria

Mental disorder which causes the likelihood of serious physical harm to himself or others.

Maximum Length of Disposition

1 year, 3 months.

Montana

Criteria

Seriously mentally ill which means suffering from a mental disorder which has resulted in self-inflicted injury to self or others or the imminent threat thereof or which has deprived the person afflicted of the ability to protect his life or health. For this purpose, injury means physical injury. No person may be involuntarily committed because he is epileptic, mentally deficient, mentally retarded, senile or suffering from a mental disorder unless the condition causes him to be seriously mentally ill.

Maximum Length of Disposition

One year. Thereafter, commitment proceedings must be initiated again.

Nebraska

Criteria

Mentally ill dangerous person who poses a substantial risk of serious harm to himself or others.

Mentally ill dangerous person shall mean any mentally ill person or alcoholic person who presents:

(1) a substantial risk of serious harm to another person or persons in the near future, as manifested by evidence of recent violent acts or threats of violence by placing others in reasonable fear of harm, or

(2) a substantial risk of serious harm to himself within the near future, as manifested by evidence of recent attempts at or threats of, suicide or serious bodily harm, or evidence of inability to provide for his basic human needs, including food, clothing, shelter, essential medical care or personal safety.

Maximum Length of Disposition

Indeterminate.

Nevada

Criteria

A person who is mentally ill and who exhibits observable behavior that he is likely to harm himself or others if allowed to remain at liberty, or that he is gravely disabled.

Maximum Length of Disposition
  6 months.

New Hampshire

Criteria
  Person in such mental condition as a result of illness as to create a potentially serious likelihood of danger to himself or others.
  "Mental illness" means a substantial impairment of emotional processes or of the ability to exercise conscious control of one's actions, or of the ability to perceive reality or to reason, which impairment is manifested by instances of extremely abnormal behavior or extremely faulty perceptions. It does not include impairment primarily caused by: (a) epilepsy; (b) mental retardation; (c) continuous or noncontinuous periods of intoxication caused by substances such as alcohol or drugs; dependence upon or addiction to any substance such as alcohol or drugs.

Maximum Length of Disposition
  2 years.

New Jersey

Criteria
  Person so afflicted with mental disease that he requires care and treatment for his own welfare or the welfare of others or of the community.

Maximum Length of Disposition
  Indeterminate.

New Mexico

Criteria
  Client with mental disorder that presents a likelihood of serious harm to himself or others, the client needs and is likely to benefit from proposed treatment consistent with least restrictive alternative.
  "Mental disorder" means a substantial disorder of the person's emotional processes, thought or cognition which grossly impairs judgment, behavior or capacity to recognize reality.
  Likelihood of serious harm to oneself means that it is more likely than not that in the near future the person will attempt to commit suicide or will cause serious bodily harm to himself by violent or other self-destructive means including but not limited to grave passive neglect as evidenced by behavior causing, attempting or threatening the infliction of serious bodily harm to himself.
  Likelihood of serious harm to others means the person will inflict serious, unjustified bodily harm on another person or commit a criminal

sexual offense as evidenced by behavior causing, attempting or threatening such harm, which behavior gives rise to a reasonable fear of such harm from said person.

Maximum Length of Disposition
   One year.

New York

Criteria
   Person who has a mental illness for which care and treatment as a patient in a hospital is essential to such person's welfare and whose judgment is so impaired that he is unable to understand the need for such care and treatment.

   Mental illness for which immediate inpatient care and treatment in a hospital is appropriate and which is likely to result in serious harm to himself or others; "likelihood of serious harm" shall mean:

   (1) substantial risk of physical harm to himself as manifested by threats of or attempts at suicide or serious bodily harm or other conduct demonstrating that he is dangerous to himself; or

   (2) a substantial risk of physical harm to other persons as manifested by homicidal or other violent behavior by which others are placed in reasonable fear of serious physical harm.

Maximum Length of Disposition
   2 years.

North Carolina

Criteria
   Mentally ill, mentally retarded or inebriate person who because of an accompanying behavior disorder is dangerous to himself or others, or is mentally retarded and because of accompanying behavioral disorder, is dangerous to others.

   a. "Dangerous to himself" shall mean that within the recent past:
   1. The person has acted in such manner as to evidence:
   I. That he would be unable without care, supervision, and the continued assistance of others not otherwise available to exercise self control, judgment, and discretion in the conduct of his daily responsibilities and social relations, or to satisfy his need for nourishment, personal or medical care, shelter, or self-protection and safety; and
   II. That there is a reasonable probability of serious physical debilitation to him within the near future unless adequate treatment is afforded. A showing of behavior that is grossly irrational or of actions which the person is unable to control or of behavior that is grossly inappropriate to the situation

or other evidence of severely impaired insight and judgment shall create a *prima facie* inference that the person is unable to care for himself; or

2. The person has attempted suicide and that there is reasonable probability of suicide unless adequate treatment is afforded under this Article; or

3. The person has mutilated himself or attempted to mutilate himself and that there is a reasonable probability of serious self-mutilation unless adequate treatment is afforded under this Article.

b. "Dangerous to others" shall mean that within the recent past, the person has inflicted or threatened to inflict serious bodily harm on another or has acted in such a manner as to create a substantial risk of serious bodily harm to another and that there is a reasonable probability that such conduct will be repeated.

Maximum Length of Disposition
90 days.

North Dakota

Criteria
Mentally ill persons requiring treatment.

"Mentally ill person" means an individual with an organic, mental, or emotional disorder which substantially impairs the capacity to use self-control, judgment, and discretion in the conduct of personal affairs and social relations. Does not include mentally retarded.

"Person requiring treatment" means either:

a. A person who is mentally ill, an alcoholic or a drug addict and who as a result of such condition can reasonably be expected within the near future to intentionally or unintentionally seriously physically harm himself or another person and who has engaged in an act or acts or made significant threats that are substantially supportive of this expectation; or

b. A person who is mentally ill, an alcoholic or a drug addict and who as a result of such condition is unable to attend to his basic physical needs, such as food, clothing or shelter that must be attended to for him to avoid serious harm in the near future, and who has demonstrated that inability by failing to meet those basic physical needs.

Maximum Length of Disposition
90 days.

Ohio

Criteria
Mentally ill person who creates a substantial risk of physical harm to himself or others, or who would benefit from treatment.

(A) "Mental illness" means a substantial disorder of thought, mood, perception, orientation, or memory that grossly impairs judgment, behavior, capacity to recognize reality, or ability to meet the ordinary demands of life.

(B) "Mentally ill person subject to hospitalization by court order" means a mentally ill person who, because of his illness:

(1) Represents a substantial risk of physical harm to himself as manifested by evidence of threats of, or attempts at, suicide or serious self-inflicted bodily harm;

(2) Represents a substantial risk of physical harm to others as manifested by evidence of recent homicidal or other behavior, evidence of recent threats that place another in reasonable fear of violent behavior and serious physical harm, or other evidence of present dangerousness;

(3) Represents a substantial and immediate risk of serious physical impairment or injury to himself as manifested by evidence that he is unable to provide for and is not providing for his basic physical needs because of his mental illness and that appropriate provision for such needs cannot be made immediately available in the community; or

(4) Would benefit from treatment in a hospital for his mental illness and is in need of such treatment as manifested by evidence of behavior that creates a grave and imminent risk to substantial rights of others or himself.

Maximum Length of Disposition
Two years.

Oklahoma

Criteria

A person who has a mental illness and in the near future can be expected to intentionally or unintentionally harm himself or others or is unable to care for his basic physical needs.

(c) "Mentally ill person" means any person afflicted with a substantial disorder of thought, mood, perception, psychological orientation or memory that significantly impairs judgment, behavior, capacity to recognize reality or ability to meet the ordinary demands of life;

(o) "Person requiring treatment" means either:

(1) A person who has a demonstrable mental illness and who as a result of that mental illness can be expected within the near future to intentionally or unintentionally seriously and physically injure himself or another person and who has engaged in one or more recent overt acts or made significant recent threats that substantially support that expectation; or

(2) A person who has a demonstrable mental illness and who as a result of that mental illness is unable to attend to those of his basic physical

needs such as food, clothing or shelter that must be attended to in order for him to avoid serious harm in the near future and who has demonstrated such inability by failing to attend to those basic physical needs in the recent past; but

(3) Person requiring treatment shall not mean a person whose mental processes have simply been weakened or impaired by reason of advanced years, a mentally deficient person or a person with epilepsy unless the person also meets the criteria set forth in this paragraph. However, the person may be hospitalized under the voluntary admission provisions of this act if he is deemed clinically suitable and a fit subject for care and treatment by the person in charge of the facility.

Maximum Length of Disposition
    Indeterminate.

Oregon

Criteria
    Mentally ill person who is dangerous to himself or others or is unable to provide for his own basic personal needs. A mentally ill person means a person who, because of a mental disorder, is either:
    (a) dangerous to himself or others; or
    (b) unable to provide for his basic personal needs and is not receiving such care as is necessary for his health or safety.

Maximum Length of Disposition
    180 days.

Pennsylvania

Criteria
    A severely mentally disabled person who poses a clear and present danger to others or himself.
    (a) Whenever a person is severely mentally disabled and in need of immediate treatment, he may be made subject to involuntary emergency examination and treatment. A person is severely mentally disabled when, as a result of mental illness, his capacity to exercise self-control, judgment and discretion in the conduct of his affairs and social relations or to care for his own personal needs is so lessened that he poses a clear and present danger of harm to others or to himself.
    (1) Clear and present danger to others shall be shown by establishing that within the past 30 days the person has inflicted or attempted to inflict serious bodily harm on another and that there is a reasonable probability that such conduct will be repeated. If, however, the person has been found

incompetent to be tried or has been acquitted by reason of lack of criminal responsibility on charges arising from conduct involving infliction of or attempt to inflict substantial bodily harm on another, such 30-day limitation shall not apply so long as an application for examination and treatment is filed within 30 days after the date of such determination or verdict. In such case, a clear and present danger to others may be shown by establishing that the conduct charged in the criminal proceeding did occur, and that there is a reasonable probability that such conduct will be repeated. For the purpose of this section, a clear and present danger of harm to others may be demonstrated by proof that the person has made threats of harm and has committed acts in furtherance of the threat to commit harm.

(2) Clear and present danger to himself shall be shown by establishing that within the past 30 days:

(i) The person has acted in such manner as to evidence that he would be unable, without care, supervision and the continued assistance of others, to satisfy his need for nourishment, personal or medical care, shelter, or self-protection and safety, and that there is a reasonable probability that death, serious bodily injury or serious physical debilitation would ensue within 30 days unless adequate treatment were afforded under this act; or

(ii) The person has attempted suicide and that there is a reasonable probability of suicide unless adequate treatment is afforded under this act. For the purposes of this subsection, a clear and present danger may be demonstrated by the proof that the person has made threats to commit suicide and has committed acts which are in furtherance of the threat to commit suicide; or

(iii) The person has substantially mutilated himself or attempted to mutilate himself substantially and that there is the reasonable probability of mutilation unless adequate treatment is afforded under this act. For the purposes of this subsection, a clear and present danger shall be established by proof that the person has made threats to commit mutilation and has committed acts which are in furtherance of the threat to commit mutilation.

Maximum Length of Disposition
90 days. Up to one year if criminal charges involving dangerous acts.

Rhode Island

Criteria
A person who is so insane as to be dangerous to the peace or safety of the people of the state or so as to render his restraint and treatment necessary for his own welfare.

Maximum Length of Disposition
Indeterminate.

South Carolina

Criteria

A person who is mentally ill, needs treatment and because of his condition:

(1) lacks sufficient insight or capacity to make responsible decisions with respect to his treatment; or

(2) there is a likelihood of serious harm to himself or others.

Maximum Length of Disposition

Indeterminate.

South Dakota

Criteria

Mentally ill person who lacks sufficient understanding and capacity to meet the ordinary demands of life or is dangerous to himself or others. The term "mentally ill" as used in this title includes any person whose mental condition is such that his behavior establishes one or more of the following:

(1) He lacks sufficient understanding or capacity to make responsible decisions concerning his person so as to interfere grossly with his capacity to meet the ordinary demands of life; or

(2) He is a danger to himself or others.

Maximum Length of Disposition

Indeterminate.

Tennessee

Criteria

A person is mentally ill and poses a likelihood of serious harm and is in need of care and treatment.

"Likelihood of serious harm" means:

(1) A substantial risk of physical harm to the person himself as manifested by evidence of threats of, or attempts at, suicide or serious bodily harm; or

(2) A substantial risk of physical harm to other persons as manifested by evidence of homicidal or other violent behavior or evidence that others are placed in a reasonable fear of violent behavior and serious physical harm to them; or

(3) A reasonable certainty that severe impairment or injury will result to the person alleged to be mentally ill as manifested by his inability to avoid or protect himself from such impairment or injury and suitable community resources for his care are unavailable.

Maximum Length of Disposition

Indefinite.

Texas

Criteria

A person who is mentally ill and requires hospitalization for his own welfare and protection or the welfare and protection of others.

Mentally ill person means a person whose mental health is substantially impaired.

Maximum Length of Disposition
Indefinite.

Utah

Criteria

(a) The proposed patient has a mental illness; and

(b) Because of the patient's illness the proposed patient poses an immediate danger of physical injury to others or self, which may include the inability to provide the basic necessities of life, such as food, clothing, and shelter, if allowed to remain at liberty; and

(c) The patient lacks the ability to engage in a rational decision-making process regarding the acceptance of mental treatment as demonstrated by evidence of inability to weigh the possible costs and benefits of treatment; and

(d) There is no appropriate less restrictive alternative to a court order of hospitalization.

"Mental illness" means a psychiatric disorder as defined by the current *Diagnostic and Statistical Manual of Mental Disorder* which substantially impairs a person's mental, emotional, behavioral or related functioning.

Maximum Length of Disposition
Indeterminate.

Vermont

Criteria

(17) "A person in need of treatment" means a person who is suffering from mental illness and, as a result of that mental illness, his capacity to exercise self-control, judgment, or discretion in the conduct of his affairs and social relations is so lessened that he poses a danger of harm to himself or others;

(A) A danger of harm to others may be shown by establishing that:

(i) he has inflicted or attempted to inflict bodily harm on another; or

(ii) by his threats or actions he has placed others in reasonable fear of physical harm to themselves; or

(iii) by his actions or inactions he has presented a danger to persons in his care.

(B) A danger of harm to himself may be shown by establishing that:

(i) he has threatened or attempted suicide or serious bodily harm; or

(ii) he has behaved in such a manner as to indicate that he is unable, without supervision and the assistance of others, to satisfy his need for nourishment, personal or medical care, shelter or self-protection and safety, so that it is probable that death, substantial bodily injury, serious mental deterioration or serious physical debilitation or disease will ensue unless adequate treatment is afforded.

(14) "Mental illness" means a substantial disorder of thought, mood, perception, orientation or memory, any of which grossly impairs judgment, behavior, capacity to recognize reality, or ability to meet the ordinary demands of life, but shall not include mental retardation.

Maximum Length of Disposition
Indeterminate.

Virginia

Criteria
A person who (a) presents an imminent danger to himself or others as a result of mental illness, or (b) has otherwise been proven to be so seriously mentally ill as to be substantially unable to care for himself, and (c) that there is no less restrictive alternative to institutional confinement and treatment and that the alternatives to involuntary hospitalization were investigated and were deemed not suitable.

Maximum Length of Disposition
180 days.

Washington

Criteria
(1) A person who has threatened, attempted, or inflicted: (a) physical harm upon the person of another or himself, or substantial damage upon the property of another, and (b) as a result of mental disorder presents a likelihood of serious harm to others or himself; or

(2) Such person was taken into custody as a result of conduct in which he attempted or inflicted harm upon the persons of another or himself, and continues to present, as a result of mental disorder, a likelihood of serious harm to others or himself.

(3) Such person has been determined to be incompetent and criminal charges have been dismissed and has committed acts constituting a felony, and as a result of a mental disorder, presents a substantial likelihood of repeating similar acts. In any proceeding pursuant to this subsection it shall not be necessary to show intent, willfulness or state of mind as an element of the felony; or

(4) Such person is gravely disabled.

"Gravely disabled" means a condition in which a person, as a result of mental disorder: (a) is in danger of serious physical harm resulting from a failure to provide for his essential human needs of health or safety, or (b) manifests severe deterioration in routine functioning evidenced by repeated and escalating loss of cognitive or volitional control over his or her actions and is not receiving such care as is essential for his or her health or safety.

"Mental disorder" means any organic, mental or emotional impairment which has substantial adverse effects on an individual's cognitive or volitional functions.

"Likelihood of serious harm" means either: (a) A substantial risk that physical harm will be inflicted by an individual upon his own person, as evidenced by threats or attempts to commit suicide or inflict physical harm on one's self, (b) a substantial risk that physical harm will be inflicted by an individual upon another, as evidenced by behavior which has caused such harm or which places another person or persons in reasonable fear of sustaining such harm, or (c) a substantial risk that physical harm will be inflicted by an individual upon the property of others, as evidenced by behavior which has caused substantial loss or damage to the property of others.

Maximum Length of Disposition
180 days.

West Virginia

Criteria

Mental illness, retarded or addicted and is likely to cause serious harm to himself or to others. Mental illness means a manifestation in a person of significantly impaired capacity to maintain acceptable rules of functioning in the areas of intellect, emotion and physical well-being.

"Likely to cause serious harm" refers to a person who has:

(1) A substantial tendency to physically harm himself which is manifested by threats of or attempts at suicide or serious bodily harm or other conduct, either active or passive, which demonstrates that he is dangerous to himself; or

(2) A substantial tendency to physically harm other persons which is manifested by homicidal or other violent behavior which places others in reasonable fear of serious physical harm; or

(3) A complete inability to care for himself by reason of mental retardation; or

(4) Become incapacitated.

Maximum Length of Disposition
2 years.

Wisconsin

Criteria
(1) A person who is mentally ill, drug dependent, or developmentally disabled and is a proper subject for treatment: and

(2) Is dangerous because the individual:

(a) Evidences a substantial probability of physical harm to himself or herself as manifested by evidence of recent threats of or attempts at suicide or serious bodily harm;

(b) Evidences a substantial probability of physical harm to other individuals as manifested by evidence of recent homicidal or other violent behavior, or by evidence that others are placed in reasonable fear of violent behavior and serious physical harm to them, as evidenced by a recent overt act, attempt or threat to do . . . serious physical harm;

(c) Evidences such impaired judgment, manifested by evidence of a pattern of recent acts or omissions, that there is a . . . substantial probability of physical impairment or injury to himself or herself. The probability of physical impairment or injury . . . *is not* substantial under this subparagraph if reasonable provision for the subject individual's protection is available in the community, . . . if the individual is appropriate for placement under s. 55.06 or, in the case of a minor, if the individual is appropriate for services or placement under s. 48.13(4) or (11). The subject individual's status as a minor does not automatically establish a . . . substantial probability of physical impairment or injury under this subparagraph; or

(d) Evidences behavior manifested by recent acts or omissions that, due to mental illness, he or she is unable to satisfy basic needs for nourishment, medical care, shelter or safety without prompt and adequate treatment so that a substantial probability exists that death, serious physical injury, serious physical debilitation or serious physical disease will imminently ensue unless the individual receives prompt and adequate treatment for this mental illness.

Maximum Length of Disposition
One year.

Wyoming

Criteria

A person is mentally ill based on evidence of recent overt acts, or threats. A mentally ill person means a person who presents an imminent threat of physical harm to himself or others as a result of a physical, emotional, mental or behavioral disorder which grossly impairs his ability to function socially, vocationally or interpersonally and who needs treatment and who cannot comprehend the need for or purposes of treatment and with respect to whom the potential risk and benefits are such that a reasonable person would consent to treatment.

Maximum Length of Disposition

Indeterminate.

BIBLIOGRAPHY

CHAPTER 1

BOSWORTH, PATRICIA. *Diane Arbus: A Biography.* New York: Alfred A. Knopf, 1984.

BOWERS, MALCOLM B. *Retreat from Sanity.* New York: Human Sciences Press, 1974.

CAVETT, DICK. Interview on "The Larry King Show," radio station WOR. November 19, 1985.

CHERRY, LAURENCE. "The Good News about Depression." *New York Magazine,* June 2, 1986.

CLAYTON, PAULA J. "The Epidemiology of Bipolar Affective Disorder." *Comprehensive Psychiatry* 22 (January/February 1981):31–43.

DSM–III: Diagnostic and Statistical Manual of Mental Disorders, 3rd ed. Washington, DC: American Psychiatric Association, 1980.

GALLAGHER, WINIFRED. "The Dark Affliction of Mind and Body." *Discover,* May 1986.

GOLDSTEIN, MICHAEL J., BRUCE L. BAKER and KAY R. JAMISON. *Abnormal Psychology.* Boston: Little, Brown and Company, 1980.

HAMILTON, IAN. *Robert Lowell: A Biography.* New York: Vintage Books, 1982.

HAVENS, LESTON. *Making Contact.* Cambridge: Harvard University Press, 1986.

KAPLAN, BERT. *The Inner World of Mental Illness: A Series of First Person Accounts of What It Was Like.* New York: Harper & Row, 1964.

KNAUTH, PERCY. *A Season in Hell.* New York: Harper & Row, 1975.

LICKEY, MARVIN E., and BARBARA GORDON. *Drugs for Mental Illness.* New York: W. H. Freeman and Company, 1983.

MCGHIE, ANDREW, and JAMES CHAPMAN. "Disorders of Attention and Perception in Early Schizophrenia." *British Journal of Medical Psychology* 34 (1961):103–16.

ROVNER, SANDY. "Down but Not Out." *Washington Post,* February 12, 1986.

TUCKER, JONATHAN B. "The Scary Ups and Downs of Manic-Depression." *Cosmopolitan,* April 1985.

U.S. DEPARTMENT OF HEALTH AND HUMAN SERVICES. *Mood Disorders: Pharmacologic Prevention of Recurrences* (Consensus Development Conference Consensus Statement). Volume 5, April 1984.

VONNEGUT, MARK. *The Eden Express.* New York: Holt, Rinehart, and Winston, 1975.

WALSH, MARYELLEN. *Schizophrenia: Straight Facts for Family and Friends.* New York: William Morrow, 1985.

WHYBROW, PETER C., HAGOP S. AKISKAL and WILLIAM T. MCKINNEY, JR. *Mood Disorders: Toward a New Psychobiology.* New York: Plenum Press, 1984.

CHAPTER 2

AKISKAL, HAGOP S. "The Bipolar Spectrum: New Concepts in Classification and Diagnosis." In *Psychiatric Update: The APA Annual Review,* Volume 2, 271–92, ed. Lester Grinspoon. Washington, DC: APA Press, 1983.

AKISKAL, HAGOP S., ARMEN H. DJENDEREDJIAN and RENATE H. ROSENTHAL. "Cyclothymia Disorder: Validating Criteria for Inclusion in the Bipolar Affective Group." *American Journal of Psychiatry* 134 (1977):1227–33.

ANDREASEN, NANCY. "Affective Flattening and the Criteria for Schizophrenia." *American Journal of Psychiatry* 136 (July 1979):944–47.

ANDREASEN, NANCY. *The Broken Brain.* New York: Harper & Row, 1984.

BLEULER, EUGEN. *Dementia Praecox or The Group of Schizophrenias.* New York: International Universities Press, 1950.

BROCKINGTON, I. F., and J. P. LEFF. "Schizoaffective Psychosis: Definitions and Incidence." *Psychological Medicine* 9 (1979):91–99.

CARLSON, GABRIELLE A., and FREDERICK K. GOODWIN. "The Stages of Mania." *Archives of General Psychiatry* 28 (February 1973):221–28.

COHEN, STEPHEN M., et al. "Relationship of Schizoaffective Psychosis to Manic-Depressive Psychosis and Schizophrenia." *Archives of General Psychiatry* 26 (June 1972):539–46.

DISALVER, STEVEN C., and KERRIN WHITE. "Affective Disorders and Associated Psychopathology: A Family History Study." *Journal of Clinical Psychiatry* 47 (April 1986):162–69.

DSM–III: Diagnostic and Statistical Manual of Mental Disorders, 3rd ed. Washington, DC: American Psychiatric Association, 1980.

DUNNER, DAVID L., and RONALD R. FIEVE. "Clinical Factors in Lithium Carbonate Prophylaxis." *Archives of General Psychiatry* 30 (1974):229–33.

DUNNER, DAVID L., and NORMAN E. ROSENTHAL. "Schizoaffective States." In *The Psychiatric Clinics of North America,* Volume 2. Philadelphia: W. B. Saunders Company, 1979.

ENDICOTT, JEAN, and ROBERT L. SPITZER. "Use of the Research Diagnostic Criteria and the Schedule for Affective Disorders and Schizophrenia to Study Affective Disorders." *American Journal of Psychiatry* 136 (January 1979):52–56.

FEIGHNER, JOHN P., ELI ROBINS, SAMUEL GUZE et al. "Diagnostic Criteria for Use in Psychiatric Research." *Archives of General Psychiatry* 26 (January 1972):57–63.

HARROW, MARTIN, LINDA S. GROSSMAN et al. "Thought Pathology in Manic and Schizophrenic Patients." *Archives of General Psychiatry* 39 (June 1982):665–71.

HATSUKAMI, DOROTHY K., JAMES E. MITCHELL and ELKE D. ECKERT. "Eating Disorders: A Variant of Mood Disorders?" In *The Psychiatric Clinics of North America,* Volume 7. Philadelphia: W. B. Saunders Company, 1984.

HIMMELHOCH, JONATHAN. "Mixed States, Manic-Depressive Illness, and the Nature of Mood." In *The Psychiatric Clinics of North America.* Volume 2. Philadelphia: W. B. Saunders Company, 1979.

JAMPALA, V. CHOWDARY. "Anorexia Nervosa: A Variant Form of Affective Disorder?" *Psychiatric Annals* 15 (December 1985):698–704.

JOYCE, PETER R. "Age of Onset in Bipolar Affective Disorder and Misdiagnosis as Schizophrenia." *Psychological Medicine* 14 (1984):145–49.

KENDELL, R. E. "Reflections on Psychiatric Classification—For the Architects of DSM–IV and ICD–10." *Integrative Psychiatry* 2 (March–April 1984):43–47.

KENDELL, R. E., J. E. COOPER et al. "Diagnostic Criteria of American and British Psychiatrists." *Archives of General Psychiatry* 25 (August 1971):123–30.

KLERMAN, GERALD L., GEORGE E. VAILLANT et al. "A Debate on DSM–III." *American Journal of Psychiatry* 141 (April 1984):539–53.

LICKEY, MARVIN E., and BARBARA GORDON. *Drugs for Mental Illness.* New York: W. H. Freeman and Company, 1983.

LORANGER, ARMAND, and PETER M. LEVINE. "Age of Onset of Bipolar Affective Illness." *Archives of General Psychiatry* 35 (November 1978):1345–48.

MAJ, MARIO. "Evolution of the American Concept of Schizoaffective Psychosis." *Neuropsychobiology* 11 (1984):7–13.

MELLOR, C. S. "First Rank Symptoms of Schizophrenia." *British Journal of Psychiatry* 117 (1970):15–23.

POPE, HARRISON G. "Distinguishing Bipolar Disorder from Schizophrenia in Clinical Practice: Guidelines and Case Reports." *Hospital and Community Psychiatry* 34 (April 1983):322–28.

POPE, HARRISON G., and JOSEPH F. LIPINSKI, JR. "Diagnosis in Schizophrenia and Manic-Depressive Illness: A Reassessment of the Specificity of 'Schizophrenic' Symptoms in Light of Current Research." *Archives of General Psychiatry* 35 (1978):811–22.

POPE, HARRISON G., JOSEPH F. LIPINSKI, JR. et al. "Schizoaffective Disorder: An Invalid Diagnosis? A Comparison of Schizoaffective Disorder, Schizophrenia, and Affective Disorder." *American Journal of Psychiatry* 137 (August 1980):921–27.

PROCCI, W. R. "Schizoaffective Psychosis: Fact or Fiction?" *Archives of General Psychiatry* 33 (October 1976):1167–77.

ROTH, M. "Classification of Affective Disorders." *Pharmakopsychiat* 11 (1978):27–42.

ROY-BURNE, PETER P., RUSSELL T. JOFFEE, THOMAS W. UHDE and ROBERT M. POST. "Approaches to the Evaluation and Treatment of Rapid Cycling Affective Illness." *British Journal of Psychiatry* 145 (1984):543–50.

SCHNECK, JEROME M. *A History of Psychiatry.* Springfield, IL: Charles C. Thomas, 1960.

SPITZER, ROBERT L., and JANET B. W. WILLIAMS. "Classification in Psychiatry." In *Comprehensive Textbook of Psychiatry,* 4th ed., ed. Harold I. Kaplan and Benjamin J. Saddock, 591–613. Baltimore: Williams & Wilkins, 1985.

SPITZER, ROBERT L., JEAN ENDICOTT and ELI ROBINS. "Research Diagnostic Criteria." *Archives of General Psychiatry* 35 (June 1978):773–78.

SPITZER, ROBERT L., JANET B. W. WILLIAMS and ANDREW E. SKODEL. "DSM–III: The Major Achievements and an Overview." *American Journal of Psychiatry* 137 (February 1980):151–64.

TAYLOR, MICHAEL A., and RICHARD ABRAMS. "Manic-Depressive Illness and Good Prognosis Schizophrenia." *American Journal of Psychiatry* 132 (July 1975):741–42.

TAYLOR, MICHAEL A., and RICHARD ABRAMS. "The Phenomenology of Mania." *Archives of General Psychiatry* 29 (October 1973):520–22.

TORREY, E. FULLER. *Surviving Schizophrenia.* New York: Harper & Row, 1983.

WHYBROW, PETER C., HAGOP S. AKISKAL and WILLIAM T. MCKINNEY, JR. *Mood Disorders: Toward a New Psychobiology.* New York: Plenum Press, 1984.

CHAPTER 3

BASKIN, YVONNE. *The Gene Doctors.* New York: William Morrow, 1984.

EGELAND, JANICE A. "Amish Study, III: The Impact of Cultural Factors on Diagnosis of Bipolar Illness." *American Journal of Psychiatry* 140 (January 1983):67–71.

EGELAND, JANICE A. "Amish Study, V: Lithium-Sodium Countertransport and Catechol O-Methyltransferase in Pedigrees of Bipolar Probands." *American Journal of Psychiatry* 141 (September 1984):1049–54.

EGELAND, JANICE A. "Bipolarity: The Iceberg of Affective Disorders?" *Comprehensive Psychiatry* 24 (July/August 1983):337–44.

EGELAND, JANICE A. "Genetic Studies of Affective Disorders among Amish." National Institute of Mental Health Grant Application, February 1986.

EGELAND, JANICE A. Telephone conversation with Demitri Papolos, July 21, 1986.

EGELAND, JANICE A., and ABRAM M. HOSTETTER. "Amish Study, I: Affective Disorders among the Amish, 1976–1980." *American Journal of Psychiatry* 140 (January 1983):56–61.

GERSHON, ELLIOT S., and J. I. NURNBERGER, JR. "Inheritance of Major Psychiatric Disorders." Amsterdam: Elsevier, North-Holland Biomedical Press, 1982.

GERSHON, ELLIOT S., JOEL HAMOVIT, JULIET J. GUROFF et al. "A Family Study of Schizoaffective, Bipolar I, Bipolar II, Unipolar, and Normal Control Probands." *Archives of General Psychiatry* 39 (October 1982):1157–67.

HOSTETTER, ABRAM M., JANICE A. EGELAND and JEAN ENDICOTT. "Amish Study, II: Consensus Diagnosis and Reliability Results." *American Journal of Psychiatry* 140 (January 1983):62–66.

KEVLES, DANIEL J. "Annals of Eugenics." *New Yorker,* October 8, 15, 22, 29, 1980.

KIDD, KENNETH K., JANICE A. EGELAND et al. "Amish Study, IV: Genetic Linkage Study of Pedigrees of Bipolar Probands." *American Journal of Psychiatry* 141 (September 1984):1042–48.

KOLATA, GINA. "Huntington's Disease Gene Located." *Science* 222 (November 1983):913–15.

KOLATA, GINA. "Manic-Depression: Is It Inherited?" *Science* 232 (May 2, 1986):575–76.

MAUGH, THOMAS H. "Is There a Gene for Depression?" *Science* 214 (December 1981):1330–31.

MENDLEWICZ, JULIEN, and JOHN D. RAINER. "Adoption Study Supporting Genetic Transmission in Manic-Depressive Illness." *Nature* 268 (July 1977):327–29.

NADI, SUSAN N., JOHN I. NURNBERGER, JR. and ELLIOT S. GERSHON. "Muscarinic Cholinergic Receptors on Skin Fibroblasts in Familial Affective Disorder." *New England Journal of Medicine* 311 (July 1984):225–30.

NURNBERGER, JOHN I., and ELLIOT S. GERSHON. "Genetics of Affective Disorders." In *The Neurobiology of Mood Disorders.* Baltimore: Williams & Wilkins, 1984.

SCHAEFFER, PHYLLIS. "Molecular Genetics to Help Understand Psychiatric Illness." *Clinical Psychiatry News,* (November 1985).

SCHLESSER, MICHAEL A., and KENNETH Z. ALTSHULER. "The Genetics of Affective Disorder: Data, Theory, and Clinical Applications." *Hospital and Community Psychiatry* 34 (May 1983):415–21.

TSUANG, MING T. "Genetic Counseling for Psychiatric Patients and Their Families." *American Journal of Psychiatry* 135 (December 1978): 1465–74.

TSUANG, MING T., and RANDALL VANDERMEY. *Genes and the Mind: The Inheritance of Mental Illness.* New York: Oxford University Press, 1980.

WALDHOLTZ, MICHAEL. "Probing the Cell: Help from a Handy 'Riflip.' " *Wall Street Journal,* February 3, 1986.

WATSON, JAMES D. *The Double Helix.* New York: New American Library, 1968.

WEISSMAN, MYRNA, et al. "Psychiatric Disorders in the Relatives of Probands with Affective Disorders." *Archives of General Psychiatry* 41 (January 1984):13–21.

WENDER, PAUL H., and DONALD F. KLEIN. *Mind, Mood, and Medicine.* New York: Farrar, Straus & Giroux, 1981.

WEATHERALL, D. J. *The New Genetics and Clinical Practice.* New York: Oxford University Press, 1985.

CHAPTER 4

ALBERS, H. ELLIOT, RALPH LYDIC, PHILIPPA H. GANDER and MARTIN C. MOORE-EDE. "Role of the Suprachiasmatic Nuclei in the Circadian Timing System of the Squirrel Monkey. I. The Generation of Rhythmicity." *Brain Research* 300 (1984):275–84.

ATKINSON, MARTHA, DANIEL F. KRIPKE and SANFORD R. WOLF. "Autorhythmometry in Manic-Depressives." *Chronobiologia* 2 (1975):325–35.

BALDESSARINI, ROSS J. "An Overview of the Basis for the Amine Hypothesis in Affective Illness." *Archives of General Psychiatry* 32 (1975):1087–93.

BALDESSARINI, ROSS J. *Chemotherapy in Psychiatry,* rev. ed. Cambridge: Harvard University Press, 1985.

BANERJEE, SHAILESH P., LILY S. KUNG, STEPHEN J. RIGGI and SUBIR K. CHANDA. "Development of Beta-Adrenergic Receptor Subsensitivity by Antidepressants." *Nature* 268 (1977):455–56.

CHARNEY, DENNIS S., and DAVID B. MENKER. "Receptor Sensitivity and the Mechanism of Action of Antidepressant Treatment: Implications for the Etiology and Therapy of Depression." *Archives of General Psychiatry* 38 (1981):1160–75.

COPPEN, ALEC. "Defects in Monoamine Metabolism and Their Possible Importance in the Pathogenesis of Depressive Syndromes." *Psychiatricet et Neurologic Scandinavia* 34 (1959):105–7.

CZEISLER, CHARLES A., JAMES S. ALLAN, STEVEN H. STROGATZ et al. "Bright Light Resets the Human Circadian Pacemaker Independent of the Timing of the Sleep-Wake Cycle." *Science* 233 (August 8, 1986):667–71.

DIAGRAM GROUP. *The Brain: A User's Manual.* New York: Perigee, 1982.

FARAVELLI, CARLO, GIAMPAOLO LA MALFA and SALVATORE ROMANO. "Circadian Rhythm in Primary Affective Disorder." *Comprehensive Psychiatry* 26 (July/August 1985):364–69.

FULLERTON, DONALD T., FREDERICK J. WENZEL, FRANCIS N. LORENZ and HAROLD FAHS. "Circadian Rhythm of Adrenal Cortical Activity in Depression." *Archives of General Psychiatry* 19 (December 1968):675–88.

HAUGER, RICHARD L., and STEVEN M. PAUL. "Neurotransmitter Receptor Plasticity: Alterations by Antidepressants and Antipsychotics." *Psychiatric Annals* 13 (May 1983):399–407.

HAURI, PETER, DORIS CHERNIK and DAVID HAWKINS. "Sleep of Depressed Patients in Remission." *Archives of General Psychiatry* 1 (1974):386–91.

HOBSON, J. ALLAN. *Dreamstage: An Experimental Portrait of the Sleeping Brain.* Hoffmann-La Roche, 1977.

HOFFMAN, KLAUS. "The Role of the Pineal Gland in the Photoperiodic Control of Seasonal Cycles in Hamsters." In *Biological Clocks in Seasonal Reproductive Cycles,* ed. B. K. and D. E. Follet. Bristol: J. Wright, 1981.

JANOWSKY, AARON, FUMIHKO OKADA, HAL D. MANIER et al. "Role of Serotinergic Input in the Regulation of the Beta-Adrenergic Receptor-coupled Adenylate Cyclase System." *Science* 218 (November 1982):900–901.

JOYCE, PETER R. "Neuroendocrine Changes in Depression." *Australian and New Zealand Journal of Psychiatry* 19 (1985):120–27.

KANDEL, ERIC R., and JAMES H. SCHWARTZ. *Principles of Neural Science.* New York: Elsevier/North-Holland, 1981.

KATCHALSKY, AHARON K., VERNON ROWLAND and ROBERT BLUMENTHAL. *Dynamic Patterns of Brain Cell Assemblies.* Cambridge: Massachusetts Institute of Technology, 1974.

KAUFMAN, I. CHARLES, and LEONARD A. ROSENBLUM. "Depression in Infant Monkeys Separated from Their Mothers." *Science* 155 (1967):1030–31.

KETY, SEYMOUR S. "A Biologist Examines the Mind and Behavior." *Science* 132 (December 23, 1960):1861–70.

KRIEGER, DOROTHY T., and JOAN C. HUGHS, eds. *Neuroendocrinology.* Sunderland, MA: Sinauer Associates, Inc., 1980.

KRIPKE, DANIEL F., DANIEL J. MULLANEY, MARTHA ATKINSON and SANFORD WOLF. "Circadian Rhythm Disorders in Manic-Depressives." *Biological Psychiatry* 13 (1978):335–51.

KUPFER, DAVID J., and ELLEN FRANK. *Depression.* A "Current Concepts" publication, The Upjohn Company, 1981.

LICKEY, MARVIN E., and BARBARA GORDON. *Drugs for Mental Illness.* New York: W. H. Freeman and Company, 1983.

LINGJAERDE, O. "The Biochemistry of Depression: A Survey of Monoaminergic Neuroendocrinological and Biorhythmic Disturbances in Endogenous Depression." *Acta Psychiat Scanda, Supplement* 302 (1983):36–51.

MENDLEWICZ, J., G. HOFFMAN, P. LINKOWSKI et al. "Chronobiology and Manic-Depression: Neuroendocrine and Sleep EEG Parameters." *Advanced Biological Psychiatry* 11 (1983):129–35.

MOORE-EDE, MARTIN C. "Physiology of the Circadian Timing System: Predictive Versus Reactive Homeostasis." *American Journal of Physiology* 250 (1986):735–52.

MOORE-EDE, MARTIN C., FRANK SULZMAN and CHARLES A. FULLER. *The Clocks That Time Us.* New York: Oxford University Press, 1982.

PAYKEL, E. S., ed. *Handbook of Affective Disorders.* New York: The Guilford Press, 1982.

POST, ROBERT M., and JAMES C. BALLENGER, eds. *Neurobiology of Mood Disorders.* Baltimore: Williams & Wilkins, 1984.

SACHAR, EDWARD J., LEON HELLMAN, HOWARD P. ROFFWARG et al. "Disrupted 24-Hour Patterns of Cortisol Secretion in Psychotic Depression." *Archives of General Psychiatry* 28 (1973):19–26.

SCHILDKRAUT, JOSEPH. "Catecholamine Hypothesis of Affective Disorders." *American Journal of Psychiatry* 122 (1965):509–22.

SCHWARTZ, WILLIAM J., STEVEN M. REPPERT, SHARON M. EAGAN and MARTIN C. MOORE-EDE. "In Vivo Metabolic Activity of the Suprachiasmatic Nuclei: A Comparative Study." *Brain Research* 274 (1983):184–87.

SIEVER, LARRY, and FRIDOLIN SULSER. "Regulations of Amine Neurotransmitter Systems." *Psychopharmacology Bulletin* 20 (1984):500–504.

TEICHER, MARTIN A., JANET LAWRENCE, NATACHA BARBER et al. "Circadian Activity Rhythms in Geriatric Depression." Poster presented at the American Psychiatric Association Convention, 1986.

VAN PRAAG, HERMAN M. "Neurotransmitters and CNS Disease." *Lancet* 2 (December 1982):1259–63.

WEHR, THOMAS A., and FREDERICK K. GOODWIN. "Biological Rhythms and Psychiatry." In *American Handbook of Psychiatry,* Volume 7, 2nd ed. Boston: Basic Books, 1980.

WEHR, THOMAS A., and FREDERICK K. GOODWIN, eds. *Circadian Rhythms in Psychiatry.* Pacific Grove: The Boxwood Press, 1983.

WEITZMAN, E. D. "Chronobiology of Man." *Human Neurobiology* 1 (1982):173–83.

WEVER, RUTGER A. "Phase Shifts of Circadian Rhythms Due to Shifts of Artificial Zeitgebers." *Chronobiologia* 7 (1980):303–27.

WHYBROW, PETER C., HAGOP S. AKISKAL and WILLIAM T. MCKINNEY, JR. *Mood Disorders: Toward a New Psychobiology.* New York: Plenum Press, 1984.

CHAPTER 5

ACKERKNECHT, ERWIN H. *A Short History of Medicine*. Baltimore: Johns Hopkins University Press, 1982.

AMERICAN PSYCHIATRIC ASSOCIATION. "Tardive Dyskinesia: Summary of a Task Force Report of the American Psychiatric Association." *American Journal of Psychiatry* 137 (October 1980):1163–72.

ANDREASEN, NANCY C. *The Broken Brain*. New York: Harper & Row, 1984.

BALDESSARINI, ROSS J. *Chemotherapy in Psychiatry,* rev. ed. Cambridge: Harvard University Press, 1985.

BALLENGER, JAMES C., and ROBERT M. POST. "Carbamazepine in Manic-Depressive Illness: A New Treatment." *American Journal of Psychiatry* 137 (July 1980):782–90.

BASSUK, ELLEN, and STEPHEN SCHOONER. "Rampant Dental Caries in the Treatment of Depression." *Journal of Clinical Psychiatry* 39 (February 1978):163–65.

BODANIS, DAVID. *The Body*. Boston: Little, Brown and Company, 1984.

BRESSLER, RUBIN. "Treating Geriatric Depression." *Drug Therapy* (September 1984):35–50.

BUNNEY, WILLIAM E., and BLYNN L. GARLAND. "Lithium and Its Possible Modes of Action." In *The Neurobiology of Mood Disorders*. Baltimore: Williams & Wilkins, 1984.

CADE, JOHN F. "Lithium Salts in the Treatment of Psychotic Excitement." *Medical Journal of Australia* 1:195 (September 1949):349–52.

CAMMER, LEONARD. *Up from Depression*. New York: Pocket Books, 1969.

CHASNOFF, IRA J., JEFFREY W. ELLIS and ZACHARY S. FAINMAN. *Family Medical Guide*. New York: William Morrow and Company, 1983.

CHIU, E., B. DAVIES and R. WALKER. "Renal Findings after Thirty Years on Lithium (Letter to Editor)." *British Journal of Psychiatry* 143 (1983): 424–25.

DAWBER, RODNEY, and PETER MORTIMER. "Hair Loss During Lithium Treatment." *British Journal of Dermatology* 125 (1982):124–25.

DOMINGUEZ, ROBERTO A. "Evaluating the Effectiveness of the New Antidepressants." *Hospital and Community Psychiatry* 34 (May 1983): 405–7.

EMRICH, H. M., T. OKUMA and A. A. MULLER, eds. *Anticonvulsants in Affective Disorders*. Amsterdam: Elsevier Science Publishers, 1984.

FREUD, SIGMUND. *Analysis Terminable and Interminable*. Volume 23, standard ed. London: Hogarth Press Ltd., 1937.

GOODMAN, LOUIS S., and ALFRED GILMAN, eds. *The Pharmacological Basis of Therapeutics*. New York: Macmillan Publishing Co., 1975.

GREIST, JOHN H., and JAMES W. JEFFERSON. *Depression and Its Treatment*. Washington, D.C.: American Psychiatric Press, 1984.

HAILEY, ARTHUR. *Strong Medicine.* Garden City: Doubleday & Company, 1984.

HENINGER, GEORGE, and DENNIS CHARNEY. "Research Issues and Models to Better Understand the Mechanism of Action of Treatments for Affective Illness: The Role of Lithium." Symposium presented at the American College of Neuropsychopharmacology, December 1986 Washington meeting.

HUGHES, JENNIFER, B. BARRACLOUGH and W. REEVE. "Are Patients Shocked by ECT?" *Journal of the Royal College of Medicine* 74 (April 1981): 283–85.

JAMISON, KAY R., ROBERT H. GERNER and FREDERICK K. GOODWIN. "Patient and Physician Attitudes Toward Lithium." *Archives of General Psychiatry* 36 (July 1979):866–69.

JAMISON, KAY R., et al. "Clouds and Silver Linings: Positive Experiences Associated with Primary Affective Disorders." *American Journal of Psychiatry* 137 (February 1980):198–202.

JEFFERSON, JAMES W. "Lithium Carbonate-Induced Hypothyroidism: Its Many Faces." *JAMA* 242 (July 1979):271–72.

JEFFERSON, JAMES W., and JOHN H. GREIST. *Primer of Lithium Therapy.* Baltimore: Williams & Wilkins, 1977.

JEFFERSON, JAMES W., JOHN H. GREIST and DEBORAH L. ACKERMAN. *Lithium Encyclopedia for Clinical Practice.* Washington, DC: American Psychiatric Association Press, 1983.

JULIEN, ROBERT M. *A Primer of Drug Action,* 2nd ed. San Francisco: W. H. Freeman and Company, 1981.

KLINE, NATHAN S. *From Sad to Glad.* New York: G. P. Putnam Sons, 1974.

KLUG, JULIE. "Benefits of ECT Outweigh Risks in Most Patients." *Clinical Psychiatry News* 12 (June 1984).

KRIPKE, DANIEL L., LEWIS L. JUDD et al. "The Effect of Lithium Carbonate on the Circadian Rhythm of Sleep in Normal Human Subjects." *Biological Psychiatry* 14 (1979):545–48.

LAHR, M. B. "Hyponatremia During Carbamazepine Therapy." *Clinical Pharmacologic Therapies* 37 (1985):693–96.

LICKEY, MARVIN E., and BARBARA GORDON. *Drugs for Mental Illness.* New York: W. H. Freeman and Company, 1983.

LIPINSKI, JOSEPH F., and HARRISON G. POPE. "Possible Synergistic Action Between Carbamazepine and Lithium Carbonate in the Treatment of Three Acutely Manic Patients." *American Journal of Psychiatry* 139 (July 1982):948–49.

LIPINSKI, JOSEPH F., GEORGE S. ZUBENKO et al. "Propranolol in the Treatment of Neuroleptic-Induced Akathesia." *American Journal of Psychiatry* 141 (March 1984):412–15.

LITOVITZ, GARY L. "Contact Lenses and Antidepressants" (Letter to Editor). *Journal of Clinical Psychiatry* 45 (April 1984):188.

LOPPMAN, STEVEN. "A Comparison of Three Types of Lithium Release Preparations." *Hospital and Community Psychiatry* 34 (February 1983): 113–14.

MUNIZ, CARLOS E., RONALD B. SALEM and KENNETH L. DIRECTOR. "Hair Loss in a Patient Receiving Lithium." *Psychosomatics* 23 (March 1982):312–13.

PRIEN, ROBERT F. *Information on Lithium.* Rockville: U. S. Government Printing Office, 1981.

PUZYNSKI, STANISLAW, and LUCJA KLOSIEWICZ. "Valproic Acid Amide in the Treatment of Affective and Schizoaffective Disorders." *Journal of Affective Disorders* 6 (1984):115–21.

QUITKIN, FREDERIC, ARTHUR RIFKIN and DONALD F. KLEIN. "Monoamine Oxidase Inhibitors." *Archives of General Psychiatry* 36 (July 1979):749–60.

RABKIN, JUDITH G. "Opinions about Mental Illness: A Review of the Literature." *Psychological Bulletin* 77 (March 1972):153–71.

RESTAK, RICHARD. *The Brain.* New York: Bantam Books, 1984.

SCHATZBERG, ALAN F., and JONATHAN O. COLE. *Manual of Clinical Psychopharmacology.* Washington, DC: American Psychiatric Press, 1986.

SCHOU, MOGENS. "Lithium Perspectives." *Neuropsychobiology* 10 (1983): 7–12.

SCHOU, MOGENS. *Lithium Treatment of Manic-Depressive Illness,* 2nd ed. Basel: Karger, 1983.

SCHOU, MOGENS. "Practical Problems of Lithium Maintenance Treatment." In *Chronic Treatments in Neuropsychiatry,* ed. Dargut Kemali and Georgio Racagne. New York: Raven Press, 1985.

SWAZEY, JUDITH P. *Chlorpromazine in Psychiatry.* Cambridge: MIT Press, 1974.

TORREY, E. FULLER. *Surviving Schizophrenia.* New York: Harper & Row, 1983.

VAN PUTTEN, THEODORE, PHILIP R. A. MAY and STEPHEN R. MARDER. "Response to Antipsychotic Medication: The Doctor's and the Consumer's View." *American Journal of Psychiatry* 141 (January 1984):16–19.

VICTOR, BRUCE S., NAN A. LINK, RENEE L. BINDER and IRIS R. BELL. "Use of Clonazepam in Mania and Schizoaffective Disorders." *American Journal of Psychiatry* 141 (September 1984):111–12.

CHAPTER 6

Seasonal Affective Disorders

BEGLEY, SHARON, and WILLIAM J. COOK. "The Sad Days of Winter." *Newsweek,* January 14, 1985.

DONALDSON, SUSAN R. "The Dawn's Early Light: Remedy for Depression?" *Biological Therapies in Psychiatry* 7 (July 1984):25.

DONALDSON, SUSAN R. "Seasonal Affective Disorder and Phototherapy: A Brief Review." *Psychiatric Times,* April 1985.

KRIPKE, DANIEL F., S. CRAIG RISCH and DAVID S. JANOWSKY. "Lighting Up Depression." *Psychopharmacology Bulletin* 19 (1983):526–30.

"Light" (Talk of the Town). *New Yorker,* January 14, 1985.

PARKER, GORDON, and STEPHEN WALTER. "Seasonal Variation in Depressive Disorders and Suicidal Deaths in New South Wales." *British Journal of Psychiatry* 140 (1982):626–32.

REITER, RUSSELL J. "The Pineal Gland: An Intermediary Between the Environment and the Endocrine System." *Psychoneuroendocrinology* 8 (1983):31–40.

ROSENTHAL, NORMAN E., ALFRED J. LEWY, THOMAS A. WEHR et al. "Seasonal Cycling in a Bipolar Patient." *Psychiatry Research* 8 (1983):25–31.

ROSENTHAL, NORMAN E., DAVID A. SACK, CHRISTIAN GILLIN et al. "Seasonal Affective Disorder: A Description of the Syndrome and Preliminary Findings with Light Therapy." *Archives of General Psychiatry* 41 (January 1984):72–79.

WEHR, THOMAS A., and FREDERICK K. GOODWIN. "Biological Rhythms and Psychiatry." In *American Handbook of Psychiatry,* 2nd ed. Vol. VII: *Advances and New Directions,* ed. Silvano Arieti and James Brodie. New York: Basic Books, 1981.

WEHR, THOMAS A., FREDERICK K. GOODWIN, ANNA WIRZ-JUSTICE et al. "48-Hour Sleep-Wake Cycles in Manic-Depressive Illness." *Archives of General Psychiatry* 39 (May 1982):559–65.

Depression in Children and Adolescents

ANNELL, ANNA-LISA. "Lithium in the Treatment of Children and Adolescents." *Acta Psychiatrica Scandinavica* 207–Suppl. (1969):19–33.

BASSUK, ELLEN L., STEPHEN C. SCHOONOVER and ALAN J. GELENBERG, eds. *The Practitioner's Guide to Psychoactive Drugs,* 2nd ed. New York: Plenum Medical Book Company, 1984.

BERG, IAN, ROY HULLIN, MICHAEL ALLSOP et al. "Bipolar Manic-Depressive Psychosis in Early Adolescence." *British Journal of Psychiatry* 125 (1974):416–17.

BIEDERMAN, JOSEPH, DAVID GASTFRIEND, MICHAEL S. JELLINEK and ALLAN GOLD-BLATT. "Cardiovascular Effects of Desipramine in Children and Adolescents with Attention Deficit Disorder." *Journal of Pediatrics* 106 (June 1985):1017–20.

BIEDERMAN, JOSEPH, KERIM MUNIR, DEBRA KNEE et al. "A Family Study of Patients with Attention Deficit Disorder." Submitted for publication, 1985.

BROZAN, NADINE. "Life after a Son's Suicide: One Family's Struggle." *New York Times,* January 13, 1986. Section B.

CANTWELL, DENNIS P., and GABRIELLE A. CARLSON, eds. *Affective Disorders in Childhood and Adolescence—An Update.* New York: Spectrum Publications, 1983.

CONNORS, C. KEITH, and THEODORE PETTI. "Imipramine Therapy of Depressed Children: Methodologic Considerations." *Psychopharmacology Bulletin* 19 (1983):65–69.

CYTRYN, LEON, DONALD H. MCKNEW, JR., and WILLIAM E. BUNNEY. "Diagnosis of Depression in Children: A Reassessment." *American Journal of Psychiatry* 137 (January 1980):22–25.

DSM–III: Diagnostic and Statistical Manual of Mental Disorders, 3rd ed. Washington, DC: American Psychiatric Association, 1980.

Economic Fact Book for Psychiatry. Washington, DC: American Psychiatric Association, 1983.

GELLER, BARBARA, JAMES M. PEREL, EDWARD F. KNITTER et al. "Nortriptyline in Major Depressive Disorder in Children: Response, Steady-State Plasma Levels, Predictive Kinetics, and Pharmacokinetics." *Psychopharmacology Bulletin* 19 (1983):62–65.

GREENBERG, ROSALIE. "Adolescent Suicide." *Fair Oaks Psychiatry Letter* 3: 12 (December 1985):67–70.

JEFFERSON, JAMES W., and JOHN H. GREIST. *Primer of Lithium Therapy.* Baltimore: Williams & Wilkins, 1977.

KASHANI, JAVAD, and JOHN F. SIMONDS. "The Incidence of Depression in Children." *American Journal of Psychiatry* 136 (September 1979): 1203–5.

KASHANI, JAVAD, ARSHAD HUSAIN, WALID O. SHEKIM et al. "Current Perspectives on Childhood Depression: An Overview." *American Journal of Psychiatry* 138 (February 1981):143–53.

KESTENBAUM, CLARICE. "Children at Risk for Manic-Depressive Illness: Possible Predictors." *American Journal of Psychiatry* 136 (September 1979):1206–8.

MALMQUIST, CARL P. "Depressions in Childhood and Adolescence (Part I)." *New England Journal of Medicine* 284 (April 1971):887–93.

PFEFFER, CYNTHIA R. "Suicidal Tendencies in Children and Adolescents." *Medical Aspects of Human Sexuality* 20 (February 1986):32–35.

STROBER, MICHAEL, JACQUELINE GREEN and GABRIELLE CARLSON. "Phenomenology and Subtypes of Major Depressive Disorder in Adolescence." *Journal of Affective Disorders* 3 (1981):281–90.

WELLER, ELIZABETH B., and RONALD A. WELLER, eds. *Major Depressive Disorders in Children.* Clinical Insights Series. Washington, DC: American Psychiatric Association, 1984.

YOUNGERMAN, JOSEPH, and IAN A. CANINI. "Lithium Carbonate Use in Children and Adolescents: A Survey of the Literature." *Archives of General Psychiatry* 35 (February 1978):216–24.

Affective Disorders in the Elderly

BASSUK, ELLEN L., STEPHEN C. SCHOONOVER and ALAN J. GELENBERG, eds. *The Practitioner's Guide to Psychoactive Drugs,* 2nd ed. New York: Plenum Medical Book Company, 1984.

BRESSLER, RUBIN. "Treating Geriatric Depression: Current Options." *Drug Therapy* (September 1984):35–50.

BUTLER, ROBERT N. "Psychiatry and the Elderly: An Overview." *American Journal of Psychiatry* 132 (September 1975):893–900.

GOODSTEIN, RICHARD K. "The Diagnosis and Treatment of Elderly Patients: Some Practical Guidelines." *Hospital and Community Psychiatry* 31 (January 1980):19–24.

MAYEUX, RICHARD, and WILMA G. ROSEN, eds. *Advances in Neurology.* Volume 38: *The Dementias.* New York: Raven Press, 1984.

PAYKEL, E. S., ed. *Handbook of Affective Disorders.* New York: The Guilford Press, 1982.

REIFLER, BURTON V., ERIC LARSON and RAY HANLEY. "Coexistence of Cognitive Impairment and Depression in Geriatric Outpatients." *American Journal of Psychiatry* 139 (May 1982):623–26.

ROOSE, STEVEN P., STANLEY BONE, CATHERINE HAIDORFER et al. "Lithium Treatment in Older Patients." *American Journal of Psychiatry* 136 (June 1979):843–44.

SCHATZBERG, ALAN F., BENJAMIN LIPTZIN, ANDREW SATLIN and JONATHAN O. COLE. "Diagnosis of Affective Disorders in the Elderly." *Psychosomatics* 25 (February 1985):126–31.

SCHATZBERG, ALAN F., ed. *Common Treatment Problems in Depression.* Washington, DC: American Psychiatric Press, 1985.

SHAMOIAN, CHARLES A. "Assessing Depression in Elderly Patients." *Hospital and Community Psychiatry* 36 (April 1985):338–39.

SHAMOIAN, CHARLES A., ed. *Treatment of Affective Disorders in the Elderly.* Washington, DC: American Psychiatric Press, 1985.

SHRABERG, DAVID. "The Myth of Pseudodementia: Depression and the Aging Brain." *American Journal of Psychiatry* 135 (May 1978):601–3.

TAYLOR, ROBERT L. *Mind or Body: Distinguishing Psychological from Organic Disorders.* New York: McGraw-Hill, 1982.

WELLS, CHARLES E. "Pseudodementia." *American Journal of Psychiatry* 136 (July 1979):895–900.

Pregnancy and Affective Disorders

ANATH, JAMBUR. "Side Effects in the Neonate from Psychotropic Agents Excreted Through Breast-Feeding." *American Journal of Psychiatry* 135 (July 1978):801–5.

BALDESSARINI, ROSS J. *Chemotherapy in Psychiatry,* rev. ed. Cambridge: Harvard University Press, 1985.

BASSUK, ELLEN L., STEPHEN C. SCHOONOVER and ALAN J. GELENBERG, eds. *The Practitioner's Guide to Psychoactive Drugs,* 2nd ed. New York: Plenum Medical Book Company, 1984.

GOLDFIELD, MICHAEL, and MORTON R. WEINSTEIN. "Lithium in Pregnancy: A Review with Recommendations." *American Journal of Psychiatry* 127 (January 1971):64–69.

JEFFERSON, JAMES W., and JOHN H. GREIST. *Primer of Lithium Therapy.* Baltimore: Williams & Wilkins, 1977.

NURNBERG, H. GEORGE. "Treatment of Mania in the Last Six Months of Pregnancy." *Hospital and Community Psychiatry* 31 (February 1980): 122–26.

NURNBERG, H. GEORGE, and JOAN PRUDIC. "Guidelines for Treatment of Psychosis During Pregnancy." *Hospital and Community Psychiatry* 35 (January 1984):67–71.

REMICK, RONALD A., and WILLIAM L. MAURICE. "ECT in Pregnancy." *American Journal of Psychiatry* 135 (June 1978):761–62.

TARGUM, STEVEN D., YOLANDE B. DAVENPORT and MARIAN J. WEBSTER. "Postpartum Mania in Bipolar Manic-Depressive Patients Withdrawn from Lithium Carbonate." *Journal of Nervous and Mental Disease* 167 (1979):572–74.

WEINSTEIN, MORTON R., and MICHAEL D. GOLDFIELD. "Cardiovascular Malformation with Lithium Use During Pregnancy." *American Journal of Psychiatry* 132 (May 1975):529–31.

CHAPTER 7

ANDERSON, CAROL M., GERARD F. HOGARTY and DOUGLAS J. REISS. "Family Treatment of Schizophrenic Patients: A Psychoeducational Approach." *Schizophrenia Bulletin* 6 (1980):490–502.

BECK, AARON T., STEVEN D. HOLLON, JEFFREY E. YOUNG et al. "Treatment of Depression with Cognitive Therapy and Amitriptyline." *Archives of General Psychiatry* 42 (February 1985):142–48.

BENSON, ROBERT. "The Forgotten Treatment Modality in Bipolar Illness: Psychotherapy." *American Journal of Psychiatry* (November 1975): 634–37.

BOFFEY, PHILIP M. "Psychotherapy Is as Good as Drug in Curing Depression." *New York Times,* May 14, 1986.

BURNS, DAVID D. *Feeling Good.* New York: New American Library, 1980.

BURSTEN, BEN. "Medication Nonadherence Due to Feelings of Loss of Control in Biological Depression." *American Journal of Psychiatry* 142:2 (February 1985):244–46.

CONNELLY, CATHERINE ECOCK, YOLANDE B. DAVENPORT and JOHN I. NURNBERGER. "Adherence to Treatment Regimen in a Lithium Carbonate Clinic." *Archives of General Psychiatry* 39 (May 1982):585–88.

DAVENPORT, YOLANDE B., MARVIN L. ADLAND, PHILIP W. GOLD et al. "Manic-Depressive Illness: Psychodynamic Features of Multigenerational Families." *American Journal of Orthopsychiatry* 49 (January 1979):24–35.

FRANK, ELLEN, and DAVID J. KUPFER. "Maintenance Treatment of Recurrent Unipolar Depression: Pharmacology and Psychotherapy." In *Chronic Treatments in Neuropsychiatry,* ed. D. Kemali and G. Racagni. New York: Raven Press, 1985.

FRANK, ELLEN, and DAVID J. KUPFER. "Psychotherapeutic Approaches to Treatment of Recurrent Unipolar Depression: Work in Progress." *Psychopharmacology Bulletin* 22 (1986):558–63.

GOODWIN, FREDERICK K., ROBERT H. GERNER and KAY R. JAMISON. "Patient and Physician Attitudes toward Lithium." *Archives of General Psychiatry* 36 (July 1979):866–69.

KLERMAN, GERALD L. Telephone conversation with Janice Papolos, May 20, 1986.

KLERMAN, GERALD L., MYRNA M. WEISSMAN, BRUCE J. ROUNSAVILLE and EVE S. CHEVRON. *Interpersonal Psychotherapy of Depression.* New York: Basic Books, 1984.

LEO, JOHN. "Talk Is as Good as a Pill." *Time Magazine,* May 26, 1986.

MAYO, JULIA A., RALPH A. O'CONNELL and JOHN D. O'BRIEN. "Families of Manic-Depressive Patients: Effects of Treatment." *American Journal of Psychiatry* 136 (December 1979):153–9.

MURPHY, GEORGE E., ANNE D. SIMONS, RICHARD D. WETZEL et al. "Cognitive Therapy and Pharmacotherapy." *Archives of General Psychiatry* 41 (January 1984):34–41.

PAPOLOS, DEMITRI F. "The Psychoeducational Approach to Major Affective Disorders." Presentation to the American Family Therapy Association, June 1984.

RUNCK, BETTY. "Conference Recommends Pharmacologic Prevention of Recurring Mood Disorders." *Hospital and Community Psychiatry* 35 (September 1984):871–73.

YESS, JAMES P. "What Families of the Mentally Ill Want." *Community Support Service Journal* 2 (n.d.).

CHAPTER 9

BERNHEIM, KAYLA F., and ANTHONY F. LEHMAN. *Working with Families of the Mentally Ill.* New York: W. W. Norton and Company, 1985.

BOHAN, PATRICK. "A Call to Advocate." *Sibling Bond* 3 (Winter 1984).

BROWN, BERYL. "Growing Up." *Sibling Bond* 5 (Winter 1985).

JOHNSON, JULIE. "Great Expectations: A Sibling Experience." *Mental Health Advocate* 22 (April/May 1983).

TORREY, E. FULLER. *Surviving Schizophrenia.* New York: Harper & Row, 1983.

WALSH, MARYELLEN. *Schizophrenia: Straight Talk for Family and Friends.* New York: William Morrow, 1985.

CHAPTER 10

APPLEBAUM, PAUL S. "Civil Commitment: Is the Pendulum Changing Direction?" *Hospital and Community Psychiatry* 33 (September 1982): 703–4.

CAMMER, LEONARD. *Up from Depression.* New York: Pocket Books, 1969.

CHODOFF, PAUL. "The Case for Involuntary Hospitalization for the Mentally Ill." *American Journal of Psychiatry* 133 (May 1976):496–501.

DURAM, MARY L., HAROLD D. CARR and GLENN L. PIERCE. "Police Involvement and Influence in Involuntary Civil Commitment." *Hospital and Community Psychiatry* 35 (June 1984):580–4.

ENNIS, BRUCE J. *Prisoners of Psychiatry.* New York: Harcourt Brace Jovanovich, 1972.

ENNIS, BRUCE J., and RICHARD D. EMERY. *The Rights of Mental Patients.* New York: Avon Books, 1978.

GOLEMAN, DANIEL. "States Move to Ease Law Committing Mentally Ill." *New York Times,* December 9, 1986 (section C).

GOTS, RONALD, and ARTHUR KAUFMAN. *The People's Hospital Book.* New York: Avon, 1978.

HARBIN, HENRY T., ed. *The Psychiatric Hospital and the Family.* New York: Spectrum Publications, 1982.

HOSPITAL AND COMMUNITY PSYCHIATRY SERVICE. *Rights of the Mentally Disabled: Statements and Standards.* Washington, DC: American Psychiatric Press, 1983.

KORPELL, HERBERT S. *How You Can Help.* Washington, DC: American Psychiatric Press, 1984.

LAURINO, MARIA. "A Growing Madness: Breakdown at Manhattan State." *Village Voice,* August 7, 1984.

MAGGIO, ELIO. *The Psychiatry-Law Dilemma: Mental Health Versus Human Rights.* New York: Vantage Press, 1981.

MATTSON, MARLIN R. "Quality Assurance: A Literature Review of a Changing Field." *Hospital and Community Psychiatry* 35 (June 1984):605–15.

MCFARLANE, WILLIAM R. "Family Therapy in the Psychiatric Hospital." In *The Psychiatric Hospital and the Family,* ed. Henry T. Harbin. New York: Spectrum Publications, 1982.

McPhee, John. "Family Doctors." *New Yorker,* July 23, 1984.

Park, Clara Claiborne, with Leon N. Shapiro. *You Are Not Alone.* Boston: Little, Brown & Company, 1976.

Rosenblatt, Aaron. "Concepts of the Asylum in the Care of the Mentally Ill." *Hospital and Community Psychiatry* 35 (March 1984):244–50.

Roth, Loren H. "A Commitment Law for Patients, Doctors, and Lawyers." *American Journal of Psychiatry* 136 (September 1979):1121–26.

Sadoff, Robert L. *Legal Issues in the Care of Psychiatric Patients.* New York: Springer Publishing Company, 1982.

Schwartz, Harold I., Paul S. Applebaum and Richard D. Kaplan. "Clinical Judgments in the Decision to Commit." *Archives of General Psychiatry* 41 (August 1984):811–15.

Sheehan, Susan. *Is There No Place on Earth for Me?* New York: Vintage Books, 1983.

Sidel, Victor W., and Ruth Sidel, eds. *Reforming Medicine.* New York: Pantheon Books, 1984.

Skodol, Andrew E., Robert Plutchik and Toksoz B. Karasu. "Expectations of Hospital Treatment." *Journal of Nervous and Mental Disease* 168 (March 1980):70–74.

Stone, Alan A. "Recent Mental Health Litigation: A Critical Perspective." *American Journal of Psychiatry* 134 (March 1977):273–79.

Sullivan, Ronald. "Limits Ease on Committing the Mentally Ill." *New York Times,* July 15, 1985.

Szasz, Thomas S. *Psychiatric Slavery.* New York: The Free Press, 1977.

Torrey, E. Fuller. *Surviving Schizophrenia.* New York: Harper & Row, 1983.

Tucker, Gary J., and Jerrold S. Maxmen. "The Practice of Hospital Psychiatry: A Formulation." *American Journal of Psychiatry* 130 (August 1973):887–91.

CHAPTER 11

American Society of Internal Medicine. *Understanding and Choosing Your Health Insurance.* Washington, DC, 1984.

Ammer, Christine, with Nathan T. Sidley. *The Common Sense Guide to Mental Health Care.* Brattleboro: The Lewis Publishing Company, 1982.

Andrulis, Dennis P., and Noel A. Mazade. "American Mental Health Policy: Changing Directions in the 80's." *Hospital and Community Psychiatry* 34 (July 1983):601–6.

Center for Health Policy Studies. *Mandated Mental Health Benefits under Private Insurance: A Review of State Laws.* Prepared for the National Institute of Mental Health, December 1983.

CORNACCHIA, HAROLD J., and STEPHEN BARRETT. *Shopping for Health Care.* St. Louis: The C. V. Mosby Company, 1982.

FREUDENHEIM, MILT. "Prepaid Means Less Paid in Medical Plans." *New York Times,* November 25, 1984.

GREENLEY, DIANNE. "Insurance and Other Third-Party Coverage for Persons Who Are Mentally Ill: Issues and Possibilities." Report written for the National Alliance for the Mentally Ill, February 1986.

HARRINGTON, GERI. *The Medicare Answer Book.* New York: Harper & Row, 1982.

MUSZYNSKI, SAM, JO BRADY and STEVEN S. SHARFSTEIN. *Coverage for Mental and Nervous Disorders: Summaries of 300 Private Sector Health Insurance Plans.* Washington, DC: American Psychiatric Press, 1983.

PEAR, ROBERT. "Conferees Agree on Bill to Revise U. S. Disability Law." *New York Times,* September 15, 1984.

PEAR, ROBERT. "Proposals for Mentally Disabled Ease Eligibility for U. S. Benefits." *New York Times,* December 8, 1984.

SHARFSTEIN, STEVEN, SAM MUSZYNSKI and EVELYN MYERS. *Health Insurance and Psychiatric Care: Update and Appraisal.* Washington, DC: American Psychiatric Press, 1984.

U. S. DEPARTMENT OF HEALTH AND HUMAN SERVICES. *Social Security Handbook.* SSA Publication No. 05-10135, July 1984.

U. S. DEPARTMENT OF HEALTH, EDUCATION AND WELFARE. *Disability Evaluation under Social Security: A Handbook for Physicians.* HEW Publication No. (SSA) 79-10089, August 1979.

CHAPTER 12

ARNSTEIN, HELENE S. *What to Tell Your Child about Birth, Death, Illness, Divorce and Other Family Crises,* rev. ed., Indianapolis: The Bobbs-Merrill Company, 1974.

HOLDEN, CONSTANCE. "Giving Mental Illness Its Research Due." *Science* 232 (May 30, 1986):1084–85.

NATIONAL DEPRESSIVE AND MANIC DEPRESSIVE ASSOCIATION. "Fact Sheet on Mental Illness." Insert in press kit, May 1986.

INDEX

Electroconvulsive therapy. *See* ECT
Elevated mood, in mania, 31
Eligibility: for disability insurance, 223–24; for Medicare, 220–21; for Supplemental Security Income, 224–25
Eliot, T. S., 18
Emergency intervention in mania, 174–78
Emotional reactions, 57
Employers, information of mood disorders, 234–36
Employment health insurance, 214–16
Endep (amitriptyline), 108
Endocrine secretion cycles, 73
Endocrine systems, 66
Endorphins, 59
Energy: excess, in mania, 5; loss, in depression, 7, 29
Ennis, Bruce, 188
Environment, and mood disorders, 45–46, 50–51
Epidemiology of mood disorders, 51–52
Epinephrine, 67, 68
Epstein's anomaly, 135
Eskalith, 93
Eskalith CR, 92, 93
Estrogen: and depression, 130; and mania, 32
Euphoric mood states, 7
Evaluation of hospitals, 194–96

Face, involuntary movements, 101, 103
Family counselors, fees of, 159
Family history, 33, 35; and cyclothymia, 40; and eating disorders, 42; and mood disorders, 7, 44–54; and psychiatric disorders, 43; of suicide, 171
Family members: and affective disorders, 161, 167–83; and care after hospitalization, 212; of depressed patients, 144–49, 185
Fatigue, 43; in children, 125; in depression, 29; lithium and, 95, 97
Fawcett, Jan, 88
FDA (Food and Drug Administration), restrictions on lithium, 91
Fear, lithium toxicity symptom, 134
Federal funding for research, 238
Feighner, John, 28
Fetal distress, lithium and, 135
Fieve, Ronald, 37
Fight or flight response, 58, 67–68, 81, 82
Financial mismanagement, 172, 173
First-dollar coverage, 216
5-hydroxyindoleactic acid (5-HIAA), and suicide, 171–72
Flagyl, and lithium, 97
Flight of ideas, in mania, 16, 31
Florida: commitment laws, 267; support groups, 255, 261

Fluid loss, lithium and, 93
Fluphenazine (Prolixin, Permitil), 100, 101; in pregnancy, 136
Folic acid deficiencies, 130
Food and Drug Administration (FDA), restrictions on lithium, 91
Foods to avoid with MAOIs, 113
For Ayes Only, 220
Formation of support group, 250–53
Foundations, research funds, 239
Frank, Ellen, 148
Fraternal twins, 44–45
Freud, Sigmund, 27, 87
Frustration, of manic children, 127
Funding of psychiatric research, 238, 239
Future, sense of, in depression, 11

GABA, 59; and ECT, 118
Gait, unsteady, lithium and, 97
Galen, 89, 120
Gastric problems, 12, 94; in children, 125
Geigy pharmaceutical firm, 105
Generic names of drugs, 100
Genes, studies of, 47–50
Genetic counseling, 52–54
Genetic markers, 44–54, 84, 162
Georgia: commitment laws, 267; support groups, 255, 261
Gerhard, Daniela, 48, 50
Glaucoma, narrow-angle, 109, 133
Glutamic acid, 60
Goiter, 91
Goodwin, Frederick, 34, 157
Gout, lithium treatment for, 89
Grandiosity, 21; in cyclothymia, 39; in mania, 31; of manic children, 127; in mixed state, 39
Gravely disabled, legal definitions, 265, 266, 268, 269, 284
Greenberg, Rosalie, 127
Group health insurance, 214–16
Growth hormone, 73
Guilt feelings, 43; in depression, 7, 11, 12, 29, 123; of family members, 169
Gusella, James, 48–50
Guthrie, Woody, 48
Guze, Samuel, 27

Hair loss, lithium and, 96
Haldol (haloperidol), 99, 100, 101; in pregnancy, 136
Haldol decanoate, 100
Hallucinations, 22–23; in depression, 13, 30, 123; in mania, 31, 34, 173; of schizophrenia, 34; treatment of, 100, 104
Hallucinogenic drugs, 32
Haloperidol (Haldol), 99, 100, 101; in pregnancy, 136

COPYRIGHT
ACKNOWLEDGMENTS

ABOUT THE AUTHORS

Demitri F. Papolos, M.D., is Assistant Professor of Psychiatry at the Albert Einstein College of Medicine and the Director of Inpatient Psychiatry at Montefiore Medical Center in New York. He is the coordinator of the teaching program on affective disorders for the psychiatric residency training program at the Albert Einstein College of Medicine and is currently involved in several areas of research, most notably that of treatment-resistant depressions. Dr. Papolos developed the family psychoeducational approach to affective disorders. He is a diplomate in neurology and psychiatry and is in private practice in New York City.

Janice Papolos has written on a broad range of subjects for national magazines such as *Newsweek, McCall's* and *High Fidelity*. She is a staff writer for *Chamber Music Magazine*. Her first book, *The Performing Artist's Handbook,* has become a standard reference in the classical music field. Janice Papolos is a member of the American Society of Journalists and Authors.